Raymond L. Aaron
President

RAYMOND AARON
GROUP

W9-CTA-851

Dear Fellow Canadian:

It is embarrassing to admit that as Canadians we probably know more great Americans than we know great Canadians.

Is it a national lack of self confidence? Is it our fate to limp through history with a country-wide poor self-image that stretches from sea to sea? Before meeting Dick Drew, I might have sadly accepted such a thought.

But this wonderful book finally shatters that myth. We are a country of vibrant history. We are a country of extraordinary achievement. We are a country of boundless successes. Dick Drew has devoted his professional career to setting the record straight. Through the medium of radio and now also in this book, he salutes Canadians who have made a difference in their community, in the country and in the world.

And I salute him for his tireless effort in uncovering these Canadian Achievers and in bringing their successes to light for us all to savour.

I am honoured to have been selected for inclusion in his radio broadcast and in this book. To be inserted as the very last story is the perfect place for a contrarian like me!

I resonate with all Canadians in thanking Dick Drew for producing this valuable Canadian asset.

With great respect,

Raymond

482 Queen Street
Newmarket, Ontario
Canada L3Y 2H4
Telephone: 1-416-853-3600
Facsimile: 1-416-853-3658

What Is "The Canadian Achievers"?

"The Canadian Achievers" is Canada's only national network radio program produced by, for and about Canadians. It is heard daily, coast to coast, on a network of 150 leading Canadian radio stations.

Each day, I share with my listeners the story of a living Canadian who is achieving his or her goal. The emphasis is placed on human achievement, focusing on Canadians from all walks of life and every corner of the country. My series is committed to demonstrating the proof that Canadians, regardless of their field of endeavour, are reaching exciting goals and achieving levels of success as great or greater than anyone else.

If you're not already a believer, I invite you to read this book and become one. These are the same authentic stories I tell on radio, 260 new stories each year. Since launching *"The Canadian Achievers"* in February of 1985, I have never run short of exciting stories about the achievements of living Canadians—and never will, because Canada is a country of achievers.

THE CANADIAN ACHIEVERS

HOW **THEY** DID IT
HOW **YOU** CAN DO IT
WHY **YOU** SHOULD DO IT

DICK DREW

Stories from
the Radio Series

Canadian Cataloguing in Publication Data

Drew, Dick.
The Canadian Achievers

Based on the radio series: The Canadian Achievers.
Includes index.
ISBN 0-9695229-0-8

1. Canada--Biography. 2. Success--Canada--Biography. 3. Achievement motivation. I. Title.
FC25.D74 1991   920.071   C91-091367-6
F1005.D74 1991

Drew Publications
202 - 2006 Main St.
Vancouver, BC
V5T 3C2

Printed and bound in Canada by D. W. Friesen & Sons Ltd.

Dedication

My radio series and this book are dedicated to the people who built this country, and those who are struggling to hold her together.

Thanks

There are not enough trees in Canada to provide the paper necessary to list all of the people I owe thanks to. And besides that, in 260 B.C. Callimachus is reported to have said "a big book is a big bore". My life and this series has been richly rewarded because of them.

I will however acknowledge my mother; Marie. My wife of 35 glorious years; Aline. Our children; Louise, Mitchell and Cameron, our son-in-law; Steve, and our daughters-in-law; Shelley and Maeve, and especially our two spectacularly gorgeous, brilliant and charming grandchildren; Kyla, 6, and her two year old terror brother, Spencer. Whenever I feel the need for intelligent conversation I phone Kyla. She puts Spencer on the extension phone and we hold a three way conversation. Within moments my world returns to normal.

Foreword

I speak from personal experience when I say repeatedly that Canada is the best country in the entire world for anyone wishing to achieve.

Canada is the one country where it doesn't matter what you're born with, it's what you do with what you're born with!

I was big for my age; I thought I knew everything there was to know. So in 1949, at age 14, I dropped out of grade 8, lied about my age, and ran away to sea on an oil tanker. It was a great life, seeing the world, meeting interesting people. Five years and thousands of miles slipped by quickly.

My life took a change one night while we were unloading crude oil in Buenos Aires, Argentina. It was 2 a.m. January 20, 1954. I was standing deck watch. When I suddenly realized I was 19 years old and although I had been travelling all over, my life was going nowhere. We were sailing the next day for Puerto La Cruz, Venezuela, to load crude oil for Portland, Maine. I decided then and there it would be my last voyage. When my ship the S.S. Esso Knoxville reached Portland six weeks later, I quit and headed for Montreal to what I thought would be a new career as the president of a large multi-national corporation. To my surprise the only job I was qualified for was pumping gas at the Shell gas station at Decarie and Sherbrooke earning 60 cents an hour plus tips.

I soon left to sell shoes at Eaton's on St. Catherines St., where I learned undying respect for shoe sales personnel, and met my future bride, the lovely Aline Gallant.

My next job was at Mappins Jewellers, but I was quickly coming to the conclusion that what I really wanted to do was to get into radio. I had always been fascinated by radio and felt I had to get into it somehow. I knew you couldn't just walk in to a station and ask for a job. Or maybe you could. But I didn't have the confidence. I needed knowledge. I enrolled at Sir George Williams College and also began taking voice and elocution lessons from well-known voice teacher, Dorothy Danford. The trouble was, she charged $10. an hour. I could only afford half an hour a week. I've often wondered how much faster my career in radio would have advanced had I been able to afford the other half hour weekly.

Finally in 1958, I got a job at CJQC, Quebec City, where I worked for one exciting year. Shortly after I left, the station ceased broadcasting. I've often wondered whether it was because of me or in spite of me.

I left CJQC for a job way out on the west coast at CJAV, Port Alberni. It was a chance to return to Vancouver and show off Aline to my family. Aline encouraged our move to British Columbia even though she, an Acadian from New Brunswick, did not at the time speak English.

We were young and foolish and full of confidence. In other words, we didn't know any better. We sold all of our furniture to Don McGowan for $200. and jammed the rest of our belongings into our aging Pontiac Coupe and headed west.

Imagine our shock when we arrived at Port Alberni to find there was no job. Economics had taken a down turn, station owner Ken Hutchison was cutting staff. We were desperate. We had no money. We were broke. In fact, we were beyond broke. I convinced Ken to let me work as a commission salesman as well as doing the morning show. Somehow we survived, and formed warm friendships there that continue today.

My big break came in October 1961 when I was offered a job at CHML in Hamilton. That changed my life. That is, an incident there put my life on a whole new course. You see, I worked at that station for 17 years. It began like this... I met station manager Tommy Darling in Vancouver. His proposition to me was this: CHML had a dynamic salesman named Vic Copps. Copps was also a Hamilton City Alderman. Tommy felt he would lose Vic eventually because he was sure Vic would run for mayor in the up-coming election. And if successful, leave the station.

Tommy liked to have backup for every situation. So he hired me as an announcer/salesman with the understanding that if Vic Copps won the election I had a permanent job. If Copps lost, I would be out of a job because Vic would remain at the station and I would be toast. I feverishly went to work on Copps campaign like I never worked in my life! On December 5, 1962, Vic Copps won, became mayor, and I had his job. (Incidentally, Vic Copps was MP Sheila Copps father.)

Among the many talented people I worked with there are Gordie Tapp, Ed Preston and Brian Costello. Each are featured in separate chapters of this book.

My tenure came to an abrupt end on May 11, 1977. By that time I was general manager. Tommy and I had a falling out and I was fired. I resolved then and there that I would never put myself in a position where I could be fired again. By 5pm that night I had formed my own company, Drew Marketing Ltd., and acquired my first client, St. Clair Productions, a radio syndication company managed by a good friend Pat Hurley. That set the mold for me and my life ahead.

I should say here that although Tommy Darling fired me I still hold him in the highest esteem. Tommy was my mentor, he made a bigger mark on my life and many other people's lives than anyone else. He passed away in 1983. And even today when faced with a personal or business decision I always wonder how Tommy would have handled it.

My life's ambition since starting in radio was to someday own my own radio station. My dream came true in 1979 when I bought radio station CKAY in Duncan, British Columbia. Aline, our three children; Louise, Mitchell, and Cameron, packed up and headed west.

I have always believed in Canada and Canadians. As a broadcaster, I wanted to somehow get the message across to everyone that Canada is a country of unlimited opportunity. So, I began interviewing Canadians who had made a mark in life through their own enthusiasm and determination. I couldn't believe how many there were. The idea for my series on Canadian Achievers arrived about four years later.

In September of 1984, Jim Edwards, a good friend and a fine broadcaster from CFRN Edmonton, was visiting me in Duncan. Jim had just been elected Conservative Federal Member of Parliament for Edmonton-Southwest. I showed him demo scripts and the rough outline of a radio series I had been working on for sometime called "The Canadian Achievers" (English); "Les Succes Canadiens" (French).

Jim's response was immediate ... *"Dick this is just what Canadians need to hear. You have got to get this message out to Canadians. It will be an encouraging message for Canadians, and a strong program for radio stations."*

I have always respected Jim as a broadcaster and a caring person. He is one of the brightest persons Canadians have ever sent to Ottawa. He belongs in the Cabinet. The message Jim and I talked about is the fact that Canada is the greatest country in the world. Canadians have the best opportunity of anyone anywhere to succeed and achieve.

On February 4, 1985, "The Canadian Achievers" and "Les Succes Canadiens" launched coast to coast on a network of English language and French language radio stations carrying the message into virtually every community in Canada.

I will always be thankful to the radio stations who broadcast my series. They share the same belief in Canada and Canadians as Jim and I and millions of others do.

You will realize what I mean when you read the Achiever Stories in this book. The encouraging letters that I receive from the Prime Minister to truck drivers, from members of Parliament to homemakers, convinced me that a book telling about living Canadian Achievers had to be written. And hopefully placed in the hands of young Canadians.

Every year thousands of Canadians become achievers through believing in themselves and in Canada.

I know from my own personal experience that anyone who truly wants to can achieve. I've done it myself. So can you. Read on, learn from them, and believe in yourself. Because in Canada you can achieve whatever goal you set for yourself.

About Dick Drew

Host, creator and executive producer of "The Canadian Achievers".

Born in Edmonton—October 2, 1934. (Libra) Raised on a small farm near Morinville, Alberta. Attended an eight grade, one room school. His family moved to Vancouver, B.C. where at age 14 he became a merchant sailor. (See Foreword)

Owner, with wife Aline of radio station "CKAY." In Duncan, B.C. and "Drew Marketing & Productions Ltd." Vancouver. Since 1981 the latter company has been involved in the ownership and production of over 4000 episodes of various network radio programs including:

ENGLISH
—"The Canadian Achievers"
—"Successful Canadians"
—"Canada's Best on the Road to the Olympics"
—"Canadian Olympic Excellence"
—"Expo '86 Report"
—"Expo '86 Update"
—"Entertainment Flash Back"
—"The Giants of Rock 'n Roll"
—"A Tribute to Roy Orbison"
—"Discovery with David Suzuki" (associate producer)

FRENCH
—"Les Succes Canadiens"
—"L'Album Olympic Canadien"
—"Noel Chez Tex".

At present a pilot is underway for a television series of "The Canadian Achievers".

Awarded the Queen's Silver Anniversary Medal for his work in community service, Dick is a life member of Kin and a Past President of Rotary.

Aline and Dick live with their dog, Shasta high on a hill in Port Coquitlam, B.C. where he does his writing from a home-based, corner office which offers a spectacular, and often distracting view of the mountains.

Table of Contents

Editorials

My First Achiever

Paul Durish

Paul Durish is the first person featured in this book because Paul is the first Canadian Achiever I recall ever working with. Although at the time you would hardly call him an achiever. We first met in 1951 when we worked together on the S.S. Imperial Fredericton, an oil tanker hauling crude oil from Venezuela to Brazil, Argentina, and other South American and Caribbean countries. Paul was an assistant cook, I was a deck hand. We were both 17 years old. We formed a friendship then that continues today. Over the years I've stood on the sidelines and watched Paul risk it all time and time again as he's moved onward and upward through the boardrooms of Bay Street, and other financial centers.

Son of an immigrant Slovak fur trapper from Hunta, Ontario, Paul ran away from home to work the oil tankers.

"I was too small to be a deckhand, so I lied a lot and they made me an assistant cook."

Back in Canada, his next job was a clerk for the Yale Lock Company, he quit when he was refused a raise from $27. a week. His boss told him: *"You are a good man, but you have an insatiable lust for money."*

If Paul had such a lust, he kept it under wraps, because the obvious qualities projected by him are charm and trust. Those traits, plus one of the oldest forms of doing business, led to his quick climb to the top of the very competitive advertising, printing and farm implement businesses.

After leaving the lock company he worked his way up the Studebaker Corporation ladder until he became International Advertising Manager. Studebaker ceased production and Durish was unemployed. He'd learned a lot about advertising and decided to start his own firm.

He rejected offers to go to work for other corporations even though he was strapped with a mortgage, wife and three young kids. Instead, at 28, he struck out on his own. With very little capital and a two month lease on a tiny downtown Toronto office, Durish & Associates was launched. His first client was Peugeot Canada. He promised to provide the French car manufacturer with creative commercials for prime time radio and television advertising. The difference from other agencies was that Durish was willing to take payment in cars, not cash.

The scheme worked very well. Peugeot was not putting out any cash, which comes out of profits. "If they owed me $3,500, they'd pay me one car, which in actual fact was worth $7,000 retail."

Paul then approached many of Canada's largest radio and television stations and bartered the cars for advertising. *"They could use the cars for news cruisers or for promotions and prizes,"* he said.

Within ten years Durish had acquired real estate, farm equipment, printing and publishing companies. He was a success. At the age of 38, when most people are looking 30 years ahead to their pension, Paul Durish, with assets of over $10 million, announced his retirement. He was going to sit back, spend time on his 52 foot yacht which he kept in the Caribbean, and enjoy the fruits of his labour. Those of us who knew him knew it wouldn't last. Paul was adamant it would. In actual fact it lasted about a year.

During that time Paul liquidated everything except his extensive land holdings. While visiting Kenya in 1978, he saw animals allowed to roam freely to the delight of the visitors watching. He decided to establish his own private game farm.

The Klahanie Wildlife Sanctuary is now home to hundreds of deer (five varieties), timber wolves, llamas, yak, buffalo, wild geese, ducks, peacocks and eight stocked fish ponds. The only fence at the 150-acre site just north of Erin, Ontario, is the one surrounding the property. The Durish family may look out of the windows of their sumptuous converted barn home and see dozens of animals intermingling in the wild.

"One day we counted eleven peacocks. We don't operate it as a zoo. Only select, invited groups come here: seniors, disabled children, school groups. My wife, Reta gives them a tour of the animals, a chance to fish, and lunch at the house."

He credits the peace and quiet and much of his success to his wife from a second marriage, Reta, who combines the talents of legal secretary, secretary, bookkeeper, wife and mother.

Durish's own formal education consisted of school at South Porcupine, St. Catherines, and Merriton in Ontario, and Millard Fillmore College in the United States. He considers ambition and innovation at least as important as formal education.

Although Paul claims he is semi-retired, he still puts in a full day's work. *"I'm really trying to slow down, I can't see spending your entire life just chasing the buck."*

What advice does he have for other entrepreneurs who would like to match his success?

"The barter system can still be used. And with Third World Countries who haven't the cash, it should be used. Our profits in the advertising business were enormous compared with the usual 15% earned by agencies using money.

"Also, learn to delegate authority. I never had an office in any of my companies. I had a secretary check every day and phone me. I made visits, but mainly I hired good people and left them alone.

"I think the banking industry is smart to lend money to small business. Banks now acknowledge that entrepreneurs are the backbone of this country's business future.

"When I started out, entrepreneurism was a bad word. Now it is THE word.

"Look for opportunity out of chaos. Then run with it."

Paul Durish is proof positive that in Canada you can achieve . . . no matter what your background is.

The Lady with a Heart

Dr. Virginia Gudas

Virginia Gudas knew from an early age growing up in Montreal that she was going to be a doctor. She didn't visualize that one day she would be the chief heart transplant surgeon at Vancouver General Hospital.

"The moment I knew I wanted to go into the field of transplantation began when Christian Barnard made medical history with the world's first heart transplant.

As for being attracted to medicine in the first place, my interest was based on two things: biology and the interaction with people. It made a good combination as far as I was concerned."

Virginia studied medicine at Memorial University in Newfoundland and at Queen's in Ontario. For 18 months she studied heart transplants at Stanford in California and at 34 years old became the chief heart transplant surgeon at Vancouver General Hospital. She also specializes in other cardiovascular and thoracic operations, such as heart-lung.

The Barnard Heart Transplant really changed her life however.

"It was back in 1967 and it boggled my mind. From that moment on I knew I had a goal, something to work towards, to achieve."

But wasn't she afraid she might fail in a field that, until then, had been pretty well the domain of men?

"It's still a predominantly male field; I'm the only female doctor involved in heart transplants in Canada. But, that's because, as so often happens, women have not had adequate role models. Also, it is very difficult for a woman to have a full time career and to be a wife and mother. These both deter many women from going into such specialized fields.

"In fact, there aren't enough women in the surgical specialties of medicine. It's not because they lack the aptitude or skill, but it is a matter of interest and how badly you want it.

"It's a cultural thing too: I'm being interviewed today by broadcasters and journalists because I am a female working in this area. I've been able to surmount all that because I did have good role models and I've forgotten the

fact that I'm a female and don't let that deter me, or make me feel any different from my male colleagues."

It's a full time job and one that keeps her hopping.

"Sometimes it's non-stop. I'm on call 24 hours a day, seven days a week for transplants in addition to my regular duties as a heart surgeon. It is stressful at times. But I enjoy what I do and I put in many hours."

Virginia, who performed British Columbia's first heart transplant in December 1988, often must go directly to the donor whose heart is to be removed. This sometimes means flying to the donor hospital. She removes the heart from the brain dead donor and has four hours to insert it in the recipient. After the lengthy operation, the patient is monitored in intensive care and Virginia goes to the Doctor's lounge to relax, hoping she won't get 'beeped' too soon.

"I like to walk and I'd love to walk all around Stanley Park but I get beeped too often and there aren't enough phones out there."

The issue that affects most doctors is the death of a patient. Although her patients are in a high-risk group compared to, say, a gallstone sufferer, it doesn't make facing the death of a patient any easier.

"I see death from the perspective of my training. We all do, whether doctor, nurse, paramedic. We are trained to expect it. It's never easy. After we have done our best, and the patient dies, what else can we do? It is particularly hard if the patient is young. If someone older dies because of rejection or infection, those are the realities of transplantation. If I've done my best, and I always try to, then I don't feel devastated by it.

"You can't work in this business without hoping that next year there'll be a better way. You keep hoping and expanding your own knowledge in that direction. Twenty years ago, when heart transplants started in the U.S. one out of every four survived. Now it's four out of five. It's only because of the improved methods of how we treat rejection and infection that we've come such a long way.

"The result is we can now return a patient to a way of life they may not have enjoyed for 20 or 30 years. We're not perfect; we're still going to lose patients, but that's part of the learning process."

Virginia has important advice for anyone planning a medical career:

"When I'm lecturing to interns who want to get into my field, I convey more by attitude than words that this is an exciting, important job. I don't consider myself a role model, but I suppose I am whether I want to be or not. I am not a chauvinist and I don't like to single out women in particular. But if I can be a good role model I'll do my best to propagate the profession. I encourage students to enter the field of bypass surgery because it is exciting. Last but not least, I think it is important in any form of work that they get enthusiastic and excited about it. I find it a great shame that many people with aptitude never really get motivated.

"If our children got a genuine interest in school, early on, we wouldn't have the high school drop-outs we now have. I'm not saying that university is the be all and the end all, but no matter what career they choose, it should be fulfilling. I think spending eight hours a day doing something that is loathsome is a punishment. The two days holiday out of seven days a week is a very small reward.

"When this heart-transplantation business I'm in becomes unenjoyable for me I will seriously look for another career. But right now, this is just what I want to be doing!" Dr. Virginia Gudas... another Canadian Achiever.

"I don't know the key to success. But I know the key to failure is trying to please everybody."
—*Bill Cosby*

An Inspiration to Everyone

David Young

In doing research for the series, I'm always being charged up by the enthusiasm and positive attitude of the people I meet. But nothing moves me more than so called handicapped people who have overcome so very much. People like Karl Hilzinger, the legless skier in the silver suit. And this amazing man, David Young. A quadriplegic, felled by polio at 19. Confined to a chair for 36 years. Unable to breath properly because his diaphragm is paralysed. Yet he's become a well known artist. He paints by holding the brush in his mouth. His seascapes are among the most beautiful you will ever see.

After he was stricken, he studied painting for 20 years. He'd never painted before. He had been a fisherman and logger living in Sointula, a fishing village off the northern coast of Vancouver Island. Later he taught painting for 18 years.

He's done over 4,000 paintings. As he says, with a smile, *"that includes the good, the bad, and the ugly."*

His paintings have been sold worldwide. Limited edition prints sell for up to 800 dollars. He does a very brisk business in cards as well. No sir, there is no holding him back. In fact, just recently he's developed a keen interest in doing etchings.

David credits his success to having a positive attitude and to being married for the past 20 years to Patricia, a charming lady from Edmunston, New Brunswick.

David may be stuck in a wheelchair but you'll never catch him sitting still. He's busy remodelling their Ladner, B.C. home to accommodate an art gallery to exhibit his and other artists works. As David says, *"I think any-body can sit back, feel sorry, and ask 'what have I got left. What can I do?'"* *"With the advent of computers a quad can do a lot if given the chance."*

That's so very true. Handicapped people can do so very much. They're proving it every day. The biggest problem they must overcome is not their physical handicap, it's our mental handicap when it comes to working with and understanding them... Canada is a better country because of the achievements of the so-called handicapped.

Retire? Me? Never!

Nathan Gold

I spoke to Nathan Gold over the phone and we agreed to meet the next morning in person.

"I'll send my car around at 7 a.m." he said. *"It's a silver four-door Mercedes, Dick. Do you think you will recognize it?"*

I told him I didn't think there would be many cars fitting that description outside my Toronto hotel at that time in the morning!

As it turned out, Nathan came along so we could chat on the way out to inspect his clothing factory north of the 401.

"I'll get my chef to whip us up some breakfast," he said. Which he did.

He was then 75, and looked amazingly fit and young for a man who had retired to a condo in Florida but got bored so he came back to Canada and started up a whole new business again. He retired in 1967 for the first time, Canada's Centennial Year, he was 55. That retirement lasted seven months before he was itching to get back into the saddle.

"I went into the fashion business almost as soon as I arrived from Poland at 14 years of age in 1926. I went from operating a sewing machine in a sweat shop to owning 10 clothing factories."

By age 55 Nathan thought he had had enough, sold the factories, headed south to his Florida condo, *"And within three days I was bored"*.

Nathan saw a chance to get back into business by buying a 50 percent interest in a 10 store chain employing 90 people. It was called Brody's Town and Country Limited. Over the next 20 years the chain grew to become 209 stores coast to coast and employing 1,300. Sales for 1991 are expected to reach $90 million.

All of this is of academic interest to Nathan Gold because at 79 he decided to retire again. He sold his 50 percent interest and retired again to his condo in Florida.

When we spoke on the phone in January 1991, he said he was once more bored with retirement and was coming back to Toronto to start *"something completely different"*.

"I haven't decided what it will be yet, but I have already opened my office and can't wait to get started. I'm too young for this retirement business."

His secret to success?

"It's simply a matter of letting the other guy worry while you're planning your next move."

Would he do it again?

"You betcha! Definitely. I enjoyed the fashion business. It's a good business to be in and my advice to young people today is to get into the clothing trade. It is always going to be with us. And it's interesting.

"Maintain a positive outlook. I always have. Hard working young people can do very well in this industry."

I asked Nathan Gold to let me know what his next venture is going to be. Whatever it is it will become another success for him.

When we first met in 1987 Nathan said he was planning a book on the clothing industry in Canada. I do hope he finds time to write it and includes several chapters of his own interesting life.

"Marry Money"
—*Max Schulman's advice to aspiring authors*

Hire Good People

David Ainsworth

When you first meet David Ainsworth of 100 Mile House in British Columbia's cariboo country, it's difficult picturing him as head of a corporate conglomerate. Nevertheless, sales in 1990 of Ainsworth Lumber Co. Ltd. reached $100 million.

"When we started up our portable sawmill outside 100 Mile House in the 1950's, we had six people working for us, including my wife, Susan. Today we employ directly or indirectly about 1,500.

"Sometimes I wonder how I got here. I remember a remark that was attributed to Lord Martin Cecil (until his death a few years ago, the leader of the Emissaries, a Christian sect very strong in 100 Mile House and area) who founded this community, that he did each day what needed to be done. Simple advice, but I guess that's what we've done."

Any secrets to pass on to entrepreneurs just starting out or thinking of starting a business or a new career?

"I think if we did anything different that might have contributed to our

success is that we were fortunate enough to find good people to work with us. I say work with us, not for us. That's the big difference.

"It wasn't all rosy. There were times when Susan and I felt like chucking it but we couldn't chuck it. We probably wanted to give up but we weren't able to!

"If you want to be a success today, you have to be able to stick. And you have to go for it. Take a chance. First of all, you have to have the ability to feel that you can take a chance. There's just as many opportunities today—perhaps more—than ever before. There doesn't appear to be, and you may have to look for them, but if you are the right sort of person, you'll find them."

After 40 years, Ainsworth Lumber has grown from that one small sawmill to become five lumber mills and several related companies. In addition, in 1990 Ainsworth landed a 25 year contract to harvest up to 330,000 cubic meters of pulpwood annually to supply a proposed $60 million oriented-strandboard plant. The timber was to be logged off crown land with the plant creating 500 direct and indirect jobs. So David Ainsworth's little sawmill operation continues to grow. Only recently, however, did the company move into the world of computers.

"We resisted it for as long as we could for the sake of what we saw as simplicity and hands-on communication. But like everything else, it just grew on us. Computerized management is a fact of life and we've just had to learn it. Some of us can't understand it very well but when I think of how we used to have to order parts for the mill, it's worth it.

"When we first came to 100 Mile House I had to go down in the evening and sit in the little old phone office and wait for my turn to make a call. Today we have a computer system that connects all our operations in Vancouver, Lillooet, Savona, Abbotsford, 100 Mile and Clinton. There's a great difference, no doubt about it. Businesses are family-run. If you can get a team to work together as well as this family has done, you have done well. I certainly can't take the credit for what we've done. I think my wife Susan should have most of the credit for all the suffering, privations and long hours she has put in.

"There were many months at the beginning where we didn't pay ourselves any salary, just took out enough to pay the bills and buy groceries. We didn't suffer, but there were lots of times we were a little bit desperate to pay the bills.

"People ask me if I had the chance to do it over would I do it differently. If we'd had more capital we might have done it differently but we didn't so I guess we'd do what we did then. We were fortunate in that we had the cooperation of the Federal Business Development Bank. We've had some form of F.B.D.B. loan now for over 30 years. Our first loan was for $60,000. Today that would be the interest for a week! We still deal with them, that's a

relationship we are proud of as well.

"I guess that's important if you are going into business today, just as it was yesterday. We have kept most of our employees and our suppliers. We treat each other with respect. If we could rely on them 30 years ago, they are probably the kind of company and people you can rely on today. We had people like A. J. Forsythe in the steel business who supported us when we needed them. There were times when he had to go to them and say we couldn't pay the bill that month. We told them the reason why: maybe the loan hadn't come through from F.B.D.B., or whatever. And they would say they'd ship it anyway and if the bill went too long they might have to charge us interest.

"It's been a mutual support system. Those kind of people deserve our support too and I hope that we have been good customers as they have been good to us."

Corporations the size of Ainsworth Lumber who are situated in small communities like 100 Mile House are fair game for everyone who needs a handout or charity. How does a home-based industry cope with all the request for funds?

"That's a difficult decision to make and one we must make all the time. Requests for donations increase every year and we have had to draw the line somewhere. We allow the use of our company helicopter for crisis use. As for donations, we try to stay with anything that deals with children. If it's for kids, we'll look at it. If it's for adults, we may not be able to look at it. The community always thinks you are big and available and we try to be, but it is not always possible."

Hiring good people and working with good suppliers is part of David Ainsworth's formula for success. Personal integrity, hard work and the willingness to take a chance are other factors. It's helped one man who used to cut trees down with an axe to become head of a conglomerate. And he says the chances of repeating his story are better than ever today! And when David Ainsworth tells you that, you've got to believe him!

Flying High Again

Cliff & Harvey Freisen

Bearskin Airlines serves northern Ontario from their base in Thunder Bay. It's owned and operated by two brothers, Cliff and Harvey Freisen. They bought the Airline in 1978. It had 5 small planes and a staff of 40. By 1985 they had 20 planes and a staff of 130 and were virtually bankrupt. They had expanded too fast. Rather than quit, they regrouped, reorganized and saved the airline. So much so that in 1988 the Ontario government and the Chamber of Commerce awarded Bearskin Airlines the Outstanding Business Achievement Award. Cliff Freisen explained when we met... *"It was tremendous to receive an award like that. It gave us a lot of confidence and it gave our management staff a lot of confidence to come from being virtually bankrupt, and then receive an outstanding business achievement award. It proves that when you work hard you can become very successful."*

The Freisen brothers now have 28 airplanes, 225 staff members and sales this year nearing the 20 million mark.

Being bankrupt is not a new story, it happens to companies all the time. The strength of Cliff & Harvey's story is that rather than declare bankruptcy, they hung in, cut expenses, and turned the airline around. Today it's one of Canada's most successful privately owned regional airlines. What is Cliff's advice for others whose company may someday face a similar situation?

"People have to be very very persistent. They have to never never give up. They have to keep going. They have to be positive. Keep a positive attitude and share a lot of the problems that you are having with your management. Keep them informed so that they can understand what is happening, because they are the people who are going to help you through."

Now that they are flying high again, what is their formula for staying up there?

"We set goals for ourselves, when we achieve those goals we set new goals. That way you continue to grow."

"One of the symptoms of an approaching nervous breakdown is the belief that one's work is terribly important."
—Bertrand Russell

He's Bringing Another New Industry to New Brunswick

Bill Stanley

There is a lovely area about an hour's drive from Saint John, New Brunswick that is called Interlake. This beautiful low-lying region is home to many creatures of the wild, particularly deer. Deer are everywhere. A lot of them in Bill Stanley's backyard. He's a deer farmer.

"Yes, there are a lot of deer out here." Bill agrees. *"But I don't farm the wild ones. The deer I farm are from New Zealand where there are approximately a million deer behind fences being farmed for breeding and venison production."*

The imported deer are called Red Deer as opposed to the New Brunswick variety of Whitetailed Deer. The two are genetically different and do not breed. There are other differences:

"The meat is more tender, less gamey and altogether very acceptable to the North American palate."

But how did a graduate in electrical engineering working as a consultant and executive for the cable television industry in Canada and the United States turn to deer farming?

"It started for me when Tony Pierce, New Zealand's Minister of Agriculture, visited New Brunswick promoting deer farming. I was intrigued and thought it might provide a new industry for this province. So I went there and saw what the New Zealanders were doing. I found deer farming is a $100 million business there. We flew all over the country, visited abattoirs, saw where diet supplements were being made from antlers, met with deer farmers and visited the areas where Red Deer were once hunted for bounty."

The result was the formation of Fundy Deer Farms Ltd. and the importation of New Zealand deer for breeding stock.

"Initially, what we have here is a breeding farm with stock to sell to other people who will in turn sell to others and through that pyramid-breeding program provide a thriving New Brunswick industry. We're already selling stock to farmers in Maine as well."

Always looking for new opportunities and doing it successfully, Bill Stanley realized the importance of allowing others to invest in his latest brainchild.

"I don't expect to make a profit for about five years while we're building up our herd. A female or 'hind' is worth about $3,000 at present but that will drop down to maybe $500 as production rises and supply meets demand. There is such a demand in the finer restaurants in North America for venison that it never has a chance to hit the supermarkets."

Aside from its unique flavour, sweeter and more refined than beef, what makes it so popular that people will pay such high prices for it?

"It is low in fat and cholesterol and ideal for people who want a high protein meat but don't want the high number of calories."

Sounds ideal. But how do the deer from New Zealand adapt to the colder Canadian climate?

"Very well indeed. No problem at all. We started off with a nucleus of 470 females and 30 stags; we now predict that by selling only the stags and retaining all the females for breeding stock, and importing more, we should have 7,500 in three years, 10,000 in six years and 20,000 in 10 years."

Forty youngsters were being born at the time of this interview. On 150 acres of fenced land, the deer look after themselves without much supervision and only occasionally have to have veterinarians assist them in calfing.

Bill Stanley is not just a deer farmer of course. Besides owning deer farms and radio stations, he is deeply involved in the cable television industry in New Brunswick, the U.S. and, more recently, in the United Kingdom. His Fundy Cable Ltd. and affiliated companies serve approximately 88,000 sub-scribers.

"But I am concentrating quite heavily on my new venture. I think that is the key to success in any business. You have to concentrate on what you are doing, and hire good people who know what they are doing."

There are other deer farm operations in Canada. Notably Canadian Fallow Deer Company in British Columbia, which has already pre-sold venison to Japan for the next five years. They raise a different type of New Zealand deer. The Red Deer on Bill's farm cannot breed with the strays that occa-sionally come up to the fences but they will breed with elk and that is why they are not allowed to be shipped past the Manitoba/Ontario border where the elk begin to roam.

Advice for the new person starting out in business?

"Do your research and make sure you have a good product and one that will fly. When we started in the cable business the regulations were very un-certain. Now it's the same with the deer industry. We have to proceed with caution, to establish profitable methods of operation, make sure we can maintain a very high quality product. This is a whole new industry for us and will take time and close monitoring through the series from breeding to meat production to exporting."

The message then is quite clear for the entrepreneur, no matter what field he or she gets into, know the product thoroughly, work with experts, con-centrate on the operation and expect to wait three, five, or even ten years be-fore you can ultimately expect success.

Bill Stanley, cable and radio station owner, deer farmer, employs about 450 people and grosses in sales about $45 million with an annual growth of about $15 million a year.

His biggest kick?

"We are just delighted for once to be able to export our technology to other countries both in the cable end of things, and our newly acquired ex-pertise in deer farming. I feel really good about that!" He's another Cana-dian Achiever.

"You can't steal second base and keep one foot on first."
—*Unknown*

Mr. Nice

Fred Davis

In 1985, I landed a contract with the Royal Bank to produce a daily network radio show called "Expo '86 Update". I phoned Fred Davis and asked if he would like to host it. We had never met. But everything I had ever heard about him was good. His reputation in the industry is so clean it's embarrassing. Fred agreed to meet and discuss it. To my everlasting joy he agreed and there began a most pleasant 41 week production assignment.

The series was heard daily coast to coast in Canada, Alaska and Washington State. We produced 205 episodes.

Fred Davis is the epitome of the words. . . . real pro, Mr. Nice, reliable, agreeable. And one I would like to create; "Mr. Arrive at the Studio Early." Unheard of in the industry.

In television today it's an achievement if a successful series lasts six or seven years before going off the air and into the land of perpetual re-runs through syndication. "Family Ties" starring Canada's Michael J. Fox, is a perfect example. However, the TV show Fred hosts "Front Page Challenge" has been on the air for 34 years. And Fred has been there since day one. Many credit the show's success and longevity to Fred's warm personality which shines through your TV set. His ability to control and keep the show moving is a large part of the show's success. Just ask its producer Ray McConnell.

Over the years Fred has had numerous offers to head south of the border. But he prefers to remain in Canada. Here he can do his own thing at his own pace and play trumpet in a band when the urge moves him.

Fred Davis. . . Mr. Nice. . . another Canadian Achiever.

The Sky's Not Her Limit

Dr. Roberta Bondar

Roberta Bondar's high school guidance counsellor in Sault Ste. Marie, told her to forget about science; she just didn't have what it takes. Many graduations later, Dr. Roberta Bondar is in intense training as Canada's first female astronaut. She is not only a distinguished and superlative scientist, but also a neurologist, pathologist and accomplished pilot.

Dr. Bondar was on the staff of McMaster University's Medical Centre in Hamilton when she flirted with curiosity by answering an intriguing ad for a job with the space program. She was one of some forty-three hundred applicants. Countless screenings, interviews and medical tests narrowed the list. Dr. Roberta Bondar was eventually chosen as one of the six members of the

Canadian astronaut program. She is currently training at the Canadian Space Agency in Ottawa, with frequent briefings at NASA's famed Mission Control in Houston.

Dr. Roberta Bondar has proved that the sky's the limit when it comes to Canadian achievement. She has also proved her high school guidance counsellor to be dead wrong about her scientific ability. I wonder what Roberta would be doing today if she had taken the counsellor's advice. She's another Canadian Achiever.

Able Walker

Norm Rolston

Experts will tell you that in order to bring a product to market successfully you must plan, evaluate, research and strategize before you even begin. None of those principles can be applied to Norm Rolston, yet two years after launching his "Able Walker" invention from the back of his van, he has run up sales of over $5 million.

"I got the idea for the Able Walker from watching my aunt Maida bending over to pick up her two canes so she could get walking," Norman says. *"It was a painful experience for her so, using old shopping carts and a stroller, soon I had a walker that she could use to hold on to, to go shopping with. Well, her friends soon needed one like it and so on, and since then, three years ago, I haven't had a day off since I built the first one.*

"There were walkers around at the time I designed mine but, they didn't have casters on the front so you could turn it. There are other features: the handholds are at the front where they give real support. And you can put on the brakes when you have to."

There have been very few brakes put on anything else in his life since Norman got his idea for the "Able Walker". From a busy office-cum-museum in Burnaby, British Columbia, his factory builds the product and salespeople fan out across the continent making life easier for people who have walking disabilities. But overcoming the skepticism of the medical profession was difficult at first:

"They had reason to be wary. Other walkers weren't safe. They toppled over too easily. But now I have doctors say to me, 'Norman I wasn't too sure about that at first. But I have no doubts about it now.' I've been told by doctors that patients they had who could never before attend their clinics come in with their "Able Walkers" confident as can be. It's the change of attitude, the independence that's been given to them. "I just borrowed some good ideas and made them come together in place."

"Able Walker" isn't Norman's first entrepreneurial venture. In 1973 he turned a crane truck into the Rolston Crane and Freight Ltd. and now owns

15 cranes and related equipment. But Able Walker takes up so much of his time (in mid-1990 he had shipped 20,000 units to places around the world) he has passed control of the crane company to his children and concentrates solely on manufacturing, sales and distribution of the walking device.

"I'm getting a lesson in geography with all these foreign sales orders coming in."

Norman shrugs off his lack of formal education. He had only a grade 7 education, but never let even that get in the way of success.

"The biggest regret in my life was not leaving school three or four years earlier. My only credential is a D.O.P.E.—Doctor of Personal Experience."

His unorthodox launching of the Able Walker nevertheless led to his first orders and ultimate success.

"My wife Myrtle and I ran off a bunch of flyers with a picture demonstrating a woman using the Able Walker. It had a few lines describing it and the price, $259.50. We stuck these flyers up in every laundromat, bulletin board, old folk's homes, rec and bingo hall from Vancouver to Saskatoon. We practically lived right out of the van. By the time we got back home to Burnaby orders were starting to roll in. And they haven't stopped since."

His unorthodox style and dress and the fact that he runs a free museum out of his business premises does not mean that he hasn't planned from the beginning to market a good product and back it with a full money-back guarantee.

"We've been fortunate to get good media coverage. And I have done my own commercials on television. But the product sells itself. I have no hesitation in saying that it is a good product."

Norman thinks of his invention almost as transportation because it makes people mobile again which reminds him that he has always had a fascination for transportation.

"My father worked for Henry Ford and he gained a great deal of knowledge from that. I have always been a great admirer of Henry Ford myself. I have a couple of Model T's in my museum and a rare Model S."

What's Norm's advice for people who want to market an invention or make a success in their own field.

"People who make a success of themselves often have to go against all odds. Like Henry Ford, or Rick Hansen, people are always telling you: it's not sensible to carry on, that will never work, if that was any good it would have been done before. Forget them.

"Believe in yourself. Your university education, not that I have any, lays a good groundwork for a beginning but it's no meal ticket. Don't forget the most important asset you have: commonsense! Build from there. Education can be a help to you but don't let it be a hindrance to you too. Some initials after your name don't mean a thing in many cases.

"I see so many things out there that need doing. Pick something that needs some work to be done on it and improve on it. As soon as I get a million of these walkers on the market, I'm moving onto other things. I have other assistive devices in mind for such places as the labour market, and in the medical field."

Common sense, enthusiasm, and keeping formal education in the proper perspective. Norman Rolston is a youthful man in his late fifties. He's young enough in spirit and heart to continue to make changes that will affect the way we live—and walk. He thinks you can do it too. And you can!

Wisdom comes more from living than from studying.

—Unknown

Everybody, Somebody, Anybody, Nobody...

Broadcast May 30, 1990

Too often we hear the expression... "that's not my job"... or... "that's not my responsibility". Well this is a story about four people named *everybody, somebody, anybody* and *nobody*. It was sent to me by a listener from Montreal who asked that I share it with you. Are you ready? Here it is. ...

It seems there was an important job to be done and *everybody* was sure that *somebody* would do it. *Anybody* could have done it, but *nobody* did it. *Somebody* got angry about that, because it was *everybody's* job. *Everybody* thought *anybody* could do it but *nobody* realized that *everybody* wouldn't do it. It ended up that *everybody* blamed *somebody* when *nobody* did what *anybody* could have done.

I want to thank the listener who sent me that story to share with you today. It seems these days we hear all too often about those four mysterious people, *everybody, somebody, nobody,* and *anybody*. Young people are being brought up to believe that letting someone else do it is the way to go. It's unfortunate that in today's busy and competitive world we're giving far too much responsibility to *everybody, somebody, anybody, and nobody.* and *nothing* happens.

"There are two kinds of problems, those that get better, and those that get worse."

—The Rt. Hon. John Turner

The Godfather of Cancon

Walt Grealis

Cancon is an abbreviation of the two words . . . Canadian Content. There's a lot of cancon on radio and television today thanks largely in part to Walt Grealis . . . founder of R.P.M. Magazine.

Twenty-five years ago, Walt recognized the need for a Canadian music industry magazine. Until then there wasn't one . . . everything came in from the States. So he started a weekly magazine called R.P.M. It's a financial success now . . . but it sure didn't make financial sense back then.

The experts told him he would fail. They said Canada's music industry wasn't large enough to support its own weekly magazine. But Walt went ahead anyway. *"The first few editions were on one page foolscap run off on an old duplicating machine."* It appeared as if the experts may have been right. Did he ever feel like quitting? *"About three times a week, but we managed to hang on."* Today, R.P.M. Magazine is very successful.

In appreciation of Walt's enormous contribution these past 25 years . . . the industry gave him a special Juno Award, and named him . . . the Godfather of Cancon.

Walt Grealis has proven the experts wrong. That's usually what happens when you have confidence in yourself and your idea. Just hang in with it and don't give up. You will achieve your goal just like Walt Grealis . . . another Canadian Achiever.

The Pumpkin King of the World

Howard Dill

When Linus of the cartoon strip sneaks out into the garden each Hallowe'en to await the arrival of "The Great Pumpkin", Peanuts and Lucy are more than skeptical that such a creature exists. They jeer. Meanwhile, in Windsor, Nova Scotia, Howard Dill is up to his neck in the largest pumpkins in the world.

They don't call Howard "The Pumpkin King of the World" for nothing. The Great Pumpkin, indeed. Howard broke the world record four years in a row and is listed in the Guinness Book of World Records. Some competitors wanted him banned from further competition. He was just too darned good.

Now, just a minute here! Who would want to grow great, orange Hallowe'en lanterns full of pulp and seeds and weighing up to 700 pounds? That's a lot of pumpkin pie!

"It's not for pumpkin pie," Howard says. *"These pumpkins are grown*

from genetically-improved seed stock. A technique I developed myself.'' On Canada's Thanksgiving Day 18 weigh-off sites around the world competed for the largest pumpkin title.

Yes, but what's the incentive?

"There's a lot of satisfaction in being called the Pumpkin King of the World. I have been successful in winning four world championships but competition is becoming stronger every year as the interest grows. There are a lot of people out there who want to be king or queen of something. Why not pumpkins?''

The largest pumpkin Howard had grown to date weighed 616 pounds and that was only good enough for second prize. A Chicago deejay auctioned the pumpkin off and proceeds went to a children's hospital in the Windy City.

There's a sidebar story to the Chicago pumpkin.

"It took longer to clear it through American customs than it took to fly it there from Nova Scotia. They brought in the drug squad because they couldn't believe it was just a pumpkin in the crate.''

Under the terms of agreement with pumpkin buyers, they may keep a few seeds, but the bulk comes back to Howard.

"The secret in growing big pumpkins is the seed, and that's my secret.''

From little pumpkin seeds large businesses grow. Howard Dill now has two farms in the United States, 10 acres in Colorado and 10 acres in California, where his Canadian seed is sent for reproduction. But his main patch is still at Windsor, 40 miles from Halifax, where he also raises fruit and beef cattle on a 100 acre farm. Although the main focus is on pumpkins, and, more particularly, the seeds that will grow world-beaters.

"I recently had a phone call from China and another from Leningrad in the Soviet Union asking about my seeds. It seems people all over the world are hooked on growing giant pumpkins.''

In the winter months, Howard and his son Danny get down to the serious job of filling mail order requests from Canada, the U.S., Britain, Holland, Japan and elsewhere. In 1990 they responded to more than 5,000 such letters. Seeds, seven to a packet, sell for $5.00. To increase the mail order business, the Dills plan to bring out a seed catalogue. They already advertise through a newsletter that extols the wisdom of buying seeds from "Atlantic Giant": *"if you want to win the Lemans, you need to drive a Ferrari, not a pick-up truck. If you want to go to the moon you need a rocket, not a pogo stick. If you want to raise a world-class pumpkin, your choice is clear: Howard Dill's Atlantic Giant.''*

According to an article in the May 1990 Financial Post, Howard Dill's annual seed production generates $1.4 million in sales.

That's a far cry from Howard's humble beginning. He got his start by following in his father's footsteps 30 years ago. His dad grew big pumpkins for a hobby. Howard saw the potential of marketing seeds from the improved variety of product he developed. At the time he began to compete in fairs and exhibitions across the continent, a 70 or 80 pounder was guaranteed a title.

The 100-pound barrier, reached in the early sixties, was the equivalent of the four-minute mile.

It was Howard's own determination and foresight that led to the breeding of the best seed in the world and why growers around the world are now clamoring for them.

A self-taught geneticist, Howard developed the species and protects the fruits of his labour by having the species patented under the U.S. Plant Variety Protection Act.

The hope of growing a giant is one thing, but how do you move the blessed thing once it takes over your garden patch?

"As there got to be more and more serious growers out there, ways and means developed to move them safely. There are pumpkin carrying devices now with five or six handles on them so that people can grab and lift the pumpkin into a half-ton truck or whatever."

Would quiet, unassuming, almost shy, Howard Dill get into this now highly-competitive business given the chance to do it again?

"Looking back to the time when I went away to the World Championships in 1976 in Ohio, I never realized what the good Lord had in store for me. I love it. It's made my life!"

It's also made him a Canadian Achiever featured in the National Geographic Magazine, the Wall Street Journal, the Old Farmers Geographic, and this book.

"You cannot achieve unless you believe."
—*D.D.*

He Overcame Oppression to Achieve His Goals

The Hon. Lincoln Alexander

Lincoln Alexander had every reason to become a bitter person. Because he was black, he had to work twice as hard to achieve half as much as the average young man his age.

Lincoln's parents came from the Caribbean around 1918, to Toronto, where blacks were banned from many places. His dad became a railway porter, his mother a maid. Lincoln was born a few years after their arrival. In 1940, the young Lincoln moved to Hamilton and took a job in a war plant.

But like most young men of the time, he wanted to serve his country. He joined the air force and became a corporal. After the war, he earned his BA from McMaster University but, because he was black, his job offer was factory work, not office work.

Undaunted, Lincoln went back to school, earned a degree in law, and began practising. Later, he ran for federal politics, lost on his first try, won the next five elections and became Canada's first black cabinet minister in 1979. On September 20, 1985, he was sworn in as Ontario's 24th Lieutenant Governor.

His Honour Lincoln Alexander... a determined individual who overcame oppressive odds to achieve his goals... another Canadian Achiever.

"Talk is cheap because supply exceeds demand."
—*Unknown*

Sam Sets Records Selling Records

Sam Sniderman

In 1937 Sam Sniderman was working in his brother's radio store on Yonge St. in Toronto. (Back then they didn't have TV) He was 17, he suggested they open a record department and he should run it. That was the beginning of 'Sam the Record Man'... a chain of 138 record stores stretching across Canada.

This year (1990) Sam will sell over 80 million dollars worth of records. The early days were darn tough. Ask Sam what he'd do differently and he'll tell you with that perennial twinkle in his eyes...

"Have a rich father or else have a big ego."

Sam readily admits to having a big ego. Life size full color cut outs of a smiling Sam greet customers in every outlet. The Canadian Recording Industry have much to thank Sam for. The door to his cluttered upstairs office is always open to Canadian talent. He's received numerous industry awards including the prestigious 'Walt Grealis Juno Award' for his support and promotion of Canadian music and Canadian artists. Their way of saying thanks to a man whose belief and support of Canadian talent has helped launch the career of many, including Anne Murray.

Sam Sniderman... another Canadian Achiever.

"Some people find oil, others don't."
—*Billionaire J. Paul Getty when asked how he became rich*

Blue Jays Head Honcho

Paul Beeston

As far as Paul Beeston is concerned, every day is Saturday for him, meaning "take me out to the ball game." Paul is president and chief operating officer of the Toronto Blue Jays of the American Baseball League. Although he says he was extremely lucky to get the position, more than luck played a part in his rise to such a responsible job, while doing exactly what he wants to do.

"I have been a sports fan all my life. I was determined one way or another to get into some end of the business. I wasn't a good enough player to make it that way, but there are other ways to make your dream job a reality."

Born in Welland, Ontario in 1945, he graduated with a B.A. from the University of Western Ontario and almost immediately began working towards his chartered accountants designation with the nation-wide firm of Coopers and Lybrand in London, Ontario. In only five short years he was made London manager.

But he still had the desire to find a job in the sports field. He jumped at the chance when approached by a group trying to attract a major league club to Toronto.

"It was a frustrating experience at first. The San Francisco Franchise that was supposed to come to Toronto decided to stay in San Francisco. I thought my dreams had gone down the drain. Subsequently a franchise was granted to Toronto under a league expansion and I was offered a job."

In fact, Paul was the first employee hired by the Jays, on May 10, 1976, only one and one-half months after the granting of the franchise. Starting as Vice President, Finance. A couple more promotions and Paul took over as president and chief operating officer in January 1989.

What advice does Paul Beeston have for young people today who might feel frustrated and scared thinking there's not much hope for them out there in the business world?

"Do the best you can do and try to be the right person at the right time. In professional sports, whether it be football, hockey or baseball, you have to pay your dues. It may mean starting at the bottom. Take any job and do it well. You may have to start out with ticket sales or working with the ground crew. Take a look at guys like Gordie Ash who started out selling tickets, worked his way through the ticket office, and is now assistant general manager. And his future is still ahead of him.

"There are guys who run the Blue Jays Marketing Department who started in the mail room.

"So, start young, work hard, everybody is not going to get the glamor job, as I did."

What a success story! Doing what you want to do and earning a lot of money as well. Of course, there's a lot of responsibility that comes with the territory. A new baseball franchise costs 95 million dollars U.S. That's just for a *new* franchise. Can you imagine what the Blue Jays are worth? In 1990 they had the best attendance record in the American league.

Paul Beeston, at 45, administers a 75 million dollar a year budget and a combined staff of over 1,300 people! That will come as a surprise to most baseball fans who think there are only 25 players, a few managers and coaches, a ticket seller here and there and some hotdog vendors.

No, it's a huge business with huge responsibilities. And Paul Beeston is showing the rest of the league how it should be done. He's another Canadian Achiever.

Her Unshakable Will to Live

Tracy Hoskins

Many of the stories of Canadian Achievers in my series deal with people who have made success of their lives in a monetary sense. This story contains no monetary value. This is a story of one person's triumph over unbelievable odds. A young woman's unshakable will to live. Her story is one of the most powerful and touching I have ever reported.

It is the story of Tracy Hoskins who realized a lifetime dream and then came back from the near dead to complete it.

The story begins 14 years ago when a nine year old girl, Tracy Hoskins from Brampton, Ontario saw the RCMP Musical Ride at the Calgary Stampede. She went backstage with her parents to inspect the horses and Mounties after the spectacle, which is renowned throughout the world. Tracy patted one of the horses and announced to her parents that she was going to be a police officer when she grew up.

"My father just smiled and thought it was a childish whim or something."

But it was no whim. Tracy kept that image of becoming a police officer alive in her mind and at 22 she joined the police force as a rookie cop in her home town of Brampton, Ontario. She was accepted in May 1987 and barely 10 months later, on January 18, 1988 disaster struck her.

"Another officer and I were directing traffic past an accident on Steeles Avenue just east of Airport Road in Brampton. We had to keep traffic to one lane, letting one group of cars go by from each side at regular intervals.

Then someone decided he wasn't going to wait his turn and came barreling through the line up of five other cars. He hit me and set me flying 150 feet. It was a hit and run. I was in a coma for three weeks and two days so I didn't know how badly I was hurt until I regained consciousness. Apparently I had been declared dead. My parents were told I wouldn't live even if I did regain consciousness. That was changed when the doctors told my parents that I might live but I would never walk, talk, or work again.

"My injuries included a fractured skull, fractured pelvis, and compound fractures of my right leg. A bone came through the back of the leg, it was so badly broken.

"I knew how grave my injuries were when the doctors told my parents within my hearing that I had less than a 50/50 chance of recovering." Her parents were told that if Tracy did survive, she would never walk, talk or work again.

"So I said to myself, don't listen to them. You can achieve whatever you put your mind to. That's what happened. I put in mind a goal: keep going. It doesn't matter what someone else is saying to you or about you."

Twenty-eight months after Tracy Hoskins, a fighter, an achiever, was told she would likely not live, and if she did she would never walk, talk or work again, she returned to work. Tracy walks with great difficulty, and her speech is a bit slower, but she's back, fulfilling her promise made to her father. How did she feel to be going back to work after her horrendous experience and miraculous recovery?

"It was sort of unreal, like in a dream. It seemed like so long since I had been in that atmosphere. It was kind of story-like. But a good feeling; really nice."

With such a courageous attitude, what advice does Tracy Hoskins have for other people who suddenly find they have been given a poor prognosis for life?

"I would say that no matter how bad a person's prognosis is, it's what they believe in their heart and mind, particularly the heart, that is their strength. What they feel in their heart, that they can function and do is more important than what anyone else tells you."

She's another Canadian Achiever.

Couple Had the Beans for Success!

Don & Rita Stafford

In 1977, Don Stafford reached a crisis in his life. He was 46 years old and had been an advertising salesman for 20 years in his hometown of Montreal. He wanted to do something different, something for himself. He looked around for an idea.

"I sat down with my wife Rita and we discussed what we could do. We realized we both had an enormous interest in good coffee. We did some market research and discovered that Montreal had only one gourmet coffee retailer."

Don and Rita started right then to plan their own venture: The Coffee Gourmet.

"Our first business on Greene Avenue in Westmount was an ideal location," Rita says. *"We acquired a steady stream of loyal customers. After 13 years we moved to our present location on Sherbrooke Street West and continue to prosper from our regular clientele and improved walk-in trade."*

The Staffords opened a second store to market their 42 varieties of coffee in the Farmer's Market in Dollard des Ormeaux. It too was an immediate success.

Total sales for the second year of business stood at $644,000. They decided to open a store in Toronto.

"That was our first and worst mistake. We are a family-oriented business and we found that we just couldn't maintain that relationship at such a distance from each other."

Daughter Lynn now manages the Farmer's Market outlet and daughter Donna is a computer whiz in the accounting department.

What is the secret of their success?

"Learn from your mistakes. Pay attention to the customers you have. Give one-on-one service. We have retained at least 80 percent of our original clients. Since most of our trade is walk-in, the location is vital to someone planning a business of this type."

Would they do it again?

"Definitely. Very much so. We started out in the dark days when politics in Quebec were rather strained. Now, after 13 years, we are really looking forward to good times."

The Staffords are planning to expand their office coffee service and a direct mail catalogue. They have added other gourmet delicacies such as various kinds of caviar, cheeses and patés in addition to blending, grinding and refining the distinctive 52 kinds of coffee their customers have come to expect.

Don and Rita Stafford are two Canadian Achievers who proved that a mid-life crisis is not always a bad thing if it makes you move from a dull job to working for yourself—and "loving it."

"It is a good thing for a person to read books of quotations."
—*Winston Churchill*

He Made His Business Grow

Len Cullen

As a young teenager growing up in Toronto, Len Cullen cut the lawn and shovelled snow for a Mr. Weall who owned a small nursery. By age 17, Len was working full time there. At 22, he bought the business.

That was 44 years ago and there are now eight "Weall & Cullen Garden Centres" in the Toronto area, to say nothing of their world famous "Cullen Gardens" and miniature village at Whitby, Ontario, a tourist attraction that draws a half million visitors every year.

At age 65 in 1990, Len was not about to retire, but had he ever felt like chucking it in?

"I can't say I ever have. I've always really enjoyed my work. I look forward to it every day. Monday is just as nice for me as Friday."

This positive attitude has kept Len Cullen perpetually young in spirit and he thinks Canada is still a pretty good place for young people to start their own businesses in.

"I think young people in this country today can do just as well or better than I have done. And some of them are. I met a young fellow last Fall who was going to start his own irrigating business, installing sprinkler systems in lawns. He began on his own, then added another fellow and then another. He's going like a house-afire. But I could tell right away that this guy was a real hustler. He's going places.

"There's lots of opportunity in all different areas of business. But, it's important for the beginner to have some experience in their field. Work with somebody who knows his trade and learn from him. It's also important to have some capital, not a lot. Start with a small firm, whatever it may be, work hard at it and give value. That is the whole answer: give the customer more than they expect to get.

"I guess if I had to do it all over again, by and large, as far as the general business and the home life are concerned, I wouldn't change a thing. Not that I haven't had some bad moments. My most difficult decision, bar none, was when we decided to build 'Cullen Country Barns'. It was right in the middle of the 1982 recession. We needed to raise $5 million. I never had so much difficulty raising money in my life. We finally did it but it was a real toughie.

"The side of the business that I get the most fun out of is supervising or working in the gardens, pruning trees and shrubs, planting flowers and bulbs, building rockeries. Unfortunately, I don't get as much of that work as I would like because I have to shuffle paper—and I hate it. I have never been used to paperwork, always been an outdoorsman. When it comes to writing,

doing payroll or schedules, filling in forms, I shuffle as much of that off on other people as I can."

Len Cullen and his wife Connie are community-spirited and when the Divinity School at McMaster University in Hamilton needed money, Len came up with a unique idea.

"Connie and I decided we would ride our bikes from Windsor, Ontario to Quebec City. About 800 miles, to raise money for the school. I sent letters to all our friends and to all our suppliers saying that we were going on this ride and asking them to either pledge so much a mile or make a donation. They wouldn't have to pay if we didn't make it!

"We had a tremendous response. Many sent donations and made pledges. We took along a van which one of us would drive while the other pedalled the bike. I used to like to get up at 5 a.m. and head out while there was little traffic.

"After we got into the rhythm of it and got in better shape, we could go further distances every day. It took us 18 days to do the 800 miles and it was fun all the way.

"We also raised $250,000 for the Divinity School—and we're pretty pleased about that."

Should business executives take an active part in raising funds for charity or good causes, or is it enough to just write a cheque?

"Sometimes I do write a cheque when I haven't got the time to take an active role in fund-raising, but when I'm really interested in the cause, I do a lot of the work. I think it is important that leaders in the community contribute to the community because we get so much out of the area in which we live.

"And we have to put things back." Len Cullen... another Canadian Achiever.

An Amazing Young Canadian Inventor

Rachel Zimmerman

There is, in London, Ontario, an inventor named R. Zimmerman, who has won a silver medal at the Canada Wide Science Fair, money from I.B.M., a Canadian Citizenship Award, and plaudits from the Minister of State for Science and Technology. Are you picturing a silver haired old gentleman working with test tubes? Surprise!! The 'R' in front of Zimmerman stands for Rachel... a pretty, young girl who, at the age of 13 developed a computer based method of communication for people who are unable to speak or write. Rachel says with compassion... *"I developed it because these people are so isolated."*

Using an Atari 800XL computer and a large ultra sensitive power pad board, a handicapped person need only touch symbols or letters on the board to make themselves easily understood. At a touch, words can be printed, allowing the handicapped to 'leave a message'.

Originally in English, Rachel Zimmerman has adapted the program to French. Rachel Zimmerman has found that 'ability plus idea, plus compassion' is a perfect formula for success.

Canada looks forward to great things from this 18 year old Canadian Achiever. Her efforts were recognized again in 1990 when she won the YTV Achievement Award for innovation.

He Sings Up a Storm

Bryan Adams

This is a story of a young songwriter who decided he'd like to be a rock star as well. Vancouver's Bryan Adams wasn't always a rock superstar.

He and his partner Jim Vallance wrote more than forty songs in a three year period. . . most of them for Canadian rock groups. But Adams got tired of the anonymity of a composer. He possesses sexy good looks and a husky voice so he thought he'd put a band together and take to the road. It was a smart move.

In 1984, a year after turning professional singer, he won four Juno Awards, including one for top male vocalist. The mayor of Los Angeles declared 'Bryan Adams Day' after he sold out two shows at the L.A. Palladium.

His first video 'Reckless' was released in 1985 and the album from it rose to become number one on Billboard Magazine's Top 10 Chart. Aware of the fact that in order to stay on top you have to grow, Bryan Adams, at the age of 27 in 1987, decided to put some social consciousness into his songs. The result was the hit 'Into the Fire'. Although he travels extensively in the States, Bryan Adams says he will never leave Canada. He's another Canadian Achiever.

His Invention Will Save Millions of Lives

Dr. John Hopps

I was sitting next to man on a plane when the subject of the pacemaker came up. I happened to mention that the heart pacemaker was invented by a Canadian. The man turned to me and said, quite brusquely: *"the hell it was!"* Seems he had had one installed in New York and he was sure an American or a Swede had invented it.

I told him I had just interviewed one of the men who had invented the pacemaker and had the tape in my briefcase. He was then convinced, but still a bit skeptical. It's this ambivalence that still clouds the story behind the invention of this wonderful device which has saved so many people's lives and continues to keep people around the world living useful lives. Strangely enough, it also keeps its originator on the go too. I am talking about Dr. John Hopps of the National Research Council where the pacemaker was developed and where it got its name.

"There's always been a bone of contention surrounding the 'invention' of the pacemaker," Dr. Hopps says. *"In truth, no single one invented it. However, ours was the first of its kind. In 1950, we at NRC were collaborating in a hypothermia study by Dr. W.G. Bigelow at the University of Toronto. Dr. Bigelow observed that a cold heart could be triggered into activity by a mechanical or electrical stimulus. We developed a device to maintain or activate the heart beat as an adjunct to that investigation.*

"We called our device a pacemaker after nature's own pacemaker, the sinoatrial node which normally organizes the heart's rate. It appeared to be a good descriptive name for the device. Subsequently, other devices designed to control the heart beat were called pacemakers.

"Those were good times for research in Canada. I doubt very much if the pacemaker would be developed today, that's how much times have changed. Things then were much more flexible. Now our science is so circumscribed with the desire to assist industry that there is little pure research being done in the country today, particularly by the government.

"The happenstance that led to the development of the pacemaker at the N.R.C. was that we had the resources of many different divisions: biochemistry, physicists, life scientists, our own electrical engineering technology and the science library. All these in one place.

"The financial cost of the pacemaker was minimal. I can't think of anywhere else in Canada where the resources were available to make this a possibility at the time. And certainly not today."

A conservative estimate of the number of pacemakers in use in North America alone is 500,000. Dr. Hopps and his brother are two of the users!

"I had no idea when I was making my contribution to the development of the pacemaker that one day I would owe my own life to it! As for my brother, I wrote and demanded that he pay me a royalty, but he refused to cough up!" He said it with a smile.

Many people who learn about the pacemaker for the first time have misconceptions about the installation procedure and the length of time the unit will operate without having to be replaced.

"On the average, a pacemaker will last 10 years before it has to be taken out and a new one installed. It is a minor surgical procedure. The pacemakers today are designed so that the patient can go to a pacemaker clinic every

*year where it can be determined very readily what condition the unit is in:
its probable life; condition of its batteries and whether it's performing and
doing its job properly. A patient really should have no concern about a
pacemaker suddenly stopping on them.*

*"The development of the transistor was what fueled the expansion of the
pacemaker. When the transistor came along it made electrical circuitry so
that the unit could be enscapulated within the body. So it became a practical
technique. The installation is quite simple and can be performed under a local anesthetic in a special procedures suite or in the operating room. A lot
of patients say they would rather have a pacemaker installed than go to the
dentist! The replacements can often be done as an outpatient procedure."*

In 1987, Dr. John Hopps was awarded the "Order of Canada" for his
contribution toward the development of the pacemaker. How did he feel
about that event in his life?

*"I felt very proud because I am a 100% Canadian and it gave me great
pleasure to receive it. I thought it reflected the work done by the National
Research Council rather than by one individual.*

"But it was a great delight to me!" Dr. John Hopps. . . another Canadian
Achiever.

"The reverse side also has a reverse side."
—*Japanese Proberb*

They Make You Feel At Home

The Rodd Family

The Rodd family of Prince Edward Island can offer you a bed if you're
ever in the Maritimes. And if you have more than five hundred friends,
they'll put all of them up too. For more than fifty years the Rodds have been
Maritime motel owners.

In 1936, Wally and Sally Rodd started the tradition with a 16 room inn in
Charlottetown. Now their eldest son, David, oversees eight family-owned
inns of various sizes in P.E.I., New Brunswick, and Nova Scotia. The business employs more than five hundred people and pulls in around fourteen
million dollars a year. And David now takes regular sales trips to Japan
where interest in Prince Edward Island has blossomed since that country
caught on to the island-based 'Anne of Green Gables' stories.

For 50 years the Rodd family has hung on to their tradition of genial and
comfortable accommodations, and built a very successful business around
it. Making them true Canadian Achievers.

He Didn't Know Times Were Tough

John Volken

Somebody forgot to tell German immigrant John Volken that Canada was in recession in 1981 so he went right ahead and became a success. From his first small used furniture store in Vancouver, he turned "United Buy and Sell" into a huge financial success with thirty-eight stores in Canada and four in the United States. And he's still growing.

"We were an overwhelming success right from the beginning," John says. Although the company name says otherwise, United Buy and Sell deals only in new furniture. John's philosophy and method of sales is simple: *"low overhead, no commissioned sales staff, and low prices. We offer a sofa for $750 that costs us $500. Another retailer sells it for $1,500. He sells one and we sell three. He makes a $500 profit; we make $750."*

From that first east Hastings Street store and one employee, United Buy and Sell in 1990 employed 260 people with total sales of $55 million.

When John Volken first arrived in Canada from Germany he was 18 years old, on his own, and bug-eyed at the opportunities this country had to offer. But, first he had to eat, and 18 year olds eat a lot.

"I worked at fast food outlets washing dishes and in construction and on farms. Meantime I was looking around for a business to get into. I had some experience in a flower shop in Germany and I did that for a while. I found I enjoyed business. But jobs were scarce. That was in 1960, another bad year!"

John finally moved to the west coast and rented the building that would be the start of his chain. He had little capital and even today keeps financing costs as low as possible. He has a $1 million line of credit but carries no long-term debt. His aim is to sell as much merchandise as possible, as quickly as possible. John owns only one store and leases his other buildings so he can close them down when United outgrows them.

"We keep the decor simple, no frills—no gimmick is our motto. Our staff are all on the floor, managers and assistants as well, bringing in sales." John pays his sales staff well after they prove themselves. Other stores hire people with experience.

"We do the opposite. We hire young people at minimum wages for a year to learn the trade. Those who survive are disciplined with long term career commitments who can move rapidly up the ladder to all levels of management.

It gives our staff initiative to work harder and work until the job's finished."

With more than 40 stores in 1990 and 30 more on the drawing board, when will there be enough? And when will the thrill of building a furniture empire wear off?

"I don't think it ever will wear off. Everytime we open a new location it is an exciting event. Consumers welcome us and accept us with enthusiasm. You can't help but get a kick out of that. It's the thrill of being accepted as we are. I know that we are going to stay simple, although we have gone to computers now. Up to 1990 we did without them.

"I still believe that to be a success in business you have to keep things simple. To much paperwork can ruin you. We have three people at head office to handle the paperwork. Compared to my competitors that is a very small staff. The reason is that much of the paperwork is done by the managers at the stores. Our managers don't just sit in the office and 'manage,' they work."

Low overhead, well-paid and trained staff, and a huge advertising budget (well over $2 million on radio and television every year and rising), the formula seems to work for the young immigrant (he's still only 48).

"We're planning to be the McDonald's of the furniture business."

He Won 3 Grey Cups

Russ Jackson

Whenever you think you're too busy, stop for a moment and think about Russ Jackson. For 12 years, in the 50's and 60's, Russ became famous as one of Canada's most outstanding professional athletes. Winning 3 Grey Cups, seven Schenley Awards (3 most outstanding, 4 top Canadian), and named twice as Canada's Male Athlete of the Year.

In 1979, 10 years after he had retired from football, a U.S. survey of all professional football players rated Canada's Russ Jackson as the finest of all times.

What few people realized was that while Russ was doing all of this, he held a fulltime teaching position. When Russ graduated from Hamilton's McMaster University in 1958, he went right into pro football with the Ottawa Roughriders, and also right into Teachers College in Toronto.

Russ always believed in keeping busy, keeping in shape and surrounding himself with good people. Ask him what he attributes his achievements to and he'll tell you. . .

"It's self discipline. Nobody can do it for you. It has to come from within."

Russ Jackson is still quarterbacking and still passing. . . but now he's quarterbacking students and passing along to them his philosophy of achieving.

Russ is principal at John Fraser Secondary School in Mississauga. So, the next time you think you're too busy, think of Russ Jackson. . . the quarterback who won three Grey Cups while still going to school. He's another Canadian Achiever.

"Nobody has ever bet enough on the winning horse."
—*Unknown*

Their Hill is a Healthy Success

Pat & Juanita Corbett

Pat Corbett grew up in Swan River, Manitoba. After graduating from university he began to paint houses for a living. But it wasn't really what he wanted to do. When he married Juanita they decided to combine their two goals: Pat wanted to run a ski & dude ranch and Juanita wanted to operate a health resort. The result is "The Hills". A 400 acre ski, dude and health ranch, near 100 Mile House, B.C., where you can either go horse-back riding or lose a lot of extra pounds, or both.

"We sure picked the worst year to start our venture," Pat says. *"1983 was a recession time and we really had to struggle to make it work. We came so close to going bust it wasn't funny. We finally sat down with our creditors and told them we were on the verge of bankruptcy, but we wanted to stick with it. With their cooperation we managed to pull it off."*

From that shaky beginning, The Hills has become a haven for vacationers from Nova Scotia to New York, from Atlanta to L.A. from England to Germany—5,000 of them a year, turning The Hills into a $3 million asset.

"We had thoughts of quitting when we were up to our waists in mud and alligators, but we had a deep conviction that we were on the right track and were doing the right thing at the right time. So we stuck it out."

The Hills offers just about anything a seeker of a healthy vacation could wish for: good, wholesome, calorie-counted food; sauna, conducted exercise, trail riding, hay rides and fireside singalongs. There are convention facilities and banquet accommodation for up to 250 people. All this in the rolling ranchlands in British Columbia's "True West" Cariboo.

"The Germans in particular love the western atmosphere. And this is the center of the world when it comes to horses and cowboys."

The Corbetts learned valuable lessons in their first years.

"Make sure you always count the costs of starting your own business. The costs include the financial costs, the costs of commitment to your idea. Be sure that you understand that if you are going to invest a lot of money in a venture you better be prepared to be very committed with your time to make sure that your idea works."

I asked Pat if the hospitality industry is going to grow in Canada, or have we peaked in the business? Where does the future lie?

"Tourism is growing at a phenomenal rate in this country. It's soon to become the number one employer. Believe it or not, tourism is already the number one industry in the world, the largest single employer of people. In Canada, because of its super natural wilderness character, we have an asset that the world is beginning to yearn and cry for. The hospitality and tourism industries in Canada will flourish far beyond anything in effect now."

Juanita Corbett concurs with her husband's assessment of the potential for growth in the industry, especially if it is coupled with a healthy lifestyle, the goal of so many people today.

"Most of today's jobs are sit down. Everyone seems to have a more sedentary lifestyle compared to that of our parents. It's our own fault; we chose something that was slower, a little easier. Such a lifestyle has major costs: we get heavier; we lose our muscle tone and our energy level goes down. There are lots of costs for that type of living.

"And that's why many people are saying they want to feel good and look good when they are 60 years old. They don't want to be in a wheelchair or a rocking chair when they can walk, jog, ride, swim. They want to be able to do active things and feel good while doing them."

Clearly, Pat and Juanita Corbett seem to have a tiger by the tail in The Hills. They've combined a lifestyle they both enjoy with the enthusiasm necessary to make it attractive to others. Pat says tourism and hospitality are growth industries and Juanita says a healthy lifestyle is the goal of millions. Perhaps there is a spot in there for you too! They are Canadian Achievers.

World Class Mezzo Soprano

Judith Forst

Judith Forst's mother Euna always knew her daughter would be a success. She told me that from the time Judith was a little tot she was always singing and practicing piano. Euna is a very proud mother and she has every right to be because now her daughter, Judith Forst, is a world renowned mezzo soprano.

The New York Times wrote recently that Judith Forst is one of the truly world class mezzo sopranos on the operatic stage today. Success has not affected her. Married with two teenagers Judith prefers to live in a modest home in Port Moody, near Vancouver, commuting regularly to New York and Milan.

When opera lovers around the world meet Judith Forst they are usually surprised at the calmness and the fact that she lives in a small town in Canada.

How did she get to the Met?? *"A lot of hard work, practice and winning a series of competitions."*

In 1968, she sang for the famed Rudolph Bing, then head of New York's Metropolitan Opera. On hearing her sing, Bing made a move unprecedented in New York Met history . . . he signed Judith to a seven year contract. She was on her way. Her musical future assured.

Unfortunately, we tend to overlook Canada's contribution to the worlds concert stage. Most of our concert artists receive greater acclaim in other countries than they do here at home. But that's beginning to change thanks to great talents like Judith Forst . . . another Canadian Achiever.

From an Orphanage to Canada's Largest Company

Raymond Cyr

Can a young man or woman still work the long way to the top in a large corporation? It was fairly common years ago. What are the chances of an unknown taking a spot on the lowest rung and ending up running the whole show?

J. V. Raymond Cyr of Montreal did it. He was raised in a Montreal orphanage and is now president and chief executive officer of Bell Canada Enterprises Incorporated, parent company of Bell Canada, Canada's largest employer.

"I think the chances of starting with a large firm and working your way to the top are actually better today than ever before. I do think it does require a university degree. I think the old family connections which were a big part of the corporate scene years ago are much less important now.

"I think it is really up to whoever is the best to move up the ladder. It requires a lot of hard work and dedication. But I think it still can be done."

Raymond Cyr was born in 1934 in the midst of the Great Depression. His father, a Montreal truckdriver, was doing as well as anyone under the circumstances. His wages barely covered the costs of feeding five young boys and keeping a home together. But tragedy struck when his wife died while giving birth to their sixth son. Raymond's father could not cope with the loss of his wife and the burden of looking after a family of that size. He was forced to put the children in an orphanage. Raymond, at eight, was the second oldest.

"Life in the orphanage wasn't so bad. It was three meals a day and religious instruction to go with school work there at one of the Jesuit Father's

Institutions in Montreal. As a matter of fact, they were instrumental in rec-
ommending that I go back to school and to continue on to university.

"I had left the orphanage at age thirteen and had taken odd jobs until I
reached 18 and decided that the advice the fathers gave me was the best way
to go.

"I went to university and that's where everything really started."

Raymond graduated from l'Université de Montreal (Ecole Polytech-
nique) with a Bachelor of Applied Science in 1958. In that year he joined
Bell Canada as an engineer. In 1962 he entered a two-year operating engineers training program at the Bell Telephone Laboratories in New Jersey. In
1970 he was appointed Bell Canada's chief engineer in Quebec City and his
climb to the top of the corporate tower was well underway.

"We have about 120,000 people in the company now. It varies when we
buy or sell some small company. Total revenue is approximately $17 billion
Canadian."

I asked him if with such a responsible position, doesn't he wake up at
night wondering, "what the heck am I doing here"?

"It may be my own personal characteristics and it may be something that
has helped me to get where I am today but, no, I do not worry to that extent.
I may be thinking about certain events in the evening, but basically I sleep
very well. If you allow yourself to stay awake worrying about a thousand
things you can't do anything about at that moment, the stress will overtake
you."

Married to the girl he met while going to university, the father of two: a
daughter who is a doctor and son who is a programmer, Raymond believes
that in addition to the excellent advice given to him by the Jesuits, there was
one driving force that kept him moving onward and upward:

"If you want to eat, you have to work!"

Raymond Cyr, from an orphanage to one of the top corporate jobs in the
land. He's another Canadian Achiever.

"What a time . . . what a civilization."
—*Cicero* (106–43 B.C.)

Famous People Players

Diane Dupuy

When Diane Dupuy was 6 years old her mom gave her a hand puppet for a
birthday present. That was over 30 years ago. Today, Diane is probably the
world's most acclaimed and imaginative puppeteer. She's even had a movie

made of her life... by an American film company at that. Diane's troop knocks 'em dead everywhere they perform including Broadway, Las Vegas, and many countries around the world.

Diane Dupuy is the creative mastermind behind the 15 mentally handicapped performers who are the world-renown "Famous People Players". The novel idea of large, fluorescent-colored puppets dancing on a backdrop of black first occurred to Diane back in 1974.

Diane explained to me how she got the idea... *"One day I went to an institution to do a show and I couldn't get over how people were living in an institution. It really bothered me. I really felt that everybody had a contribution to make to society. There is a creative energy in all of us that needs to be explored. So, that's basically how I got the idea."*

Diane Dupuy ... proof that in Canada, talent and determination will overcome any handicap. She's another Canadian Achiever.

"Your future hasn't been written yet. No one's has. Your future is whatever you make it. So make it a good one."
—*Dr. Browne, played by Christopher Lloyd, to Marty McFly, played by Michael J. Fox.* (Back to the Future, III)

Her Art Makes Big Marks

May Marx

Today May Marx bronzes, prints, and paintings are collected all over the world. She's recognized as a talented Canadian with a master's touch for popular art. But it wasn't always like that ...

Like most struggling artists, she had to take in part time teaching jobs to pay for studio rentals and supplies. She chuckles that being a sculptor in any country is not a lucrative profession. Not unless they happen onto an ingenious idea like May did when she heard that hockey legend Wayne Gretzky had just won his umpteenth gold watch award. She wondered if Wayne and the legions of other corporate and community award winners weren't bored with silver trays and crystal knick-knacks. Wouldn't they prefer a unique and original May Marx Bronze sculpture? So she got to work in her Toronto studio and created an abstract Chrysler Logo Sculpture. Chrysler didn't buy the idea but Chairman Lee Iacocca loved it, bought it, and it still sits on his desk in New York.

Other companies soon got curious and interested. She is now kept busy supplying governments and leading corporations with her unique bronze award art sculptures. In 1988, the federal government presented a May Marx sculpture to Canadian Boxing Champion Sean O'Sullivan. Sean's mother told May that of all the awards and trophies he'd received May's had the most meaning.

Today May Marx award art has turned into a 200 thousand dollar a year income simply because she came up with a better idea for well established products. She's another Canadian Achiever.

Her Cookbooks Cook Up Huge Sales

Jean Paré

Anyone who looks in the cookbook section of a bookstore will wonder how so many cookbooks can sell. They may well say: what this country doesn't need is *another* cookbook! Nevertheless, Jean Paré of Vermilion, Alberta expects to sell a million or more in Canada every year.

"And that's a fairly conservative estimate. We now have 14 books out and sales in Canada alone exceed 5 million copies."

Jean Paré was born in a small rural town named Irma in eastern Alberta. She got into the cookbook industry after running her own catering business in Vermilion, Alberta for 18 years.

"I volunteered to cater to 1,000 people at the 50th anniversary of the Vermilion School of Agriculture (now Lakeland College). I really didn't know what I was in for. It was just a challenge and I enjoyed it. As a result of that, since it was a success, people began asking me to cater weddings, anniversaries, school graduations, business meetings.

"And over the years I began to collect an enormous number of recipes. People would ask me for them and I never turned them down and I also got some in return. I still get recipes in the mail.

"Then people started to say I should write a cookbook. I thought about it but it was really my son Grant who encouraged me. He saw the potential. I said if I wrote a cookbook it would be three feet thick and Grant said to concentrate on one thing and get that out. So I wrote "150 Delicious Squares" and within two weeks of its publication I knew I had to give up the catering business."

Jean's business was so successful she had to move into an 800 square foot office and warehouse from her test kitchen in her home. Soon she had to move to a larger place with 2400 square feet.

"Then we moved to Edmonton where we had an 8,000 square foot office and warehouse and thought we were really fixed. No way! We built our own 24,000 square foot building and we can build on to it."

Meantime the books, all under the "Company's Coming" series, were selling like hotcakes in other countries.

"We have distributors in the U.S., England, New Zealand, Australia,

Singapore, the Philippines, Barbados. And I'm sure every English-speaking person in Saudi Arabia has a copy of all of our cookbooks! Where we don't have distributors we get group orders for cases of books. We now have versions in French and we sold the right to a Mexican publisher to publish them in Spanish."

I asked Jean what she sees for the future?

"We're doing two books a year with no end in sight. I never plan to retire. In addition, our 'Company's Coming Snack Bars' are doing well. We're franchising them and they're now coast to coast. We're on the Alberta Stock Exchange and hopefully we'll soon be on the Toronto Stock Exchange."

'Company's Coming' is a real family business. From the beginning son Grant Lovig (now vice-president) worked with Jean, then daughter Gail (western marketing manager) and son Lyal joined the firm. Were there problems with having family in the business?

"My only problems are good ones! I can only wish that every family is as fortunate as I am. My children get along so well. I think one reason is they are not working side by side on the same thing. There is no arguing over whose idea is the best. Their ideas relate to what they are doing. I only wish my grandchildren could become more involved but they live too far away. Some of the older ones do come and help out when we are busy with a new release."

Jean keeps ahead of the cookbook game by taking note of what her customers want.

"We have a tally sheet in the office and when someone requests a book on a particular food, we mark it down. Pasta was very high on the request list so we brought out a book on Pasta. People seem to want to entertain at home more nowadays, which is one reason cookbooks are so popular. Also, I think there is an enormous amount of pleasure derived from making a nice-looking dish, an appetizing dish. I have a lot of cookbooks myself. While it's been said that a cook will count it lucky if she uses one recipe repeatedly out of a book she'll not begrudge the price, I am overwhelmed by the letters we get from people who say they use my recipes over and over. In our next sales of 200,000 copies of our new book we expect half will be pre-ordered. They have such faith in these books that they buy them sight-unseen."

Of the 14 books available from *Company's Coming* in 1990, what was the most popular?

"In these low-calorie and health-conscious days where salt and sugar are no-nos, you might think 'soup & sandwiches'. But no. The number one best-seller is the first book we did: 150 Delicious Squares!"

Jean Paré's goal is to place a cookbook in every home in the English-speaking world. A big goal? Not for the gentle lady from Vermilion, Alberta who proved that you don't have to live in a big city to have big ideas. She's another Canadian Achiever.

Listeners send me the nicest things. A listener in Sault Ste. Marie sent this bit of sage advice.

The results of a survey "Things People Worry About"...

—things that never happen	40%
—things they can't change	30%
—needless worry about health	12%
—petty & miscellaneous worry	10%
—real problems	8%

92% of the things people worry about are things that don't matter. I beg you. Don't waste your time worrying.

Third Time Successful

Allan Laakkonen

Allan Laakkonen is the tenacious school teacher/alderman in Thunder Bay who headed up the civic committee that wanted to bring the Nordic World Ski Championships to Thunder Bay. In 1985 they made their first bid in Vancouver, and lost. In 1988 they travelled to Istanbul to bid again, and lost. In May, 1990 they travelled to Montreaux, Switzerland—bid again, and won! In 1995 the world's attention will centre on Canada for two big weeks as Thunder Bay hosts the Nordic World Championships. Allan Laakkanen headed up all three bid attempts. I asked Allen what advice does he have for other communities bidding for major events?

"I would say that they have to be patient. Depending on what level of bid they're going for. Canadian or international, they are going to have to be tenacious. They have to put a group together that's committed to their bid. And most important, they must have a strategy."

All of his committee members work will pay off in big dollars for the region in 1995. *"It's estimated that a minimum of 38 million new dollars will come into the area. Other figures we have heard go as high as 60 million new dollars. So it's quite an impact and keep in mind, it's new money. Not recirculating old money."*

That certainly makes bidding on events well worth the effort.

Canada's First Man in Space

Marc Garneau

Marc Garneau did not spend his childhood dreaming of travelling in space. In fact, as a boy growing up in Quebec City, the son of a distinguished general, Marc thought space flight would be out of the question for Canadians for a long time.

If Marc and his family had decided to take their vacation in July, 1983, instead of staying home that month, he might not have become our first astronaut. But he was at home, and he saw the newspaper ad for candidates to apply for the Canadian Man-in-space Program. Marc was one of forty-three hundred applicants. Since he was a career navy officer, he really didn't feel he had much of a chance; many of the other applicants were pilots.

The list was whittled down to eighteen hundred, then to sixty-eight, then to nineteen, and finally, to six. Marc Garneau learned that he was to be the first Canadian to travel aboard the U.S. Space Shuttle Challenger. On October 5, 1984, the world watched as Marc Garneau blasted off and became Canada's first man in space.

Back on the ground, Marc works for the Canadian Space Agency in Ottawa. His job is to create new interest in space science among Canadians and Canadian companies, and to make sure Canada is part of the space programs of the future.

Marc Garneau... a man who challenged the odds and won.

He's Another Canadian Achiever.

"Tough times never last, but tough people do."
—*Robert H. Schuller*

The Flag is Tatooed Over His Heart

Alex Baumann

By the time he retired from world-class swimming, Alex Baumann had won two Olympic gold medals, set many world records, had taken home numerous trophies and honours, including Athlete of the Year and the Order of Canada. . . . And Alex Baumann was only 23 years old!

Before becoming a fulltime coach, Alex took time out to collaborate with his former coach, Jeno Tihanyi, on a book about swimming. Called "Swimming with Alex Baumann: A Program for Competitive and Recreational

Swimmers". It is also aimed at coaching. It was something that Alex found quite different at first.

"I started by doing some coaching with the varsity team in my hometown of Sudbury, Ontario, in 1989. I enjoy it, but it is a lot different from being in the pool. You have to become quite inventive and make up different work- outs to keep the swimmers alert and interested."

Since completing the book Alex has become a fulltime coach at Laurentian University, Sudbury.

"I was very fortunate to have Dr. Tihanyi as my coach for 14 years. He guided me along by getting the best out of me, instilling in me how to set goals for myself and disciplining me. Studies have shown that sometimes a coach has more influence than a parent or a teacher at a certain point in an athlete's life."

Good coaching and hard work are the keys to success in the water, Alex has learned.

"Eleven years of training before the first big signs of success means a large part of your life must be spent in the pool. It means getting up at 5 a.m. every morning, whether you feel like it or not, swimming up to 12 or 13 kilometers a day. Five hours of grueling effort. It can become very boring because it is repetitive. That's why I'm glad we had competitions. We got to travel a lot. See the country. My friends were swimmers too so there were some healthy rivalries that developed and I'm sure that had a lot to do with my success."

Then, at the peak of his career in 1981, a shoulder injury forced Alex to retire.

"It was a time of physical and psychological torment for me, thinking all the time that I might not ever swim competitively again."

Through long and arduous hours of rehabilitation and training, Alex re- gained the strength of his shoulder and continued to prepare for world- record times.

Alex won his first international race in 1978, then went on to win medals and break records that still stand today. The culmination of years of hard work came at the 1984 Summer Olympics in Los Angeles where he brought home two gold medals for the 200 meters and the 400 meters, Alex told me.

"It was a tremendous feeling walking into that stadium with 90,000 people cheering. Even the Americans gave me quite a lot of applause. I guess, saluting their neighbour from the north. The cheering got my adren- alin flowing and ready for the competition. There was a lot of pressure on me to win because I had two world records going in so after the first winning race was over I felt a lot of relief. The second one was easier after I had won the first."

It was a real coup for Alex because no one from Canada had won gold medals in swimming since 1912 when George Hodgson of Montreal struck gold in two events. In addition to winning the gold medals, Alex Baumann was considered the fastest individual medley swimmer in the world.

Interestingly enough, Alex did not at first take to water like the proverbial duckling.

"As a small child I liked the water all right, but I didn't want to work at swimming. I was more interested in splashing around and having a good time than in learning strokes. My mother had been a successful competitive swimmer in Czechoslovakia in the 1940's but she didn't teach me to swim until I was five years old. I think she was wise in not pushing me at an earlier age. She just let me enjoy the water."

Another thing Alex learned to enjoy was being a Canadian. Although born in Czechoslovakia, he came to Canada with his parents at a very young age. One way he wanted to show his pride in Canada was to get a flag tattooed on his chest!

"It started in 1978 when Bill Sawchuk and Graham Smith got tattooed because they were proud to be Canadians and are world record holders. When I broke the 200 meter world record in Germany in 1981 I went out and got my tattoo. I was going to the University of Indiana at the time and that made it very plain where my loyalties were."

What advice does Alex Baumann have for young swimmers and for anyone who wants to succeed?

"It is essential to set short term goals for yourself. Once you achieve those goals you can move on to others and climb up the ladder that way. I think if you take life one day at a time you get a lot of satisfaction out of it.

"Also, Dr. Tihanyi taught me to visualize myself in action every step of the way from the start, to turns and finish. You really see yourself in those positions beforehand. And that really translates into anything you plan to do in your life." Alex Baumann... a gold medal Canadian Achiever.

Fine Furniture—Wooden You Know It?

John Brown

In 1974 a young university student named John Brown decided to drop out of advanced education and look for something entirely different. He took a course in woodworking and there met a friend who shared his growing interest in making furniture.

The two refurbished some antiques, made some copies of classic Nova Scotia furniture and attracted enough customers to keep the business growing.

John's partner dropped out and John continued on his own. He worked on the production floor with the rest of the small staff and at the end of the year showed a healthy but modest $30,000 in sales. This year he'll gross over a million dollars in sales to the Atlantic Provinces and the Caribbean.

"We also plan to market in New England and the French islands of St. Pierre and Miquelon."

John's Argyle Pine Label is the backbone of Woodcraft Manufacturing Ltd., a sort of Nova Scotia original style. The plans for each piece go from the drawing board to the mill shop where the lumber is picked out, cut, assembled by hand, then it's off to the finish shop where it is lacquered and polished.

"It's not a particularly sophisticated method of making furniture but we want to maintain a high standard in our all-wood products. We have diversified as well. We make custom office furniture in a combination of architectural finishes."

John Brown of Halifax took his dream of making authentic Nova Scotia furniture from a rented country store, expanded five times until now Woodcraft Manufacturing Ltd. employs 20 in an 8,000 square foot facility near Peggy's Cove.

His secret and advice for others?

"I was lucky to get some Government sponsorship. I had proved that my product was saleable so I was bankable. I grew gradually and have managed to keep complete control of my own business."

The same theme runs through these success stories: Work hard at what you like to do. Plan before expanding. John Brown turned a summer job and what he calls a "Nova Scotia flair" in furniture styling into a million dollar business. You can do it too if you follow his formula for success.

The Sunflower King

Issy Steen

You never know when or where opportunity will strike next. Just ask Issy Steen, owner of "Sid's Sunflower Seeds" in Regina. His big break came when two strangers approached his display of sunflower seeds at a food show in New York. They said their kids enjoyed sunflower seeds and asked for a few sample packages. Issy gave them several packages, and promptly forgot the incident. Several months later they called him in Regina, told him they were in charge of licensing products for major league baseball. They asked Issy if he, for a fee, would be interested in having the license to place a major league logo on each package of seeds. It was a big step for him, but Issy agreed.

In April 1989 Issy struck a deal with the Toronto Blue Jays of the American League and Montreal Expos of the National League to allow his company, "Sid's Sunflower Seeds" to be their official supplier. This meant he could put the major league logo on his product.

To launch the campaign, the Expos held a "Sid's Day", handing a package of sunflower seeds to the first 20,000 fans through the turnstiles. The event was well-publicized before the day. Radio commercials told the public at home. At the stadium the electronic scoreboard and public address system promoted Sid's Day a week in advance. Issy said the cost of the campaign was well worth it. Being a typical risk taker Issy didn't stop there. He risked more money by signing an endorsement deal with two of the top baseball players in Canada. Dave Steib of the Blue Jays, and Buck Rogers of the Expos.

Issy Steen was born in Roumania in 1945 and came to Canada with his family at the age of three. Before moving back to Saskatchewan where his father farmed near Hoffer, the family lived in Winnipeg where they ran a grocery store. Issy went to the University of Manitoba and obtained a BA in Sociology in 1966.

He married his wife Francie the following year and the couple moved to Regina where Issy worked for a local restaurant chain. It was his experience in the fast food business that led him to Sid's.

Before his coup in grabbing the attention of the baseball fans in Canada, Issy decided that he had to take the rather inefficient little company he had purchased in 1961 and turn it into a competitive business. Growth was stymied; the Saskatchewan market was oversold so he sent his sales team out into the remaining western provinces and soon had customers there demanding more sunflower seeds. Sid's was growing faster than anything else in the Canadian snack food industry.

Meanwhile back at the plant in Regina, the latest in equipment, inspection techniques and skilled staff were being installed to keep up with the demand.

Before long Issy had the entire western market eating out of his hand, so to speak. However, central and eastern Canada remained elusive. Then came the deal with the Expos and Blue Jays and Sid's became a household name in sunflower seeds across the country. He has now signed all 24 major league baseball clubs to sell his seeds in their stadiums.

Stephen Leacock said: *"I am a great believer in luck, and I find the harder I work the more I have of it"*. Issy Steen has the same philosophy.

Since much of his business is concentrated in the eastern U.S. and California, Issy plans to open plants there. He knows he will have to decide whether to expand his Regina plant or make a move. As a young boy he used to trade in pop bottles so he could buy packages of Sid's sunflower seeds. Like the guy in the razor commercial, Issy liked the product so much he bought the company.

"I grew up thinking Sid's Sunflower Seeds was a big company," he says.

"After I bought it I found out it was a lot smaller than I thought."

That's all changed, Sid's is now the biggest company of its kind in Canada, employing 21 people and selling seven million pounds of sunflower seeds a year.

"I am a firm believer in advertising and promotion of the right kind. Thoughtfully worked out."

That plus the hard work and luck of the likes of Stephen Leacock, seems to be a winning combination for the plucky Issy Steen. Another Canadian Achiever.

"Corn sells."
—*Tommy Darling,* Canadian Broadcaster

King of the Quiz Shows

Alex Trebek

Every evening over 15 million North Americans tune in to watch Alex Trebek lead them through another round of "Jeopardy".

Born in Sudbury, July 22, 1940, Alex's father was a hotel chef, his mother a homemaker. He was packed off to a devoutly Catholic prep school where he admits he engaged in more pranks than study. Nevertheless, Trebek graduated from the University of Ottawa and with no formal training landed a job at the C.B.C.

Alex was operating a ski chalet when his friend and fellow Canadian, Alan Thicke, got him a job as host of "The Wizard of Odds" on N.B.C. When Merv Griffin launched the game quiz "Jeopardy", Trebek was chosen as the host. "Jeopardy" became a hit and the rest years later, is history.

When I asked Alex what advice he offered for hopeful achievers he thought for a moment and said, *"Get a good education, work hard, pay your dues, keep your fingers crossed so that perhaps you will get that lucky break. Also, there are things you have no control over such as your looks. So don't worry about those. Emphasize the positive. Do something about those things that you can change. But, if it's beyond your control don't worry about it."*

That philosophy has paid off handsomely for Alex. He lives in a magnificent home high up in Beverly Hills, California. He is one of the highest paid people in his profession. With his moustache somewhere between Groucho Marx and Zorba the Greek, Alex exudes charm and class. The kind of charm and class that can lead to the movie career he would like to develop. Alex still keeps his Canadian citizenship and is very close to his friends in Canada. He's another Canadian Achiever.

Being An Achiever

A listener in Lunenberg, Nova Scotia mailed me a very inspirational message and asked me to read it on my program. I was so taken by the reality of its message that I read it on my New Year's Day 1990 program. You'll notice I offered listeners a free copy if they would take it to their nearest school and post it on the bulletin board. Here is the script I read New Year's Day:

"This is the first program of the New Year and new decade. It's exciting to think about all of the wonderful achievements we can look forward to. Recently, a listener in Lunenberg, Nova Scotia mailed me an item which he asked me to share with you. I've been saving it for this first program of our new decade. Here is the item...

If you follow the crowd, you will likely get no further than the crowd.

If you walk alone, you're likely to end up in places no one has ever been before.

Being an achiever is not without its difficulties, for peculiarity breeds contempt. The unfortunate thing about being ahead of your time is that when people finally realize you were right, they'll simply say it was obvious to everyone all along.

You have two choices in life: you can dissolve into the mainstream, or you can choose to become an achiever and be distinct. To be distinct, you must be different. To be different, you must strive to be what no one else but you can be. Remember—if your mind can conceive it and your heart will believe it, eventually you will achieve it!"

I now keep this on my desk at home and refer to it often. If you would like a free copy of this inspirational item just send me a self-addressed, postage paid envelope c/o this station. Mark your letter "Canadian Achievers" I'll be happy to send it along. In fact, I'll send you extra copies if you promise to take them to your nearest school and ask them to post it on their bulletin board or print it in their student newspaper because, this is the message we must get through to all young Canadians. Happy New Year!

I was surprised by the number of letters I received from virtually every region of Canada. The most touching of all came from a blind lady in Ontario requesting permission to print it in braille.

Little did that kind listener in Lunenberg realize the positive impact his letter would have.

"They are able because they think they are able."

—*Vergil*

His Performances are Hypnotizing

Reveen

Since moving from Australia to Canada in 1962, the man they call Reveen has played in just about every city, town and hamlet in Canada, and around the world.

He astounded the entertainment world by first going to Calgary and selling out 28 consecutive performances at the Palace Theatre. Word quickly spread and Reveen was established. Reveen and his family fell in love with Canada and in 1966 they became Canadian citizens.

Reveen is recognized as one of the world's top authorities on the subject of the potential of the human mind. More than six million Canadians have attended his performances and watched as he mesmerized and hypnotized people from the audience. He's a fascinating man, this Canadian Achiever Peter Ryan ... the man they call Reveen.

Hotels & Airports Spell Success

Arthur Hailey

Arthur Hailey is now one of the world's best selling authors. His eleven novels have sold more than 150 million copies in 35 countries and 30 languages. Eleven movies, including "Hotel", "Black-Out", "Wheels", and the "Airport" series, were made from his books. His latest novel "The Evening News" (1990) was an immediate blockbuster.

Hailey emigrated from England to Canada in 1947. At first he couldn't get a job on a newspaper so he worked as a real estate salesman and an advertising executive. His big break came in 1956 when the CBC broadcast his first teleplay, "Flight Into Danger", the story of food poisoning aboard an airliner that affects both passengers and crew.

That story became a movie called "Zero Hour", then became the first of his best-sellers, "Runway Zero Eight".

Where does he get the ideas for his best-sellers?

He told me he got the idea for "Airport" while being shown around a new section of the Toronto Airport (now terminal one) by it's designer, John Parkin.

"John was telling me and my young son Stephen about some of the various difficulties the flights were encountering. We stood on the roof watching the planes take off into the winter night, I suddenly thought: when I finish Hotel, there's my new subject."

"I can't open a newspaper without coming up with half a dozen possible

subjects. Selecting the right one, or course, is the trick. Some of my ideas have come from other people. "Strong Medicine" about the pharmaceutical industry, was the idea of a publisher's editor in New York. At first I didn't think much of the idea but I trusted the man's judgment and when I looked into the background of the industry I found it one of the most fascinating, and one of the most successful too.

"The Evening News", my latest book (1990) was completely my own idea."

Some authors worry about a book once it is on the shelves. Arthur doesn't.

"By the time it's published, I know it's the best I can do. If you hate it, blame me; if you like it, praise me. It's irrevocable; it's done. Why worry when you can get on with the next one?"

What is the key to his success? How is it that his novels are all best-sellers while other writers' work sit on a back shelf and don't quite make it with the public?

"When I do a book—and this is why they are successful—the story is all. Even though I bring other ingredients in, they have to count for something. If something doesn't relate to the story, I leave it out.

"I always say in the course of my story, if I can tell the readers something about what goes on in the institutions I write about, that's fine. But if it is not relevant and doesn't move the story along, I don't use it.

"I learned one or two things when I was writing for television: keep it lean and tight. Cut out those surplus words. There are very few pieces of writing that cannot be improved by that policy of cutting.

"Early on in my writing career, a TV producer told me that the motto I should have hanging over my desk should be: conflict! conflict! conflict! that's what keeps the story going, keeps people interested. So there are three things: lean and tight, cut and conflict."

What about sex, I asked?

"Yes, sex is important. It's part of life. But you don't drown your story in it. You put it on like pepper and salt. A sprinkle here and there."

Another question that always comes up when Arthur Hailey is interviewed, or even by people at cocktail parties, is about the movies made from his books. How much influence does he have when Hollywood goes to work on his latest creation?

"I have no influence at all on the films made from my novels. I couldn't even get a part for a girl I knew who I thought was perfect for a role.

"It's a producer/director's medium. They have the last word."

Authors, even those as successful as Arthur Hailey, can be influenced by book reviewers. He has a positive thought about that too.

"I've never had a good review in The New York Times *that I can think of. There's nothing gets a book off to a better start than a bad review in the*

New York Times. I once said: 'They're writing reviews and I'm writing books'."

Although Arthur has had quadruple bypass surgery, his health has been generally good and his energy level obviously high.

"There are days when I say—why me? Why have I been so lucky? I'm still dazed, but I try to keep a sense of proportion. I just enjoy what I'm doing. That's the key to life."

Arthur Hailey, another Canadian Achiever.

"Writing is easy. All you do is stare at a blank sheet of paper until drops of blood form on your forehead."

—Gene Fowler

Big Success From Big Pond

Rita MacNeil

Canada is having a conspicuous love affair with 43-year-old singer-composer Rita MacNeil from Big Pond, Cape Breton Island. This big, beautiful lady, who loves to belt out songs in her stocking feet, can't read a note of music, nor play an instrument. What she can do is compose songs from her life experiences and sing them with such pure, sweet, down-home honesty, that audiences are drawn into a magical world of togetherness with her.

Part folk, part country, part pop, she has a spell binding way of making a hall packed with people feel simply wonderful.

It took a few years for Canadians to discover this Atlantic treasure. Life was often lean for her during those years. At one point, she 'cleaned house' for the elite instead of singing for them. In fact, at one point, she told me: *"I was ready to quit singing all together. I was so poor I had difficulty buying gas for my car to travel to out of town engagements."* But recognition was ahead. Small engagements led to big tours; soon she was wowing them all across Canada ... in Japan ... the United Kingdom ... and at Expo '86.

This charming mother of two will never run out of fans because she sings 'of' and 'to' the common people, and there are so many of us to appreciate that. And when she invites her concert audiences or television viewers *"to drop in for tea next time you're in Big Pond"* ... she sincerely means it.

Rita MacNeil... another Canadian Achiever.

"He that is overcautious will accomplish little."

—Schiller

A Father of Confederation

The Hon. Joey Smallwood

Joseph Robert (Joey) Smallwood didn't start out to be a Father of Confederation, in fact the thought probably never occurred to young Joey Smallwood. He had dropped out of school at age 15, but picked up an education working as a reporter for newspapers in St. John's, Halifax, Boston and New York. He may be the only Canadian Premier ever to have worked on the New York Times.

In the U.S. at age 24 he campaigned on behalf of the Progressive Party's candidate for President.

Four years later he was in England campaigning for the Labor Party. Back in Newfoundland in 1928, he was a campaign manager. . . then lost his first attempt to win a seat four years later.

For the next seven years Joey was "Joe the Barrelman", spinning homespun stories on the radio in St. John's.

In those days Newfoundland was an independent country. But dirt-poor. Joey Smallwood said the only way to help the people of Newfoundland get into the 20th century was unity with Canada. He campaigned hard for provincial status. . . and when the vote was taken it was a squeaker. . . only 52 percent in favor.

Joey Smallwood was chosen to lead the Liberal Party of Newfoundland and in April 1949 he led Newfoundland into Canada.

He claims: *"I went into politics because no one else would accept the challenge of bringing Newfoundland into Confederation."*

His proud boast is that he's the first Premier of Newfoundland and the only living Father of Confederation.

Joey Smallwood, a Canadian like you, who had a dream and made it work.

"A government which robs Peter to pay Paul can always depend on the support of Paul."
        —George Bernard Shaw

He Makes Us Proud to be Canadian

Mel Hurtig

Five years ago Edmonton publisher Mel Hurtig made Canadians sit up and take notice when he published the 3 volume set "The Canadian Encyclopedia". Mel established a record by selling 155,000 sets in 3 months.

Canadians snapped up the sets because finally we had an encyclopedia of our own. Well he's done it again. Only this time bigger and better. It's called "The Junior Encyclopedia of Canada". All new, all Canadian. Designed specifically for Canadian children to learn about the important role Canada has played over the years.

Did you know that the world's oldest burial site is right here in Canada? Did you know that the first oil well in North America was right here in Canada? Kerosene was invented by a Canadian? No longer do Canadian children have to rely on Canadianized versions of foreign publications. This isn't a commercial for the Junior Encyclopedia but it is an endorsement for the important role it can play in helping Canadian children, parents and educators have a better understanding of this great country. Canadians have been responsible for many important discoveries: rocket fuel, the synthesizer, the pacemaker, 5 pin bowling and of course ice hockey.

We could fill a book listing all of our achievements. In fact we are. That's what this book of *"Canadian Achievers"* is all about.

His Corn Sells

Gordie Tapp

When Gordie Tapp worked at radio station CHML in Hamilton, Ontario, the station manager Tommy Darling, gave him an important piece of advice: "Corn Sells".

At that time, Gordie was doing a jazz show called "What's on Tapp?". He loved jazz.

Tommy Darling was putting together a program called "Main Street Jambouree" with a very young country singer named Tommy Hunter, and one of Canada's very best honky-tonk piano players ever, Maurice Beaulieu. Tommy wanted Gordie to play the roles of a number of country characters. Despite the fact that Gordie could do almost any kind of accent from proper British to country bumpkin, he resisted.

"So Tommy Darling told me it was his way, or the highway", Gordie recalls. So he did the corn. And country corn became the most important item in his entertainment career.

Several years later "Main Street Jamboree" with Gordie Tapp moved to CBC-TV and became "Country Hoedown". Years later it became "The Tommy Hunter Show". In 1969 Gordie was asked to join the cast of a new U.S. television series being put together by two expatriot Canadian Achievers, Johnny Aylesworth and Frank Peppiatt.

"They wanted me as a writer and performer. I jumped at the chance." Now, 22 years later, he's still writing and starring in it. "Hee Haw" is one

of the most successful, longest running, syndicated series ever, proving what Tommy Darling said 35 years earlier, "corn sells".

I asked Gordie if he ever thought that he would step from being a sort of bandmaster of jazz to cousin Clem.

"I never did. I'm sure I had illusions of grandeur—that I would become a star in radio (television hadn't begun at that time). But I never thought for a moment that I would end up as a country comedian. But, I guess the roots were there. The thought was there. I'm glad it happened."

In October, 1989, Gordie Tapp was accorded the highest accolade that a Canadian country performer can receive: installation to the Canadian Country Music Hall of Fame.

"You know, you receive accolades from audiences, and that is very rewarding. But when you are saluted by your peers, I guess that's the ultimate. I was pretty thrilled, especially when they put my picture on the wall."

For anyone to stay on top for 30 years in the tough business of entertainment takes a certain amount of luck, courage, and more. What's Gordie's staying power?

"I don't know if there is a secret, but probably the whole thing just came to me naturally. I was sort of the class clown. I used to get in trouble for imitating the teachers in school, and our minister in church. Maybe the secret is that I am a student of people. Somehow I manage to do the kind of humor that people enjoy.

Although he maintains a home in Canada and one in Florida, Gordie earns the bulk of his income in the United States. However, he has never moved there entirely and continues to remain a Canadian citizen.

"You would be surprised at the number of Canadians who are successful in the States who are still Canadian citizens. I know lots of them. I am also flattered and proud that the Americans have accepted me. I pay taxes in both countries so I feel I am keeping up my obligations.

"It's wonderful being a Canadian. Because of my work I spend nine months of the year in the U.S., but my family is here and many of my friends. I like to come home and visit them, and keep up on what's going on. A lot of famous Canadians in the U.S. still do come home."

For many Canadian performers attracted to the U.S., the goal is better money.

"I would say that is true. But it's only part of it. Probably more so it's the challenge. The opportunity to show them that we are as good as they are, or anybody is. That for me is the attraction. That's why so many talented Canadians go to the U.S. They have reached the pinnacle of success in this country and are anxious to prove they can do it there too. And that's exactly what it is: a bigger market."

Gordie has worked with other Canadians who are world-famous country music entertainers. They seem to project a kind of good clean fun: Tommy Hunter, Ann Murray and Hank Snow.

"Tommy's a very disciplined performer. He always arrives on the set on time and knows his lines. He is a very private person and has a wonderful home life. I live just up the road from him. I kid him that I'm going to drop by some time to borrow a cup full of money.

"Ann Murray is very professional. A wonderful lady. I've watched her and her husband on the set. You don't have to visit people in their homes to know what they are like. Ann is loved not only in this country but also very much in the States.

"Hank Snow is also very professional." Gordie and I visited him backstage at the Grand Ole Opry several years ago. Hank was in his dressing-room practising the songs he was going to sing, even though he must have performed them a thousand times before.

"I guess if I were to offer advice to anyone breaking into show business, it is to work hard. Very hard. Learn your craft. Study. Remember the old story about the hippie standing on the corner in New York when a guy comes by and asks how do you get to Carnegie Hall? The hippie replies: 'Practice, Man, Practise'."

"There is no great genius without a mixture of madness."
—*Aristotle*

He Set a World Running Record

Al Howie

In 1971, Al Howie decided to quit smoking and improve his health. He was 30 years old and really out of shape. Al started jogging. Never one to do things half way he was soon entering and winning marathon races, including setting the North American record for the 24 hour race in July 1981 at Ottawa. But it was in New York City in 1989 that Al Howie won the grand-daddy of them all. The 1300 Mile, or 2100 Kilometre New York Marathon. Al ran it in a world record time of 17 days, 8 hours and 25 minutes. To fully understand his remarkable achievement, it's equivalent to running 75 miles (125 km) each day for 17 days. Newspapers and television programs around the world showed Al crossing the finish line with a smile on his face and a Canadian flag held high.

Al's not in it for the money—in fact there is no money—he pays his own expenses.

In these days of mega-million-dollar sports contracts, it's refreshing to meet an athlete who wants to achieve for the sake of achieving—Al Howie—another Canadian Achiever.

She Wants Future Generations to Live Here

Lorraine Johnson

Canada has a disgraceful record when it comes to damaging the environment: we use more energy per capita than any other country in the world. We produce more garbage than any other country studied. Canadians have the lowest recycling rate of any country studied. We consume the second highest amount of water, our output of sulphur dioxide (major contributor to acid rain) is higher than that of the United States and, our per capita output of carbon dioxide (major greenhouse gas) is second only to the U.S.

So what are we doing about it now that these startling revelations are becoming known? Lorraine Johnson has made it a life goal to bring this awareness to more and more people.   She wants to make a difference and wants the rest of us to help. Her book "Green Future: How to Make a World of Difference" is a gloomy prediction of what will happen if we don't smarten up in our attitude towards global warming, acid rain, garbage disposal and other issues that are becoming critically important to us all.

"I decided to write the book when I was working as an editor at Penguin Books in the summer of 1988. That was an incredibly hot year, creating droughts everywhere. That event, the extended heat wave, brought home to me the importance of the environmental issues I had been reading about in the newspaper.

"I wondered if this was the global warming that we had been warned about. So it led me to ask the question: 'What can I do about this? How can I make a positive difference?' And I decided to write a book about it. I couldn't find a book that already existed that would give me those answers. While there are a few environment books that have come out recently, each has a very different focus. There's a consumer guide, for example, mine isn't so much a consumer guide as a handbook on the issues and the actions that people can take."

Did Lorraine grow up with an awareness of the importance of recycling and re-using and conservation of our resources?

"My father was involved in recycling and that had an influence on my attitude. Very little was wasted in our household and that instilled in me an awareness of the importance of conservation.

"Granted, conservation in those days was mainly for economic reasons. In the household where I grew up, commonsense ruled. So we saved electricity and water to save money. But whatever the reason, and it is still valid, we weren't wasting resources.

"My book is full of suggestions on how we can all make a positive difference, through the products we buy, the way we run our households, the way we run our offices.

"One of the positive aspects that is becoming apparent in Canada is the number of kids who are educating their parents on environmental issues. I see kids constantly asking their parents questions about recycling and other concerns. I think this is a wonderful thing because it is the youth of the world today who will have to confront these issues.

"The days of rampant consumerism are on their way out. I don't think there will be a resurgence of the kind of incredible consumerism that we experienced in the 50's and again in the 70's. The big issue right now is the animosity felt by some environmentalists to big corporations who are jumping on the bandwagon to cash in on what groups like Friends of the Earth have been advocating for years. Some groups are a bit suspicious of that involvement."

We are always hearing about acid rain. What is it and what can we do about it?

In Canada we have at least 14,000 biologically dead lakes, and that is a low estimate because obviously not all lakes have been studied.

"The job for us as individuals is to keep up the pressure on the governments; we can also assist by using less energy every day, thus reducing the amount of energy and acid rain our power plants create. We can use our cars less, use public transit, cycle or walk.

"As I said, if we want as individuals to reduce the risk of further global warming we have to consider how efficiently we heat our homes, the amount we drive our cars. We can use energy efficient appliances; there are hundreds of commonsense ways to conserve energy."

I asked Lorraine if Canadians should be concerned about the destruction of the rain forests in Brazil?

"Yes. At least one species of life form—animals, birds, flora—is being destroyed every day that the forests are being burned down. Their habitat is going. The other way we are affected is the way the rain forest impacts on the global climate. Those trees absorb carbon dioxide and release oxygen. They also regulate the water cycle that goes through the Amazon to the ocean.

"That's how the rain forest destruction affects us all. That's why we use the slogan: think globally: act locally. To get a local view of a global problem, garbage, take a trip to your local dump and see the incredible amount of material thrown out. You may have thought you solved your garbage problem by throwing it into the trash can. Out of sight, out of mind. But it hasn't gone away!

"Even in Ontario where 69% of the population is now participating in the blue box program, only about 2% of the garbage we produce is diverted from the dump. We have to also rely on two other principles: reduce and reuse."

Lorraine Johnson is someone who is doing something positive to change our world. She is a Canadian Achiever who has a lifetime goal: to make the rest of us aware of the incredible importance of thinking globally: acting locally.

He Makes Christmas Live

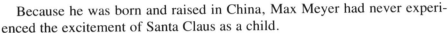

Max Meyer

Because he was born and raised in China, Max Meyer had never experienced the excitement of Santa Claus as a child.

His family returned to Germany where, as a young man, he joined the Merchant Navy. When his ship visited Vancouver he fell in love with Canada and wanted to live here. He applied to immigrate and was accepted. He got a job as a bus driver in Vancouver, and it was while serving in this capacity that the spirit of Christmas inspired Max to unusual heights. Long after his career as a reliable bus driver had been established, Max decided to spend Christmas week dressed as the Santa Claus he had missed out on knowing for so many years. He purchased candy canes for his passengers and led them in Christmas song as they wended their way along Max's west end bus route. Everyone loved the idea; everyone, that is, except the company that employed him.

Max was told to stop such frivolity. His behaviour, he was told, was unbecoming, and it was against company policy to drive the bus while out of uniform. When Max refused to stop spreading his Christmas cheer, the company threatened to fire him. Max was undaunted. The company threatened to transfer him to another route. When Max's passengers heard about the disagreement they raised such a fuss that Max was finally allowed to continue in his role as Jolly Old St. Nick. He continued to act as Santa every Christmas thereafter, right up until his retirement.

Even though Max no longer drives a bus, he still dons whiskers and suit each Christmas season to spread a little cheer at Vancouver area hospitals, senior citizen homes and the huge ferries that travel back and forth to Vancouver Island. This Christmas (1990), Max and his two helpers gave out over 20 thousand candy canes. Mostly at his own expense and without any remuneration.

Max Meyer. . . a real live Canadian Santa Claus. He's another Canadian Achiever.

"He started to sing as he tackled the thing that couldn't be done, and he did it."

—Edgar A. Guest

The Sailor Who Now Owns the Fleet

Jim Lane

In 1949 Jim Lane was 12 years old growing up in Vancouver. Jim was a big kid for his age and because of his size he got a summer job as a deck hand on a tug boat and quickly fell in love with the sea. At age 14 he quit school and went to sea full time.

Over the years he worked hard, studied and got his Masters ticket, saved his money, and eventually acquired 10% of the towing company. But that didn't satisfy him so he sold his shares, levered a bank loan, bought his own tug boat, and started his company, "Mariner Towing". That was in 1979. Now Mariner Towing Company is one of the most active on the west coast.

His three tug boats 'Sea Lane', 'Storm Crest' and 'Tugger Lane' are always busy towing barges up and down the Inside Passage from Olympia, Washington, to Port Hardy, B.C. and all points in between.

In 1989 Jim made world headlines when he donated the services of the 'Sea Lane' to tow the world's largest hockey stick from the Expo '86 site in Vancouver Harbor, under Lions Gate Bridge and across Georgia Strait to Duncan on Vancouver Island.

Today at 54, Jim is easing up a little. He lives with his wife Ellen on a Gulf Island. His sister Irene and brother Irv run the office. Son, Jim Jr., does bull work on one of the tugs learning the tricks of the trade. Jim deserves to take it easy, after all he's been hard at it for 42 years, it's time he eased up the slack a little.

Quebec's Young Entrepreneur

David Lauzon

Twenty-seven year old David Lauzon of Papineauville, Quebec near Ottawa, is truly a remarkable Achiever: the youngest of eight children, David lost a leg in a motorcycle accident when he was 17 years old. But he didn't let that deter him from becoming successful.

"My parents were very encouraging and that was a very important factor in my success. I was a very mature 21 year old, and when I saw my friends going off to university to spend four years getting an engineering degree or whatever, I was busy working to save money to buy my own business."

David saved up $5,000 and rented a sawmill that was involved mainly in turning raw lumber into wood flooring. In five years he built "David Lauzon Limited" from annual sales of $100,000 to a projected $3 million in 1991, making him Papineauville's second largest employer.

His business acumen was recognized by the Federal Business Development Bank on October 17, 1990 in Toronto when David was awarded the Young Entrepreneur Award for Quebec. The 12 winners, one from each Province and Territory, received their awards at the launching of 1990's Small Business Week.

Born in Notre-Dame-de-la-Paix, David is that town's most successful son. In selecting him, the jury could not overlook David's remarkable entrepreneurial spirit. His mill's system of production is organized in such a way that all scrap is recovered and no waste is dumped into the environment. Since launching his business, David has captured almost 60 percent of the local market.

"I know we are experiencing bad market conditions today but we are keeping our heads up and know that things will return to normal soon. The world needs wood products and we are looking after our local markets too."

Which does not mean David will limit his scope to sales in Montreal and Toronto, but hopes to one day sell in foreign countries such as England and China. The woodflooring mill sells to wholesalers, homeowners and contractors who install and varnish floors.

David is well known in Papineauville for his involvement in social and community activities. Every year he participates in a summer job creation program for the disabled. He contributes to local assistance campaigns and is active in the Chamber of Commerce and business groups in his area.

When I asked his advice to other handicapped persons who want to go into business? He replied simply:

"I begin work at 5 a.m. and I work until 7 or 8 p.m. every day but Sunday. I guess my advice would be to work, work, work."

David Lauzon, a credit to his community and indeed a credit to Canada. We need more young entrepreneurs like him. He's another Canadian Achiever.

Native Musical Genius

John Kim Bell

John Kim Bell, a Mohawk Indian, was born on the Kahnawake Reserve near Montreal 37 years ago but left with his mother when he was three years old. If he had stayed on the reserve, his great musical talent might never have been discovered.

"After the trouble on the reserve in 1990, I'm glad I left when I did."

John studied piano and violin and by the age of 18 was conducting orchestras on Broadway. He was also pianist to popular singers and rock groups including the Australian group of Saturday Night Fever Fame, the Bee Gees.

On the classical side, in 1980 he became apprentice conductor of the Toronto Symphony.

John Kim Bell was the first North American Indian to reach such heights in the music world. But he never forgot his roots. Back in Canada he discovered that native artists were not receiving Canada Council Grants to develop their talents, so he established the Canadian Native Arts Foundation and dedicated himself to giving native children opportunities for specialized education and training in the performing, crafted and visual arts.

John Kim Bell, a Canadian Achiever, recipient of the Order of Canada, helping other Indian kids to develop their talents.

Don't Be Afraid... You Can Do It!

... [broadcast Friday, Jan. 25/91]
If you're like me, and you probably are, you go into each new year with a feeling of excitement looking forward to the challenges and opportunities a new year will place before you. If you're like me, and you probably are, you even made a list of all the things you resolved you would do once the new year finally arrive. We even give the list a name, we call it our list of New Year's Resolutions. How is your list coming along? Have you given up any of them yet? If they now seem too challenging, remember what David Lloyd-George said ... "Don't be afraid to take a big step if one is needed. You can't cross a chasm in two small steps". If you told yourself last year that you were going to do something this year, then do it... you can. You can do whatever you set your mind to. Remember, don't be afraid to take a big step if one is needed. You can't cross a chasm in two small steps. I read recently that going through life is like riding in a car. Are you moving along or is the car moving and you're just sitting there? That's a good question. You can bet that the Canadian Achievers I talk about everyday on this program are not just sitting there letting a car take them along life's highway. No sir, you can bet they're in full control driving the car. You still have time to start and achieve your 1991 goals. But don't procrastinate, time is flying by. 1991 is already nearly 1/12th over. Before you know... it'll be time to work on your 1992 resolutions.

"You can't beat winning."
—*John Bassett III*

Internationally Famous Singer/Songwriter

Gordon Lightfoot

Gordon Lightfoot's story is the story of a Toronto guitar player who became an international singing songwriting star.

Born in Orillia, Ontario, October 17, 1939, music has been part of Gordon Lightfoot's life almost from the start. At age 11 he was a singer in the church choir, at 13 he was winning music festivals that gave him the right to sing in Toronto's Massey Hall, and at age 16 he was teaching himself to play the guitar. He spent his early years performing in bars and coffee houses, singing his own songs as well as those of others.

One of his first big breaks was an invitation to join the cast of 'Country Hoedown' as a dancer, then later as a singer. This brought him to the attention of TV viewers across Canada. Despite the fact that television gives him exposure to Canadians, Gordon shies away from it. He doesn't think he projects as well on the tube as he does on stage or on records. He'll tell you that a lot of his personal life is in the music he writes. For example, a lost love is behind his hit "If You Could Read My Mind."

His first big hit "In the Early Morning Rain" has been recorded by many major recording artists including Elvis Presley. He's published over 300 songs and released 25 albums. His songs have been translated and recorded in 12 different languages.

An extremely proud Canadian, he still lives in Canada recording, and collecting royalties from his songs. Gordon Lightfoot, a Canadian like you, had a dream and made it work. He's another Canadian Achiever.

"Well begun is half done."
—*Horace*

A High School Drop Out Who Achieved

Brian Tracy

Brian Tracy is known world-wide as a leading authority on the development of human potential and personal effectiveness. His peak performance seminars have been attended by over 600,000 people. His motivational tapes and video tapes are produced in five languages, sold around the world, and followed religiously by millions.

Brian Tracy's gross income in 1990 exceeded $10 million. Not bad for a high school dropout from Charlottetown, Prince Edward Island.

Brian is a living example of the power that's within everybody. Proof that a sincere desire to achieve will overcome any background.

"We have a family joke. I was born during the war, my mother said that since there was nothing else to do on P.E.I. they decided to have me!"

It wasn't a bad decision, if becoming such a phenomenal success is any yardstick by "Spud Island's" criteria.

"I must admit, I didn't have an impressive beginning. I failed out of high school and then began a succession of labouring jobs: washing dishes, digging wells, working in sawmills and on farms. By the time I reached 20, I realized if I didn't do something soon, nothing was ever going to change for me."

So Brian set out on a lifelong study of what it is that makes some people successes while others fail.

"Why is it some people make more money, are healthier, have nicer relationships? It was an obsessive world-wide search for success and achievement in all its various aspects. After about 10 or 15 years I began to apply these principles to my own life—with some success, and began sharing these ideas with other people, first individually, then in small groups. Later I addressed seminars and large public audiences."

Now one of the most successful public speakers in the English language, Brian speaks to more than 100,000 people a year. His audio and video cassettes on success in business and relationships are the best selling of their kind in the world.

I asked Brian, why are some people more successful than others?

"The major ingredient in success comes down to this one word: responsibility. Most people don't realize that they are totally responsible for everything that happens to them. Once a person understands that and accepts that, they can't make any more excuses. They have to become responsible.

"The next step is to say, here's my goal, my aim. Here's where I want to go."

Brian relates the story of a man who came to a seminar of his in Toronto:

"He told me he had never thought about responsibility and setting goals. He'd been a car salesman for years. He was like everyone else he knew, always broke. After hearing me speak he made a decision to design a financial plan in which he would save 10% of his earnings and reach his goal in five years. He achieved his goal in three years and almost immediately was offered the opportunity to buy a Chrysler dealership. Now he had the experience, the knowledge for money. He bought the dealership and three years later he was a millionaire. When he had accepted responsibility, made a goal, made a plan and went to work on it, he became successful."

Money may be many people's goals in life, but what of those who want to achieve in other areas? Can this advice work for them?

"In order for us to be truly happy and to enjoy peace of mind, we have to

feel that our lives are making a difference. We are making a contribution of some kind. Success means achieving a happiness or inner peace by doing something that you love to do and doing it very well. Making a difference in the world!"

What about age? Is there a limit to the time that a person can still achieve goals and make a difference?

"Some people get turned on to their potential when they're fifteen, others at fifty-five. Numerous people are now going back to university in their 40's and 50's to get medical and architectural degrees to start new careers and professions. Colonel Sanders was a short-order cook until the highways department in Kentucky re-routed traffic around his cafe. A few months later he received his first social security cheque. The two incidents, loss of job and getting old, spurred him on instead of shutting him down. He got angry. He told himself he was tired of living like that so he cashed that cheque and bought some pots and pans and went out to sell his own secret chicken recipe.

"He wasn't very successful at first. One thousand restaurant owners turned him down before he sold his first rights to use his formula. Surprisingly, it was in Toronto! They promised to pay five cents a chicken to the Canadian Red Cross and that was the beginning for Colonel Harlon Sanders, who was a multi-millionaire within the next ten years and one of the most familiar figures in the world. Colonel Sanders didn't get started until he was 65!

I told Brian that one of the problems with motivational seminars and tapes seems to be that people come away full of vim and vigor and good intentions but the feelings leave them and the tapes end up in a drawer, unused. How does a person keep cranked up?

"That is the most critical question in the whole field of human success, achievement and motivation. How to get going and stay going?

"The secret to success is not to bite off more than you can chew. People who make big resolutions usually fail. A big resolution is too enormous; it's like eating an elephant. You can eat an elephant but you have to do it a bite at a time."

What does Brian Tracy, successful high school dropout recommend to young people starting out?

"The most important thing I learned as a young man and all through my years is to select something you enjoy, don't just take whatever job that comes along. Go out and interview employers rather than have them interview you. See what they have to offer. You should get a kick out of your work. Something that will make you happy to do, not just to get a pay cheque.

"Commit yourself to paying any price, to going any distance. Commit yourself to being the best. If you become really excited by what you're do-

ing, you'll be paid more, you'll be respected more and you'll derive more satisfaction and pleasure. And—you'd be able to control your whole destiny!''

Following Brian Tracy's advice has helped many people become Canadian Achievers.

His 'Family Ties' are Canadian

Michael J. Fox

In the final scene of the movie 'Back to the Future III', Dr. Brown, played by Christopher Lloyd, tells Marty McFly, played by Michael J. Fox, *"your future hasn't been written yet, no one's has. Your future is whatever you make it. So make it a good one."* That scene may have been pure fiction, but the advice is pure reality. Michael J. Fox is making his future a good one.

The 'J' in Michael J. Fox doesn't stand for anything in particular. Michael put it there a few years ago when he learned that he was not the only Michael Fox looking for acting jobs in Los Angeles. He certainly needn't worry any more about confusion over his name.

Born in Edmonton, June 9, 1961, Michael J. Fox was a smash hit with his starring roles in the three 'Back to the Future' movies and the TV show 'Family Ties', now in syndication. Even though he was older, Michael played a teenager several years younger in those hit shows.

His career got its start on the strength of Michael's ability to portray a character much younger than himself. When he was fifteen years old he landed the part of a ten-year-old in the television show 'Leo and Me', a role he played for two years.

At the suggestion of movie greats Art Carney and Maureen Stapleton, Michael decided to try looking for work in Los Angeles. It didn't take Los Angeles long to realize that these veteran actors knew their stuff: Michael J. Fox had talent.

Michael J. Fox now lives in Los Angeles, even though he maintains real 'Family Ties' with Vancouver. His movie 'The Secret of My Success' is something of a misnomer: it's no secret that talent is the foundation for this Canadian Achiever's skyrocketing career.

"A pro is someone who makes it look easy."
—Paul Henderson

A Canadian Gift To Hollywood

Genevieve Bujold

Several years ago Aline and I were vacationing in Acapulco, Mexico. Our travel agent had booked us into "Los Brisas", a lovely resort high in the hills offering a spectacular view of the harbour. Unknown to us was the fact that the annual Mexico Film Festival was on. Many International stars were staying at our resort.

We arrived late at night and went to bed. Imagine our surprise the following day at lunch to see James Mason, Adam West, and Genevieve Bujold among the people lunching in the dining room. Several days later, during a quiet moment around the pool, Aline and I introduced ourselves to Genevieve and complimented her on her achievements. She seemed genuinely pleased to meet fellow Canadians whom she could relate with.

Her story is one of great pride, since she is now regarded as one of the world's great actresses. But it's doubtful that many of the students attending the Hochelaga Convent in Montreal in the 1950's imagined that a future movie star was in their midst. When Genevieve Bujold finished her twelve years at that school, she went directly into the Conservatory of Arts in Montreal. Three more years of schooling prepared her for a professional acting career. As she says, *"A diploma can't get you work in the theatre, but a part can!"*

By the time she was twenty-four, Genevieve was in Paris to accept a major award. The following year she was nominated for an Emmy. Two more years saw her win a Golden Globe award in Hollywood and an Academy Award nomination for her role in "Anne of a Thousands Days".

In 1972, Canada finally caught up with the rest of the entertainment world, and named Genevieve Bujold "The Most Outstanding Performer in Canada."

Genevieve Bujold, a Canadian like you. She had a dream and made it work. She's another Canadian Achiever.

He'll Help You Achieve

Art McNeil

This Canadian Achiever believes there is a five-year-old child in all of us who is crying to be let out. The trouble is, five-year-olds can be a pain sometimes if they aren't given their own way. And do you give your direction to a five-year-old child?

R. A. "Art" McNeil is founder and president of *The Achieve Group In-*

corporated*, a Canadian company that specializes in developing skills in people. Art was director of sales and marketing for Bell Canada and later for the Edmonton Telephone Company. In 1977 he retired to found a company in Edmonton called *"The Achieve Group"*. His goal was to help employees and employers understand what it takes to achieve.

Art's company is now centered in Mississauga, Ontario after first starting out in Edmonton. At time of writing, "The Achieve Group" had six offices, 35 employees and sales of $7 million a year! Art collaborated with Dr. Tom Peters, co-author of "In Search of Excellence", in the development of an action sequel to the book. He also wrote his own best-selling "The 'I' of the Hurricane", and "The V.I.P. Strategy", (both with Jim Clemmer) and is an internationally recognized speaker on leadership and service quality.

"You don't have to be a rocket scientist to realize there are changes happening in every part of the world. We are now getting to an era as we enter the 21st century where people with the product are going to win and those without are going to lose. It's as simple as that. We're looking at a world where the Asian trading block and the European trading block are really going to put it to us. Unless we shape up and get skilled and discover what it is that we can do better than anyone else we are going to get beat. When you see yourself getting beat, you get energized real fast!"

But isn't it true, I asked Art, that more than ever, heads of corporations are sending their executives and employees to seminars to learn how to manage other people and make changes that will benefit the company?

"Companies have all these big elaborate plans but they don't know how to manage day to day affairs. The major innovation that I've noticed is that executives are starting to understand that their customer is the non-management employee. The real link that connects the server with the served is all wrong. The problem is with the manager and the managed, not with the server and the customer.

"The first thing is to uncover the core value that everyone in the organization believes in. Things like innovation; responsiveness; quality; integrity. Something that brings the five-year-old in all of us alive and says: 'Yes, I want to belong. I want to win. This is the kind of organization I am prepared to put my commitment behind.'"

So what is it that Canadians have that no one else has?

"Around the world Canadians are known for being trustworthy. Trust is a value. We are a value-giving society. We don't recognize it as much as the rest of the world does. We also have discipline, unlike the Americans who get all excited about something but don't know where to take their energy.

---

* There are several companies in Canada using the world 'Achieve' in their corporate title. None form part of 'The Canadian Achievers' Group.

We Canadians are institutional in our thinking. We're terribly disciplined and organized and have a way of taking what we believe in at a slower pace to make it work. Whereas the Americans tend to get an idea and go off like a sky rocket in every direction with no discipline."

If we must improve and become innovative to stay at least abreast of the competition from Europe and Asia, what must we do?

"The world is changing so fast that you have to develop a system within your organization that continually improves. People will take a system that is not working, change it, and a year later change it again and they are still out of step. Innovation is absolutely necessary, but innovation by itself is chaos. You must have a clear notion of where you are going and what to believe in.

"In a study of 90 top leaders in the fields of business, academe, sports and the arts it was concluded that these leaders had visions or intentions that are compelling and pull people along with them. Intensity coupled with commitment is magnetic."

"When I first started out in the business, I wanted to find out what it was that prevented people from taking action. They knew what they wanted but they didn't know how to do it. Action, not talk produces excellence. After a lot of research I discovered it was an absence of skill camouflaged with a lot of defence mechanisms. They will not own up to the fact that they have a skill deficiency and use all kinds of methods to disguise it and may not even know they are doing it. My advice is, when in doubt, skill out. Practice skills and you create empowerment. The routine is quite simple: to be successful in the nineties, make sure your value space is clear, and practice your skills."

What about that five-year-old in all of us? Is he/she in there gumming up the works all the time?

"It's true! And at every level. One thing I have learned in dealing with executives is that they are just like confused kids. They have a need to know people care; they go into traumas; they'll overwork and overplay and when you need them most they are too tired to be at their best. Five-year-olds are not concerned about or interested in plans. No reason why they should be. If you let the five-year-old in you come out and play and dream about the future it will give you an opportunity to put up with the tremendous set of problems that beset us every day.

"That's how you can stick to your plan: you keep going back and firing up the little guy with ideas." You can have both; you can set a plan and imagine possibilities. The beauty of the paradox of dreaming and planning is not making your plan become a dream and not making your dream become a plan as the dream provides energy and the plan provides the direction.

"But because of our training, we always want to merge the two and it doesn't work. In most cases, both die."

"The world is changing too fast for most people. We are programmed in negativity before the age of five. Now everytime we hear the word 'change' we see 12 negative pictures before we see one positive one. That means if you really want to become effective as a person, you must paint pictures of the preferred future so that the vacuum between our ears is filled with something positive."

Art McNeil. . . he trains people to become Canadian Achievers.

He's Digging Up Gold

Barry Gunn

Spying on your competition is as old as the hills. You spy on them, they spy on you. A restauranteur in Lloydminster, Alberta has added a new twist on spying that is simple as suds. Yet works like a charm. 34 year old Barry Gunn owns 'Diggers Family Restaurant'. He employs 40 people. To find out what the competition is doing and stay ahead of them he pays four of his staff to go and have a nice meal once a month at a competitor's restaurant. Never the same four staff. Never the same competitor. The next morning there is a staff meeting and the four give a complete report on what they saw. Here's how Barry explained it to me. . . *"Really what it is is a way of highlighting what we are trying to drive home to our staff. All the areas in which we can improve. They get to look at some of the other operations and expose our people to what the competition is doing. It's worked very well. We visit seven competing restaurants in our market area."*

It's always the simple ideas that work the best. In this case it's working very well. Barry's restaurant will do over one million dollars in sales this year. In a city of 15 thousand people you have to admit that's very good.

Barry Gunn of 'Diggers Restaurant' is digging up gold with sharp ideas.

He's Revolutionizing Highway Resurfacing

Pat Wiley

Canada is truly a land of creative entrepreneurs. I guess it's because we are only 124 years young that we still have the explorer's sense about us, frontier mentality. Unlike most of the older countries our best and most inventive ideas are still coming from average Canadians in average sized towns and cities. Fortunately our creative curiosity hasn't yet been stifled or swallowed up by huge multi-national corporations. Canadians still keep coming up with ingenious inventions that are being accepted around the world. Unusual inventions like a device I saw while on a speaking engagement in Williams Lake, British Columbia. It's called a "Hot In Place Asphalt Recycling Machine". Its inventor is Pat Wiley, a 35 year old entrepreneur.

What is it? Well, if you're driving along the highway and see a huge machine moving along at 4km per day chewing up and eating the highway surface in one end of the machine and laying it down out the other end in the form of fresh new highway surface, stop and look because that's Pat Wiley's incredible invention.

Pat has always been an entrepreneur. He left high school to work in a welding shop; by age 21 he owned it. Then he got into asphalt resurfacing. He knew there had to be a better, faster way. Here's how Pat explained it ...

"It took us about three years or prototype testing. Now for the last couple of years we've been selling the machines quite well."

The first sale was to a Japanese company for highway resurfacing in the southern U.S. Other sales followed. Pat now has machines in several countries. When you consider that each machine sells for 2 million dollars, you quickly realize that Pat has a major invention.

"I take a great amount of pride in being an entrepreneur. In North America we need more entrepreneurs creating new products to keep up with the rest of the world."

Does he recommend entrepreneurship for everyone?

"It's not always the easiest life. Sometimes there's ups, sometimes there's downs. Sometimes you wonder if there will be a tomorrow in the business. But the rewards are great. As far as business goes there are just two kinds. There is managing a business or there is creating a new business. Certainly the most rewarding is creating a new business. People get jobs from it and you can make a lot of money. Yes I recommend it highly."

Pat's machine is revolutionizing highway and airport runway resurfacing. Buyers have come from as far away as Russia and Japan to order the machines. Pat Wiley and his small company "Artec Asphalt Recycling Systems" have become big players in the global market place. He's another Canadian Achiever.

"Critics are people who have failed."
—Anonymous

From Winnipeg to Hollywood

Mimi Kuzyk

The people of Winnipeg think of her as one of the local kids who grew up dancing in a Ukrainian folk group. People who have watched the television show "Hill Street Blues" think of her as Detective Patsy Mayo. Mimi Kuzyk is both of these things, and more.

Mimi's fourteen years of dancing with the Winnipeg group gave her a love of the stage that eventually took her to Toronto. There she waited on tables, took acting lessons and tried out for every part she could find. It all paid off a few years ago when a TV executive from the U.S. encouraged Mimi to go to Los Angeles to try her luck.

Her luck proved to be pretty good. Within just a few weeks, Mimi was offered the part of Detective Mayo on the "Hill Street Blues" series, and a starring role in the movie "Paper Castles".

Mimi has not left her background far behind. She recently travelled to Regina, Edmonton, and her home town Winnipeg, acting in a play about growing up Ukrainian in Canada. Mimi successfully continues to enjoy her love for acting in Canada and the U.S. Be it on television, film or the stage. She's another "Canadian Achiever".

He Has the Best of Both Worlds

Dr. Ron Taylor

Ron Taylor was headed for a career as an electrical engineer. He got short circuited in 1962 when he was drafted right out of the University of Toronto into baseball's major leagues as a pitcher. For the next ten years Ron had an enviable career including a World Series championship in 1969 with the New York Mets. In 1972 he felt it was time to retire and build a long term career. Instead of electrical engineering, Ron wanted to become a sports medicine physician. It meant going back to university and starting all over again. Which he willingly did.

Today Dr. Ron Taylor has the best of both world's. He practices sports medicine at his own clinic. And he keeps his hand in major league baseball as team doctor for the Toronto Blue Jays. It's the dream of most young Canadians to have a life of glamour and fun as a professional athlete. We hear about the fabulous contracts being offered youngsters, many of whom are still in high school. It's an attractive temptation to set aside formal education for the chance to grab the brass ring and its riches. But what about life after sports? *"It's difficult for a teenager to imagine he or she will ever get old, but it's a fact of life they must eventually face."*

When you consider the average career in professional sports is four years, it's easy to understand why former professional athletes like Dr. Ron Taylor are unanimous in stressing the importance of acquiring an education for life after sports.

He's the Greatest

Wayne Gretzky

What hasn't already been said or written about Wayne Gretzky. He's recognized as the greatest hockey player the world has ever seen. My interview with Wayne had been arranged by the Kings' management to take place the morning following a Vancouver Canucks/Los Angeles Kings game in Vancouver. During the game I sat with hockey legend and member of the Hockey Hall of Fame, Babe Pratt.* I asked Babe what he thought of Wayne Gretzky. Babe replied . . . *"I've seen 'em all . . . this kid is beyond compare. The best way to describe him is to say that if the good Lord had of sent somebody down to earth to show us all how this game of hockey should be played, he'd of sent Wayne Gretzky."*

Wayne is a very humble person. During our interview the next morning, I told him what Babe had said. He looked down at the floor almost embarrassed and said . . . *"Now that's pressure . . . over the years there have been so many great players in this game that it's tough to compare. The game has changed a lot, it moves ahead. I really believe that players today are much better and stronger than even when I first broke in. The Game is making progress and that's what really matters most of all."*

Number 99 Wayne Gretzky, from Brantford, Ontario, he's broken nearly every record, and won nearly every award, including being the first hockey player ever named as Sports Illustrated's "Man of the Year". On March 22/91 Wayne set another world record when he and Los Angeles Kings owner Bruce McNall paid $451,000 U.S. for a 1½ x 2½ inch 1921 baseball collectable card of Honas Wagner. And also in 1991, Wayne, along with Canadian comic John Candy and Bruce McNall, bought the Toronto Argos of the CFL!

* Two weeks later Babe Pratt died suddenly of a massive heart attack. He died doing what he liked best ... watching a hockey game in an arena.

From Cottage Industry to Franchise Chain

Gary & Vicki Lynn Bardon

Gary & Vicki Lynn Bardon of Mahone Bay, Nova Scotia, created the very successful 'Suttles and Seawinds' retail and wholesale chain from a cottage industry that concentrated mainly on handmade quilts. When they expanded their line to include clothing, business really boomed. But they decided to sell even more; franchising was the answer.

Gary, a lawyer, realized that their products did not get the same attention in a regular retail outlet handling many different manufacturers.

"It was obvious that we must accumulate as much of our product on display for the benefit of the customer to make a selection. So the dedicated store became the marketing answer for us, although the wholesale business is still very important. We saw that all Suttles and Seawinds products assembled in one store make far greater impact and sales increased dramatically."

There is another important reason for franchising even though there is less profit to the owner than obtained from his own stores:

"The franchisee puts up the capital to start with, but even more important is the on-the-spot management. Nobody is more dedicated than the person who owns the business."

The Bardon's business grew from an idea that Vicki Lynn got while working in New York for the prestigious American Home Magazine. She had gone to New York after graduating from Acadia University to study at the New York School of Interior Design. So how did she switch from interior design to fashionable clothing?

"From what I saw in the market in New York, I realized that the ladies back home were very talented and I was sure that with a little help with design and marketing they could be fairly paid for the wonderful crafts they could make in their own homes."

Vicki Lynn returned to Nova Scotia and gathered together a group of craftswomen (200 showed up at one meeting) and met with the provincial government Department of Development.

"They advised us to decide if we had anything worth selling, and have a display somewhere."

And what a display it was!

"We put together our line of quilts, pillows, place mats and other small things and in a couple of months we put on a show at the Canadian Consulate in New York. Because of my contacts, I was able to draw attention through the media and representatives from Bloomingdales and Sax Fifth Avenue. We were a success even before the show."

"Soon we got an order from the trendy Abercrombie & Fitch for

$40,000 and we had to move quickly. This was still just an idea, we didn't even have a company. The provincial government was helpful.

"With their help we found investors and a lawyer to put the company together." The lawyer became her husband and partner. *"And that's how we got going."*

Got going is right! The company moved into the clothing business right after it was seen that hand-crafted quilt and pillows became very expensive by the time they hit the retail level.

"So we had to make other things. What happened was after about a year I would do a store promotion some place wearing a dress made from one of the prints in the quilts. And people would want to buy the dress. So, we were forced to go into clothing.

"But people liked clothing with this composite of prints, quilting, textures, applique. Now that part of the business supplies 80 percent of our trade while 20 percent comes from the quilts and the little things we started with.

"From a few lady home sewers we now have more than 85 fulltime employees working in our workshops and about 100 home sewers. In 1991 we expect our revenue to be about $4 million, which calculated to retail is about $6.6 million."

Do Vicki Lynn and Gary have advice for people who think they have a good idea and want to market it, perhaps franchise it as well?

Vicki Lynn: *"The best advice I think is to believe that you can do it. Don't be deterred by all the little problems on the way. Just be persistent. A buyer at Bloomingdale's told me my middle name must be tenacious because I was so determined that I was going to sell to them that he had to give in and buy."*

Gary: *"If you are thinking of franchising, first define your product to see if it is something special. Something you can put together as an organized package to present to a prospective franchisee, one that is not too much like everybody else is doing in the market."*

Gary and Vicki Lynn have another word of advice for the would-be franchiser. . . . don't go too fast too soon.

"We did that and we lost our house in order to stay in business." The Bardon's bounced back and now have a lovely home again. After 18 years in business their Suttles and Seawinds have eight stores in Canada and a burgeoning wholesale business that sells to outlets across Canada and the United States.

After what they've been through, would they do it again?

"Definitely!"

"The person who makes no mistakes does not usually make anything."
—*Edward J. Phelps*

Kids Mean Business

Eileen Cole

Studies indicate that more women than men are setting up their own small businesses in Canada today. Lending institutions will tell you that women applying for start up loans come to them better prepared. Their pro formas are more realistic. Their business profit expectations are usually more realistic than men's. Women stand a better chance to succeed.

Eileen Cole of Elkhorn, Manitoba is part of this new business trend. Eileen is owner of a toy shop and playschool for 3 and 4 year olds in Red Deer, Alberta called, "The Children's Corner".

As a former instructor at a playschool cooperative for a number of years, and as the mother of two children, Eileen spotted the need for a quality educational toy store in central Alberta. She knew a lot about choosing toys and the value of play. What she didn't know very much about was accounting and managing staff. So, she talked to lawyers, bankers and management consultants before deciding to go for it. Seven years of planning went into her store, which opened September 1985. Eileen is really pleased with the way things have gone.

She operates with a full and part time staff of seven people. She limits enrollment at the playschool to 100 youngsters, and there is always a waiting list to enroll. Eileen told me . . .

"For years I taught school full time and then playschool for 12 years. But, I always wanted to be on my own. This is wonderful."

There'll Be No Tag Days For Him

John Ferguson

His name is engraved on five Stanley Cups. He spearheaded a hockey dynasty in Montreal that lasted from 1963 to 1971. How did John Ferguson do it I asked?

"When you get right down to it, I made it my business to be an absolutely miserable S.O.B. on the ice all of the time."

If the Montreal Canadiens had a weakness in the early sixties it was size. Too often they were being battered against the boards and checked out of action. That problem was solved when general manager Frank Selke brought John up from the American Hockey League as a sort of enforcer, or policeman. He hadn't lost a fight in the A.H.L. and lived up to his reputation during his first game in Boston. At the opening faceoff he got into a fight with Ted Green and he won. He then proceeded to score twice in that game.

After playing 500 games, scoring 145 goals, 158 assists and spending 1,214 minutes in the penalty box, the extremely aggressive forward retired from the Canadiens in 1971 to begin a new career as a businessman. But he couldn't stay away from the game he loved. He came back as coach and general manager of the New York Rangers in 1976, then as general manager of the Winnipeg Jets and finally as general manager of Team Canada. But the biggest moment of his life was being taken on by the Canadiens.

"It was like dying and going to heaven, being called into Frank Selke's office. I had come up from the American league leading in goal scoring and selected for the All-star team and Mr. Selke told me: 'Son, I am going to pay you $125 a game whether you are with the American league or with the big team, and I hope it's with the big team.' I said: 'Fine, Mr. Selke. Just give me the pen and I'll sign the contract.'

"That worked out to $8,500 per season. Pretty small peanuts compared with player's salaries now. But we didn't have any agents then and I wasn't about to negotiate with the Canadiens. I was just glad to be there."

Other hockey superstars, like Gordie Howe for example, are bitterly resentful of the poor pay they received in their early years. Is John resentful, and does the big money now attract young men to the game as much as anything else?

"Money definitely plays a big role in attracting new players. Stars are in demand and they demand good money. Thankfully the N.H.L. does not have free agency comparable to the American and National Baseball leagues. At least you can control the situation in hockey because if you don't the Madison Square Garden Group and the Los Angeles Kings are going to control hockey because of the wealth they can spend on talent.

"The downside on that—playing for the big money—is the emphasis to become a star, not a member of the team. Since the advent of agents there's no real loyalty to the teams. It's look after yourself first."

John Ferguson was a very loyal player and even in the off-season while playing for Montreal he still would not even talk to members of opposing teams. What made him so fanatical about the game?

"Hockey was my whole life from the time I was a kid. I was raised in Vancouver and at that time there were only three arenas and practice time had to be shared with the figure skaters. I used to get up at five a.m. every day and get in as much ice time as I could. I guess that was the secret of my success. I persevered. I finished high school at Vancouver Technical School then went to Melville, and played in the Saskatchewan Junior League. I kept persisting and persisting until I finally got a chance with the Canadiens. The biggest luck is to get that chance to play in the N.H.L., but don't expect to go in right away. You have to work hard and become a self-made hockey player."

Aside from being accepted by the Canadiens, what was the biggest thrill?

"Winning the Stanley Cup the first time was the most invigorating feeling anyone could ever have. But I never lost my enthusiasm for winning a second or a third. And believe me, winning it is tough to do. You never get enough of winning, but you learn to take the ups with the downs. You have to remember you will be meeting the same guys coming down as you met going up."

What advice does John have for young players?

"It's terribly expensive for parents nowadays to get a kid into minor hockey. Some people just can't afford the equipment which is tough because their boy may have great potential. I think if a player wants to get into pro hockey he should start skating as soon as he can walk.

"My best advice to young players is to stay away from drugs, they can ruin your life. I've had players succumb to them. One guy who played for me had so much talent, but he got into drugs and he went downhill fast. Now he's completely out of the game.

"Get your education and stay away from drugs. That's it."

I'm pleased to report that you will never hear of a tag day for John Ferguson. He is an astute business person whose investments have made him very wealthy. It couldn't happen to a more deserving guy.

"Canada has never had a civil war. After hockey, Canadians would probably have found it dull."

—*Jim Broshman*

No Such Thing as Handicapped

Art Wallman

Art Wallman of radio station CKSW in Swift Current, Saskatchewan admits he is pretty blunt when asked what young people today should do to get ahead in a career or business endeavour:

"Get off your butt and get it done! I don't feel the world owes me a living and I don't feel it owes anyone else one either. If you have goals, you should go after them. You can reach them regardless of the circumstances."

Art Wallman can afford to give that kind of blunt advice because he is the embodiment of grit and guts. He was born in a two-room shack near Wadina, Saskatchewan more than six decades ago, the victim of spastic paralysis. For the first nine years of his life he could only crawl on his hands and knees.

One of 10 children in a poor family, he received no formal education but taught himself to read and write and play several musical instruments.

After the failure of the family farm, the remaining brothers dispersed and Art became a ward of the Provincial Welfare Department. This was in 1950. He moved to Regina and was sent to school for the first time; he was 20 years old and in grade one. He persevered and next entered Regina College. He stayed at a boarding house and was given a $14 a month allowance. Hardly enough to have a good time on.

"To supplement my income some friends and I formed a band called 'The Happy Roamin' Rangers' and we played at dances and weddings all over the province."

Art has limited use of his legs even after more than a dozen operations at the Shriner's Hospital in Winnipeg but he manages very well on crutches.

It was while on those crutches crossing an icy street in Swift Current that his whole life changed.

Friends had told me I should try out as a radio announcer since I had a good voice and a wide knowledge of country music. I was crossing the street when I fell down. A man stopped his car and helped me up. He asked what the heck was a man on crutches doing on an icy street. I told him I was going to ask for a job at the radio station. He was aghast. 'No radio station is going to hire a cripple,' he said.

"Well I guess I fooled him. I've been in the broadcast industry now for 30 years and still going strong.

"I wrote my life story in a book called "A Good Day To Be Alive" because that's the way I feel about life. I always get a real charge out of this business of living. I don't think I've missed much in life. As a matter of fact, I have done a lot of things so-called physically-equipped people haven't done. Once you've considered the alternative, every day is a good day to be alive."

Although he had to overcome so many disabilities, Art rejects the word handicapped when applied to people like himself.

"I never felt handicapped. It is not a word in my vocabulary. I think it's a state of mind. If you want to be a failure, you can be one. If you want to be a success, you can be that too. Your disability has got to be pretty bad if you can't accomplish something out of it."

Art has received many plaques and awards for community service. He married his wife Marlene the same year the Saskatchewan Country Music Association presented him with its prestigious "Heritage Award". In November of the same year he was given the Saskatchewan Order of Merit, the highest honour the Province can bestow on one of its citizens.

It's Art's bright positive outlook on life that has allowed him to "get off his butt" and make a success of himself. His story would fill a book, and it does. I suggest you read it if you want to become as inspired as I am about this Canadian Achiever.

Tribute to Volunteers

Last year during volunteer week I read this special tribute on my program. I was astounded by the number of letters that poured in requesting a copy of the poem Here is the script as it appeared on the radio:

It's Volunteer Week in Canada. The one week of the year that it's alright for hundreds of thousands of volunteers to reach over their shoulders and pat themselves on the back. If you're a volunteer of any kind, you earned and deserve your pat on the back. Where would Canada be without you? Recently a listener sent me a cute little poem written just for volunteers. It's appropriately called... 'Yes, there is a heaven for volunteers'. I'd like to share it with you.

> (Harp Music: in the background)
> Many will be shocked to find
> when the day of judgment nears,
> there's a special place in heaven
> furnished with big recliners,
> satin couches and footstools,
> where there's no committee chairman,
> no group leaders, no car pools.
> No eager team that needs a coach,
> no bazaar and no bake sale.
> There will be nothing to staple,
> not one thing to fold or mail.
> Telephone lists will be outlawed,
> but a finger snap will bring
> cool drinks and gourmet dinners
> and rare treats fit for a king.
> Who'll serve those privileged few
> and work for all they're worth?
> Why—all those who reaped the benefits
> and not once volunteered on earth.

"Why is it", said a rich man to his minister, "that people call me stingy when everyone knows that when I die I'm leaving everything to this church?"

"Let me tell you the story of the pig and the cow," said the minister. "The pig was unpopular and the cow was beloved. This puzzled the pig. 'People speak warmly of your gentle nature and your soulful eyes,' the pig said to the cow. 'They think you're generous because each day you give them milk and cream. But what about me? I give them everything I have. I give bacon and ham. I provide bristles for brushes. They even pickle my feet! Yet no one likes me. Why is that?'"

"Do you know what the cow answered?" said the minister. "She said, 'Perhaps it's because I give while still living.'"

—*Soundings,* The Economic Press

He Got Rid of the Splinters

Bill Caldwell

Back in the 1950's, when Bill Caldwell was a 26 year old sales engineer for Monsanto in Montreal, the average Canadian bathroom had a wooden toilet seat. The careful user always watched out for splinters.

But Bill had plans to change all that. He watched the introduction of the plastic toilet seat in the United States, and saw it as a golden opportunity.

Bill quit his job December 31, 1955. The following day January 1, 1956, he started his own company... 'Moldex Ltd.' in Barrie, Ontario. Why Barrie and not Montreal where he and wife Shirley lived? Bill told me it was a simple case of... *"detailed financial research. I searched all over to find financing. The only people who would invest were my relatives in Barrie. They wanted the plant in Barrie so they could keep an eye on me and their money."*

They need not have worried. Bill's idea to get into plastics was solid gold. His plastic seats caught on, and eventually captured sixty percent of the Canadian market and a major share of the U.S. market as well as England and the Far East. Producing eleven thousand toilet seats per day.

In 1986, Bill formed another unrelated company, 'United Extrusions' of Orangeville, Ontario. United made corrugated tubing for agricultural drainage, wiring harnesses for cars, sewer pipes and other assorted products. Two years ago at age 60, Bill sold both companies for ten million dollars net. Now living in supposed retirement his wife Shirley told me... *"He's busier now than ever doing the things he's always wanted to do."* Those things include a lot of community service work and hobbies which include skiing, tennis, boating, and studying history.

Does Bill miss the ups and downs of the toilet seat business?... *"No sir... I haven't had a moment of restlessness... we winter in Florida, but return at least once a month to keep in touch. I'm on the board of two companies and that's enough."*

Bill Caldwell, the man who took the splinters out of Canadian bathrooms. Another Canadian Achiever.

For Better or For Worse

Lynn Johnston

Every day comic strip readers around the world enjoy following the trials and tribulations of the Patterson family who live in Lynn Johnston's studio near North Bay, Ontario. You see, Lynn is the woman who created the immensely popular "For Better or For Worse" which appears in more than 700 newspapers worldwide. Selected the number three choice of all cartoonists in North America.

It should be known by all that Lynn Johnston is without a doubt one of the nicest, most genuine people in the entire world. I have long been a fan of her comic strip family. When her publicist arranged our interview for Canadian Achievers, I hurried out and bought two copies of her latest book. I hoped she would autograph one for my private collection, and one for a Toronto friend of mine, Dick Moody who was recovering from a heart attack and would enjoy the humor in her book. I fully expected Lynn would scribble her signature like most famous people do. Instead she took much time and signed with an illustration, both my copy and Dick Moody's copy. Several weeks later I built up my courage and wrote asking her permission to reprint her autographed illustration and share it with you in this book. Being the gracious lady that she is . . . she agreed.

Lynn's is a success story that even Lynn still finds a bit hard to believe. In addition to the popularity of her daily comic strip, Lynn, past president of the National Cartoonist Society, has sold over 500,000 copies of her collected works in book form. Yet Lynn projects a feeling of insecurity.

"It's the insecurity that makes you good. I say to myself, I don't think I can do it for 365 days. I'm not good enough. Insecurity does make you better and makes you excell in this business."

Lynn wasn't always on top. She had struggles and some heartbreak along the way.

"But I knew almost from the beginning that I was going to be an artist for a living. I guess it began when I was asked by the elementary school to do all the place settings for a teacher's meeting. I was so thrilled! I always knew I could draw; it was almost an obsession. It was just almost like I had to do it."

It was fortunate for Lynn that she had her drawing to concentrate on because she was a lonely little girl growing up in Collingwood, Ontario and, later, in Vancouver, B.C. To get attention Lynn would do almost anything.

"My methods were rarely appropriate. No noise was too vulgar, no prank too risky, no rule went untested. And if I got a laugh, then the inevitable punishment was worthwhile."

Her irrepressible sense of humor and involvement in class shennanigans continued right through school, especially in art class in North Vancouver. Lynn and her cohorts were frustrated by the "Veddy British" teaching methods.

"Strangely enough, four of us from that class now make our living in the entertainment business and several others went to colourful careers in art and advertising."

The urge to draw and get attention finally came to fruition when she began to do cartoons. After several years of rejection, that is.

"In this business, rejection letters are something to collect. People gauge their success by the number of rejections they have received. Jim Davis, who draws Garfield, *has boxes of them. My advice to beginners is to be critical enough of your own work to know what's good and what isn't. If someone doesn't get it—do it again!"*

Lynn didn't go through the rejection slip routine.

"I did three little books on pregnancy and raising kids. These were picked up by a syndicate and they offered me the opportunity. I sent in 20 strips and they sent me a 20 year contract. This almost never happens!"

Now that she had hit the big time, it was pretty scarey.

"I was in a dilemma: on one side I was really happy; but it's terrifying to think that these people are expecting this kind of quality consistently. So the insecurity really comes in. It keeps you awake at night biting your nails and thinking, am I going to come up with another good idea?"

Where do her ideas come from?

"When cartoonists get together we always ask each other that question. I

will walk over to Sparky Schultz and ask him where he gets his ideas for PEANUTS; even he says he doesn't know! Maybe there are Vaudeville guys who passed on years ago who are sitting on your shoulder who say 'try this'—or maybe there's a mystical chemical there that you draw on and wonder sometimes if you are going to use it all up.

"There are times when something happens to you, like a death in the family or the loss of a relationship. The creative urge does dry up and the terror mounts as the deadline approaches. If I don't have six weeks written in advance, and eight weeks for the colored weekend comics, I'm in big trouble.

"And there's no escape for Christmas or family get-togethers. The six week deadline is always there and for anyone who is thinking of breaking into cartooning, they should keep that in mind. Also, we are fined $100 if our strip is late!"

Lynn admits her characters are somewhat drawn from life—her own family's life to be specific. Her dentist husband, Rod, daughter Kate and son Aaron bear an uncanny resemblance to the fictional Patterson family of the strip. However, the newest addition to the cartoon family, "April," is on her own!

Scarey, sleep-disturbing, but well worth it, says Lynn, whose collected works are sold in book form worldwide.

"I can't imagine working at any other job. It can be tough but if you are confident in your ability and you keep working at your very best, you'll succeed."

Letters of a Businessman

Kingsley Ward

Kingsley Ward is a very successful independent business person, owner of eight companies primarily in the field of health care. His son and daughter have both followed his example and chosen careers in the family business.

Kingsley, a native son of Bathurst, New Brunswick, wanted to share his business knowledge with his children. Like most parents he found it difficult to discuss business in person so he wrote them letters. In 1985, the letters were published in two books. The first "Letters of a Businessman To His Son" became an instant worldwide hit. . . translated into eight languages including Japanese. The book sold over 1 million copies. It was followed by another equally successful book "Letters of a Businessman To His Daughter". Both books have almost become business bibles. They contain the advice of a self-made businessman on how to succeed in business and life. After reading them I immediately bought copies for each of our three children who work in our family business.

As well, I sent a set to a friend whose son and daughter are with him in their family business and who I knew were having difficulties overcoming the parent/child barriers that can destroy family relationships as well as the family business. My friend's wife called shortly after and said both books had helped ease and overcome a great deal of the turmoil their family had been experiencing.

Kingsley's book acknowledges the common dream scenario of an entrepreneur starting out, building a business, then turning it over to the children to run while mom and dad clip coupons on warm sandy beaches. It sounds great and it does happen.

Kingsley's books help explain how you can make it happen for you.

His hobby is military history. In 1989, he along with Edwin Gibson, authored the book "Courage Remembered", a definitive guide to Commonwealth War Cemeteries and almost 200 war memorials. Their book was dedicated to the one and three quarter million fallen who never came back.

Kingsley Ward, sharing his success and helping others achieve through his own experiences. He's another Canadian Achiever.

Building a Chain in Japan

Tony Robins

An old saying in the radio business is... 'always do your best on the air because you never know who is listening and might offer you a better job.' Well, actually that old saying really applies to every profession.

Just ask Vancouver architect Tony Robins. Three years ago Tony designed a Japanese restaurant located on 4th Avenue called the "Shijo". As with all his projects Tony designed everything: exterior, interior, lights, chairs, even the menu.

One evening last year a Japanese businessman stopped by the restaurant for dinner. No one was aware that he was Mr. S. Kondo, owner of the Asakuma Company Ltd., a major conglomerate based in Nagoya, Japan. Mr. Kondo was enroute to San Francisco from Japan and had only stopped in Vancouver for a brief visit. He had no idea the restaurant even existed. He was out for an evening stroll, was caught by its unusual appearance, and walked in.

He was so impressed with the design and decor that he asked to meet the people responsible for its design. He was surprised to learn all of the work was the result of one person, a Vancouver Caucasian named Tony Robins.

The businessman explained to Tony that he was planning a chain of restaurants in Japan and wondered if Tony would take on the project. Tony nearly fell over when he learned the project consisted of 300 restaurants. Each with a budget of one million dollars.

Tony began work on the project immediately. Time has created some delays. The right locations in Japan are more difficult to acquire than expected. Plus, costs have increased to 1.2 million per location, causing the project to be scaled down to 200 restaurants.

The first will open in Nagoya this year (1991). Thirty will open in Tokyo and Nagoya in 1992. It's expected all 200 outlets will be operating within six years.

As Tony explained... *"The success of this project is based on the economics of scale. Once we open the first one, we have to get a number underway in order to effect cost savings."*

Tony will tell you that getting this project was... *"A little bit of luck"*. Don't you believe it. The project would never have come his way had he not designed the "Shijo" properly and then followed through with quality in every detail. Look how it paid off for him. There is a lesson there for everyone.

"Never let a problem become an excuse."
—*Robert H. Schuller*

They Walked from Russia to Canada

Richard Weber, Laurie Dexter, Max Buxton,
Chris Holloway

On a personal note, one of my other careers as a young man was working on a construction site 200 miles inside the Arctic Circle. It was 1955, Canada was building the Dew Line and as a Prairie farm boy I thought it would be fun and adventurous to work in the Arctic. Plus, the money was great. I soon learned that fun it wasn't—adventurous it was.

I quickly developed profound respect for the dangers of the Arctic. That's why I find this story of achievement so incredible: In 1988, four Canadians and nine Russians walked across the Arctic. In 91 days they walked and skiied from the most northerly point in Soviet Siberia over the North Pole to Ellesmere Island in Canada.

They bridged the Polar Arctic enduring bone-chilling temperatures as low as minus 50 celcius with 80 kilometer per hour winds.

The four Canadians were Richard Weber, a mechanical engineer from

Chelsea, Quebec; Laurie Dexter, an Anglican Minister from Fort Smith, Northwest Territories; Max Buxton, a doctor from Calabogie, Ontario and Chris Holloway, a computer consultant from Chelsea, Quebec. The four authored a book about their adventures: "POLAR BRIDGE: An Arctic Odyssey". (Key Porter Books, 1990)

Richard Weber had been skiing competitively since he was six years old and was on Canada's National Cross Country Ski Team for seven years. His Swiss-born father was an avid skiier in the mountains of his former country and his enthusiasm was passed on to his son.

Another incentive to ski across the top of the world came because his father, a geophysicist, had been three times to the North Pole on expeditions.

"I'm sure we are the only father and son who have been to the North Pole!"

In 1985 Richard heard some Americans were looking for a Canadian to join them in an expedition walking to the Pole. A year later they went from Ellesmere Island by dogsled to the Pole without any air support.

"Then in 1987 the Soviets came to Ottawa looking for me and I was very keen to go with them. This time we would go from Soviet soil to Canadian soil across the Arctic Ocean, again without any outside supply system. It was a thrilling and sometimes boring and exasperating trip. It's not like climbing a mountain because there's no high peak to look down from. The thrill was in that we went from land in the Soviet Union across a sea of ice to the Pole and then to land again in Canada. That was the only thing you could reach out and grab.

"You can't even leave a marker because the Ocean ice moves at about five kilometers a day. In 1968 my father left a bottle with a message in it at the North Pole and a year and half later it turned up in Iceland. On another expedition we left a time capsule with a reward of $5000 for the finder from one of our sponsors, Dupont, and it was recovered by fishermen two years later in Ireland!"

What was the worst part of the trip?

"The cold was expectable. It was the fog and the white-outs. You can't see where you are going and staring ahead you fall over pressure ridges, snow drifts and into holes. I found it very depressing and difficult to deal with. When the sun's out and it's 25 below, it's a nice place to travel in.

"Dealing with the Soviets was challenging. They spoke only Russian and we spoke only English. No one spoke both. But we managed. But it was obvious we came from very different cultures. While we spoke of working with and alongside Nature, they talked about victory over the ice, conquering the Arctic.

"And our equipment was different. We had wood skis; they had fiberglass. We used synthetic clothing; they had wool and cotton. We ate high fat

and they had a lot more sugar and salt. It was tricky but it worked out well in the end."

Sadly, they found the Arctic landscape no longer pristine. Traces of pollution from industry from others parts of the world were everywhere to be found.

On a happier note, the four Canadians were flown to the Kremlin where they were presented with the Order of Friendship of Nations, the highest honour the Soviets can bestow on a foreigner.

What advice does Robert Weber have for other young adventurers whether it's crossing the frigid Arctic or getting to the top in a job or business?

"Set short goals. Don't make the North Pole your goal. That's two months away. You don't even think about that. Think about today. Concentrate on what you are doing this hour, now. Don't look too far ahead. It may discourage you.

"In my talks to young people I always say you can do anything you choose to do. If you think you can do it, and it's a logical thing, you can really do anything you want to do. Chase your dreams. It's true."

Does being physically adventurous help a person in a career or business life?

"It means you have all the energy and stamina to do all the other things. It gives you discipline, drive and ambition. It gives you all the attributes to take into your business or family life."

"Failure is more frequently from lack of energy than from lack of capital."
—*Daniel Webster*

He's Bursting with Talent, Energy and Enthusiasm

Red Robinson

As a teenager growing up in Vancouver during the 50's, Red Robinson had only one desire. He wanted to become a radio announcer, nothing else. He hung around radio stations begging station managers to give him a try. It worked. . . he finally convinced one to. . . "Give the Kid a Break." He was 16. Listeners like his fresh energy and honest enthusiasm and he quickly caught on and became known as "the Technicolor Host on the Coast'.

Within 5 years, and still only 21, Red was working for the top radio station in Portland, Oregon. But he missed Canada and his friends so he returned to Canada, married Carole whom he met on a blind date, and continued his radio career in Canada.

In 1974, he and a buddy, Steve Vrlak, opened a small advertising agency. It grew to become one of the largest advertising agencies on the west coast, with a staff of 52 doing $27 million per year.

While all of this was happening, Red kept his daily morning show on radio, m-c-ing most major events in Vancouver, and hosting the annual Timmy's Telethon, consistently the most successful telethon in Canada. Seven day, 90 hour weeks were no stranger.

Then, in 1988 Red surprised everyone by selling his shares in the agency and announcing his retirement. Those of us who knew him knew it wouldn't last. Sure enough, within two weeks, Red was back in business full speed ahead.

Since 1985 it has been my great pleasure to produce over 700 episodes of various national network radio shows with Red as host. I can tell you first hand that few people bring more to the table in talent, energy, enthusiasm and honesty than Red Robinson. . .

Just as this book was going to press Red was appointed by the provincial government "Mr. Music 91". He's the ambassador for "Music 91" a major tourism initiative celebrating a year of Canadian and International music. As ambassador, he must travel extensively throughout B.C. acting as M.C. and talent co-ordinator for several hundred live music events featuring such headliners as k.d. Lang. Andre Phillipe-Gagnon, Rita MacNeil. Semi retired eh!!

A Leader in Community Service

Clifford Chadderton

Every year the Royal Bank selects one Canadian whose outstanding achievements make an important contribution to human welfare and the common good. The recipient receives one hundred thousand dollars, and a gold medal. The 1988 recipient was a man who has dedicated his entire life to just these values. Clifford Chadderton, chief executive officer of the War Amputations of Canada.

Cliff's a war amp. A victim of the Belgium Campaign in '44. After the war he worked with veterans rehab and in 1965 became chief executive officer of the War Amputations of Canada.

Over the years, he's originated many innovations including 'Champ', the child amputee program. 'Playsafe' films to show children how to play safe. And most notably the film series called 'Never Again', which portrays the horror and futility of war to young Canadians. The films are used extensively in schools. When presented the award, the judge said, "He's dedicated his life to adding spirit and hope to the lives of thousands of Canadian amputees... he's a personal and valued friend not only to his fellow war veterans but also to many parents and their children throughout Canada"... what more can be said.

Clifford Chadderton, recipient of the Royal Bank Award and this recognition as a Canadian Achiever.

The Founder of Kin

Hal Rogers

If the Rotary Club hadn't turned down Hal Roger's membership application back in 1919 because his father was a member and the club forbid two from the same profession, the Kinsmen Club might never have been started.

Hal had just come back from the First World War to his hometown of Hamilton, Ontario and he missed the companionship of his Army buddies. Born in London, Ontario Hal had been in Hamilton selling plumbing supplies from his father's store for only a short time when war broke out.

"I never made many friends in Hamilton and felt quite lonely. I talked to a fellow named Harold Phillips whom I'd seen in church and we both agreed what the city needed was a club where young men could meet and participate in club activities. Harold had been in Hamilton a little over a year and he had only met a few people too."

With two others: Trevor Thompson and H. L. "Link" Brace, plans were made to start the new club, but only Hal and Trevor Thompson stayed on, and on February 20, 1920 the first Chapter Night for the Kinsmen Club was held in the Nanking Cafe of 65 1/2 King Street East in Hamilton. Now there are over 600 Kinsmen Clubs in Canada and over 500,000 young men and women have shared the dream that Hal Rogers began. Until recently the age limit for membership was 40 years. In 1987 it was increased to 45.

Hal has resisted all attempts to make the Kinsmen Club an international organization like Rotary or Lions. He maintains that Kinsmen and the wive's Kinette Clubs should remain uniquely Canadian. (They do, however, have affiliation with other clubs worldwide.)

Over the years, the club has raised millions of dollars for community projects. Canada's Prime Minister during the Second World War, William Lyon Mackenzie King, paid tribute to the club for its service to the community:

"In time of peace, the Association gave many years of generous and unselfish service for the relief of distress in the communities where its clubs were organized. During the war years, it has created a truly splendid re-

cord, above all in the magnificent work it has done in shipping more than 50 million quarts of milk for the children in Britain."

Serious as some of their projects are, Kinsmen are not without a sense of humour. At their 1963 National Convention held that year in Hamilton, an elderly Chinese man was brought onto the stage and introduced as the owner of the cafe where the first Kinsmen met. He bowed and waved and smiled and left the hall to a standing ovation and cheers. Afterwards it was revealed that the man was just someone who agreed to play the role of the old cafe proprietor.

In January 1963 I was brought to a Hamilton Kinsmen meeting by Kin member Fel De Marchi. Fel was manager of Beaver Lumber; I was an advertising salesperson. I tried to sell him radio advertising; he tried to sell me membership in Kin. I'm happy to report we both succeeded. I was impressed by their enthusiasm and commitment to service. After several meetings I joined and still keep in touch as a Life Member of the Association.

The greatest thrill of my Kin life came on August 23, 1990 when I was invited to deliver the keynote address at their National Convention in Thunder Bay, Ontario.

Hal Rogers, a hale and hearty 92 lives in retirement in Toronto. He leaves the running of the Association he founded to younger people. However, he still crosses Canada several times each year attending Association functions. *"I only go when they ask me"*, and they ask him often. Hal enjoys telling this story of the time he attended a Kinsmen Convention: His name badge appropriately identified him as "Hal Rogers—Founder". He was brought down from any feeling of self importance he may have had when he was asked by a younger member, *"Who are you, and where's Founder?"*

As often as I've heard him tell that story I never tire of it because no story can describe the honesty of Hal Rogers better than that one.

Over the years Kinsmen and Kinette Clubs have touched, in some way or another, every community in Canada. In 1964 they took on the challenge of finding a cure for Cystic Fibrosis; since then they have raised over 16 million dollars for research. Mila Mulroney is National Chairperson for Cystic Fibrosis and works hand in hand with Kin.

Kinsmen and Kinettes, a distinctly Canadian organization that grew out of the idea that service and companionship can lead to success and happiness. Hal Rogers, another Canadian Achiever.

"The most neglected form of compensation is the six letter word . . . 'Thanks'."
—*Robert Townsend*

From Banker to Entrepreneur

Stephen Hurst

Stephen Hurst is a young man in a hurry. He was a 'Bankers Brat' who travelled with his father and family from place to place, branch to branch. And the bank life influenced him.

"It gave me a sense of mobility and practicality that I don't think I would have gotten elsewhere."

At the age of 22, Stephen was already managing a bank of his own, the Canadian Imperial Bank of Commerce in Norman Wells in the Northwest Territories. It was 1977, three years after the Yarmouth-born banker had started out in his chosen career.

"But early on I realized that I wasn't cut out for the pin stripe suit and it was not fitting well. So when an opportunity came up to go into business for myself, I jumped at it."

Stephen had been talking to a client who was in financial trouble with a lumber mill in Yellowknife, Northwest Territories. As manager of the CIBC Bank there he was now a confirmed northerner and acutely aware of the problems and opportunities.

"I told the man what his company needed was not men who could sell lumber but someone who could handle finances. The potential was there; the answer was to find the right man. He smiled and said, 'I think I'm looking at him.' So I quit my job at the bank and went home and told my wife Glenda I was going into business for myself. She was happy for me because she knew I had been chafing in the bank long enough."

Great Northern Lumber went from the gates of bankruptcy four years ago to the employing of 14 people and sales projected to be $4.3 million in 1991.

In 1989 Stephen Hurst decided to stage a Yellowknife business conference to attract money and people to the city.

"Then I decided to go beyond that and have it include the entire Northwest Territories, the idea being to attract southerners to our turf and clearly tell them we are looking for capital and skilled people. The people we called were the busiest people in the country because the busiest people are the people who get things done. They came; the project got off the ground right away. It bloomed."

That's where I first met Stephen and was knocked out by his enthusiasm and drive. When I asked him if there was still the opportunity in the north that there used to be, he replied, *"I was talking to a man of about 55 or 60 years of age who was thinking of retiring south. I asked him if there was less opportunity now than there was 25 years ago. I told him I was always pumped up by the spirit and dynamism of the north. He said, "I saw 25 years ago what you are seeing now. You're pumped up because it's real."*

Stephen took a low profile in 1990 to 'heal up' after the exhausting job of running his lumber company, co-ordinating the 'Prospects North '89' Business Conference and starting a small graphics company, Yellowknife's first and only in that line. Now he's off and running again and the conference is already being planned for the year 1992.

"We are 53,000 strong here in the territories and we consume $1.1 billion worth of goods and services, most of which comes from the south. Our territorial government is heavily mandated toward import substitution to the point where they make it worth while for contractors and suppliers to use what's here. There's too much stuff coming in from the south that we can produce here . . . and we're going to do it."

The old saying was 'go west, young man' but Stephen Hurst has proven that if you are looking for opportunity and adventure, "go northwest young man and young woman."

Big Mac . . . Big Sales

George Cohon

When George Cohon came to Canada from Chicago in 1968 to run the fledgling Canadian operations of McDonald's, he immediately fell in love with the country. He became a Canadian citizen. He later was awarded The Order of Canada for his outstanding contributions to his newly adopted country.

Never one to do things in half measures, when George was sworn in as a citizen, he had the entire Bobby Gimby band in the courtroom play "Canadaaaa". He has become a great Canada booster and contributor to worthy causes. One year he and two other major donors saved the Santa Claus Parade in Toronto from extinction:

"I figure you have to put something back into the country you live in. This country's been good to me, to my wife and children. So you find the time for that sort of stuff whether it be for Terry Fox or Rick Hansen or the Ronald McDonald Houses. You do that because you have an obligation to do it."

When George Cohon came to Canada there were six McDonald's doing about a million dollars a year. Twenty one years later there are 625 restaurants with sales of about $1.5 billion a year and growing.

"I remember opening the first one in London, Ontario. We decided to donate the opening day proceeds to a crippled children's charity. I had to go to a meeting of the agency's board to explain who McDonald's were!"

He has no need to explain who McDonald's are anymore. Not even in the Soviet Union. Under George's directorship, McDonald's of Canada signed a deal to open 20 McDonald's in the USSR, the first one opened January

1990 in Moscow's Pushkin Square, very close to Red Square. The Soviets own 51 percent and Canada owns 49 percent. What a gutsy move!

"Gutsy? I don't think so. We started on that project in 1976 and we finally did it in 1989—so I don't think of it so much as gutsy as forward-thinking. There are 280 million people in that country. On average we serve 50 thousand customers a day. In our first year we served over 15 million customers. That's over half the population of Canada. Our McDonald's there is the highest volume McDonald's of anywhere in the world."

In addition to owning part of the Soviet McDonald's, the Canadian branches train Soviet staff at branches in Toronto, Ottawa and London, Ontario.

"I used to say in jest that Burger Diplomacy would bring people together, working shoulder to shoulder and they'd be friends. And my God, it's actually happening!"

McDonald's is so famous that in a survey taken in a group of Canadian schools 70 percent of the students identified John A. MacDonald, the founder of the country, as the Hamburger King. When George Cohon was told of this he said: "Only 70 percent? We have to go after that other 30!"

We asked George if there were as many opportunities in Canada as there were when he came here in 1968.

"Almost every day some youngster out of school, not necessarily university, comes to McDonald's, works hard and becomes an owner/operator at outlets right across this country. If getting ahead means working seven days a week and giving 110 percent of your effort, you do it. I've never been much of a one to punch a time clock. I never thought of the hours I've had to work. I look forward to coming to work every day. The founder of McDonald's, Ray Kroc, had a saying: 'If you don't look forward to coming to work, you're in the wrong job.'

"Canada is such a wonderful country. In the next decade we have a rare opportunity to emerge onto the international scene. You see the space ship with the Canada spar arm on it; you see that Bombardier has contracted to build all sorts of trains in Europe. You see Olympia and York, probably the largest real estate developer in the world, changing the faces of cities all over the world. As we go into the next century I think Canada will be in a great position to affect the way the world is."

That's George Cohon, who in 21 years built the largest quick service restaurant chain in Canada employing over 60,000 people. And also the highest volume restaurant in Russia. He's another Canadian Achiever.

"It's better to attempt something and fail, than to attempt nothing and succeed."
—Unknown

A Religious Feminist?

Dr. Lois Wilson

In 1980 Dr. Lois Wilson made history in Canada when she became the first woman to be elected as Moderator of the United Church of Canada.

"It was a wonderful feeling of accomplishment and something I really enjoyed doing."

Dr. Wilson had already earned her stripes after graduating from the University of Winnipeg and taking her post-graduate work in theology. She was ordained and ministered in Thunder Bay, Hamilton and Kingston, Ontario.

In 1983 she was appointed one of seven presidents of the World Council of Churches, representing 315 Orthodox and Protestant churches worldwide. She held the position until February 1991.

Dr. Wilson is barely 153 centimeters tall but she is a remarkably tireless and spunky woman. She calls herself a Feminist and has taken strong stands in the field of human rights. A newspaper once described her as "small but dynamic" which is just as well because her duties include exhausting travel to remote corners of the world.

"I've made several trips to Chile. I was there to monitor the plebiscite, and I was in Namibia when they declared their independence from South Africa.

"I was in India for six weeks sharing our experiences as ordained women of the west."

On the day we spoke to her last, Dr. Wilson was on her way to Australia to speak on human rights and the ordination of women.

What advice does she have for other younger women who might want to follow in her footsteps?

"I don't think I have to give that advice. About 65 percent of all candidates for ordination in Canada are women."

She is not planning to retire. One project is to write children's books with a Feminist's point of view.

"I am also part of a task force on the concept of disposing of poisonous waste in Canada."

Dr. Wilson is married to a United Church minister in Toronto. With all her other duties she doesn't get much chance to preach.

"When I do I must admit I am terrified—but confident."

Dr. Lois Wilson—a Canadian Achiever and a shining example for other women who may want to reach to the highest order in the church.

Advice to bosses . . . "Polish, don't demolish".

From Seat of His Pants to Company Head

Greg Clark

It can be truly said that Greg Clark learned the farm implement business from the bottom up. He grew up on a farm near Bounty, Saskatchewan and as a youngster spent many hours sitting on the hard steel seats of tractors, hay rakes and other farm equipment. Little did he think as he rode them, that some day he would be the president of the company that makes them!

Today, Greg is President of John Deere Limited, the largest farm implement company in Canada. But the road to the presidency was a rocky one. After spending grades one to eight in a one-room schoolhouse, Greg took part of his high school instruction by correspondence because there was no transportation to the nearest high school. He stuck with his education, attended the University of Saskatchewan where he majored in agricultural engineering, then joined the John Deere Company as a trainee.

Asked if he would follow that same route today he answered enthusiastically *"Yes"!* But what are the chances for a young person doing the same thing in this new world?

"The world has changed a lot since then. I don't think young people can spring up the ladder as quickly as you could back then. The economics of the business are different. We are dealing in a shrinking market and competition is fierce. But on the plus side the universities are sending out much better trained graduates who have a keener understanding of market conditions. Their education is broader-based. Our company seeks the person who wants to get ahead. The old work ethic is still alive and well at John Deere."

Greg says it is no harder for women or minorities to rise within the company. *"If they are willing to go after the job, women have as good or better chance of reaching the top."*

Greg's own climb came through that same hard work which meant a move to Columbus, Ohio where he was sales manager in charge of five States. He returned to Canada as General Manager and now is not only the President of John Deere but also Past President of the Canadian Farm and Industrial Equipment Institute.

Greg's brother Brad took over the family farm in Bounty while Greg has a "Gentleman's Farm" in Grimsby, Ontario. This Canadian Achiever, the boy who ran tractors, now runs the company that builds them but, is still a farm boy at heart.

"Failing doesn't mean that you are a failure. It simply means you haven't succeeded yet."

—Unknown

"You Seniors Have Sure Got It!"

Morinville Rendezvous Seniors Club

The standard practice for building a community recreation hall or Senior Citizen's Centre is to call upon all the provincial government agencies possible to hand over the money, then hire a contractor to do the work. Not so with the seniors of Morinville, Alberta.

The seniors in this farming community near Edmonton wanted a recreation centre. In 1985 they approached the Provincial Government for some money. The government told them they didn't have any money for their endeavour. So what did they do? They went out and raised the money themselves.

They raised nearly half of the necessary $250,000 to build the 8,000 square foot facility. Two of the prime movers and shakers were my uncle, Peter Gibeault and Ferd Vervynck, President of the Rendezvous Senior Citizens Club:

"We raised enough money to put up the shell of the building and then the donations just started to roll in."

They raffled off a car and cleared nearly $26,000.

"We went from business place to business place and got more money. And we knocked on doors and took donations. We held an auction and took in $2,700 and the women held suppers, like the one for the curling association which raised $435."

(Incidentally, the car was won by a man from Nova Scotia who bought a ticket while visiting relatives!)

While the hall is not completely paid for yet, it will be as it is rented out regularly for weddings and other large gatherings. The Morinville Chamber of Commerce has rented a permanent office in the centre.

As Ferd Vervynck says: *"In this town we do it the old fashioned way. We work for it!"*

Do they get praise?

"People are always saying to us—you Seniors sure have got it!"

The people of this small rural community have a real spirit that would be the envy of towns and cities everywhere. As we were going to press with this book, Morinville was on the brink of entering the Guinness Book of World Records. Not to be outdone by the Vergerville Easter Egg or St. Paul's UFO Landing Pad, this town of 5,000 boasts the World's Largest Toque. The grey and burgundy stocking cap is 15 feet high and 39 feet wide at the base. It took 136 volunteers to knit it!

They Made Their Dreams Come True

Jules & Liette Dumouchel

I enjoy telling stories of successful restauranteurs. Maybe it's because I travel a lot and spend so much time in restaurants. But also, it's because there is not another business that attracts so many small investors with big dreams. A perfect example is Jules Dumouchel. 27 years ago he quit his job as a meat salesman with Canada Packers to buy a small roadside restaurant in Chateaguay, Quebec. It's called "The Rustick". He and his wife Liette pooled their meagre savings, and worked their hearts out. Chateauguay is a small community located about 20 miles from Montreal. Hardly the place you would expect to now find one of Canada's best run and busiest restaurants. When Jules and Liette bought it 27 years ago Chateaguay and the restaurant were the best kept secrets in Canada. Jules was born and raised in Chateaguay, saw potential and decided to take the plunge.

Over a pleasant dinner at 'The Rustick' one evening Jules explained. . .

"That's true. We did take a plunge. But if you like what you're doing and you have good staff and service, you should do alright. However, you must be sure to take inventory of your supplies every month, stay on top of the business and remember to deposit the days receipts in the bank. Too many restaurateurs spend the money as it comes in. Forgetting that they must pay the bills at the end of the month. That's where they go wrong. If you have good food, good service, good customers, and take care of the business, you cannot miss."

Their restaurant has undergone many expansions over those 27 years. Today it includes the main restaurant which seats 15 hundred people, a 42 unit motel, and another restaurant next door specializing in Italian food. And they employ up to 200 people.

"We expect to do over 8 million dollars in business this year." (1991) They have built their business on the tried and true formula of good food, friendly hospitality, and long hours.

"We work seven days a week and we like it. That's the only way. If you don't, somebody else will, and you're gone."

Jules and Liette Dumouchel, proof that in Canada you don't have to be in a big city to be a big success. They are Canadian Achievers.

Be Prepared
"If you have eight hours to chop down a tree, spend 6 hours sharpening your axe."
    —*Abraham Lincoln*

Canada's Top Comedy Duo

Don Harron & Charlie Farqueson

Don Harron has had many successful careers. As an actor, performing Shakespeare on Broadway and England for 12 years. As a writer, he's written among many other things, the "Libberet" for Anne of Green Gables— Canada's longest running stage musical. He's written books as Don Harron and as his fictitious character "Charlie Farqueson". Like most people in the creative field, Don's mother doubted he had a career profession. So to make things happen Don headed for New York and then England.

Since returning to Canada life's been good for Don Harron. Except when Charlie Farqueson gets in the way.

Charlie Farqueson is the comic character created years ago by Don Harron. Don is the serious guy. Charlie is the rapscallion who says things that sound very funny but, always have a deep serious meaning. On my January 1st, 1991 program, I asked Charlie Farqueson to give us his thoughts and wishes for the New Year. He looked at me wide-eyed and said...

"Well my gosh... we should make war... yessiree we should make war... war on poverty, war on pollution, war on sickness, and we should hang together... yessiree we should all hang in there together."

Universities around the world that teach Greek mythology may soon have to begin teaching Canadian mythology as written by Charlie Farqueson. His new book (Nov.90) aptly called 'Universe' is causing quite a stir. Space fans and scientists really sit up when Charlie explains that there are U.F.O.'s all around his farm near Parry Sound, Ontario. *"Yessiree, the United Farmers of Ontario, that's them there U.F.O.'s alright."*

Don Harron and Charlie Farqueson have become Canada's best known comedy duo. For 20 years, Don was a comedy writer along with Gordie Tapp on the popular syndicated TV series "Hee Haw". Charlie Farqueson was "Hee Haw's" ace news reporter delivering the news on their mythical radio station K-O-R-N.

She Got Into Tourism By Mistake

Shirley Letto

Shirley Letto got into tourism by mistake and is now one of Newfoundland's hottest travel promoters. She wants to see how far she can go promoting tourism in Newfoundland and Labrador.

24 years ago she quietly rented out a few rooms in her Labrador home to fellow teachers. Tourists heard about the rooms and the next thing she

knew, she and her husband were running a 29-room hotel with sport-fishing on the side. They now also have a summer resort in Newfoundland.

Since then, she helped set up Northern Travels, an association to promote travel in Newfoundland and Labrador (now known as the Viking Trail Tourism Association). As marketing director of the seventeen-member group, Shirley cooks up everything from bus tours to the five year marketing plan which now targets the Maritimes, the Toronto area, the eastern seaboard of the U.S., and European markets.

Though she's never been involved or trained in marketing and promotions, Shirley finds she loves the work and not only that, she's doing very well. Tourist visits to historic sites in the province are way up and the association is winning awards.

Shirley Letto was open to changing needs around her and found a way to organize and motivate others for everyone's good. She's another Canadian Achiever.

Two Guys with a Red Hot Idea

Ross Cruickshank & Keith Barnwell

Many great ideas have come from casual conversation. Here is a classic example...

It all came about when Ross Cruickshank, 36, and Keith Barnwell, 27, were sitting outside having a cold beer on a hot Ontario summer afternoon. The hot sun was too much for the styrofoam bottle holders they were using to keep their beer cold. They reasoned that a beer bottle holder filled with frozen freezer gel would do the trick. So, they set about designing what months later became "The Fridge®".

It took them 18 months and 250 thousand dollars to develop it. They ran out of cash and had to bring in partners. But they persevered and it's paying off. They moved from their backyard garage to a 10,000 square foot plant. They now employ 8 people and expect sales of over 1 million dollars. And are projecting sales of 10 million dollars over the next five years.

So, the next time you're enjoying a refreshment with friends and someone says, *"Why don't we invent a something or other..."* think of Ross Cruickshank and Keith Barnwell and their brainwave that led to "The Fridge®". That's how it all started for these two Canadian Achievers.

"Enjoy the little things in life. Because the big things don't happen very often."

—*Andy Rooney*

Mediocre?? My Foot

Broadcast January 4, 1991

While reading Dick Beddoes entertaining book of hockey anecdotes titled "Greatest Hockey Stories", I was surprised to read a quote attributed to well known Canadian novelist Robertson Davies who is reported to have said, and I quote from the book of Beddoes, "Canadians lack a capacity for excellence and achievement. They value mediocrity". If Robertson Davies did in fact say that, then I feel sorry for him and any other person who feels that way. (By the way, Dick Beddoes does not agree with Davies. Thank goodness)! Anyone who feels that way has not been listening to this program. There are millions of Canadians out there achieving in every field imaginable: medicine, science, education, the arts, sports, you name it. There is not one profession, respectable or otherwise, that you will not find Canadians either leading the way in or playing an important role. I'm not just talking about the Wayne Gretzkys, Ann Murrays, Robert Batemans, Arthur Haileys and Rick Hansons. I'm talking about the millions of Canadians whose names don't ring a bell but, whose achievements are the contributing factor that continues to make Canada and Canadians the most respected and envied nation in the world. Mediocre ?? my foot. I'm darn proud of the achievements of Canadians. I know you are too.

Music is His Life

Ed Preston

In 1962, when I arrived at CHML, Hamilton, the station music director was a quiet, bright red-headed guy with the biggest most brilliant smile the world had ever seen. Twenty-nine years later, some of the red hair has lost its lustre, but the smile remains the same. And his career reflects the opportunity that one can develop in Canada.

Before his radio days, Ed played drums in a band and sold records in a store. He left radio to join RCA Victor Records, and his career took off. . .

"I got in on the ground floor as a regional promotion guy calling on radio stations and record shops, became regional sales manager, then national promotion manager, then Canadian V.P. & GM of The Record Division. I wasn't shooting for the top job. It was just one of those things. It just grew. Everything just fell into place at the right time."

Ed makes it sound so easy. But Ed wanted his own record company, with his own major artists. So he left RCA to join Tembo Music Inc. where his good friend Roger Whittaker was his first major artist. Ed is the President and GM of the company and executive producer of many of Roger Whittaker's albums. Another of Ed's recording artists is Carroll Baker, "Canada's Queen of Country Music."

Ed Preston has come a long way from selling records in a record shop. And it couldn't happen to a nicer guy. If you're wondering how to get a recording contract, here's Ed's advice. . .

"I think its always best to stay within the region you live. Use a local studio to cut a demo, and prepare a brief bio with photos. Then send it around to record companies and music publishers. When someone hears it and feels there is real potential, they might be willing to offer a contract."

She Turned Silver Into Gold

Elizabeth Manley

When Ottawa's Elizabeth Manley gave her dazzling performance at the Calgary '88 Olympics the crowd stood and cheered for what seemed like hours.

Since winning the silver medal that night she's gone on to a career that has included. . . *"all kinds of things. I'm now with Ice Capades travelling all over the country, I've had television specials, movie screen tests, I could go on for about four hours describing the wonderful things that have happened to me since the Olympics."*

Her income this year will exceed one million dollars. And yet it nearly didn't happen. At 17, Elizabeth Manley gave up. She quit. *"Well I got to a situation in my career where I didn't think I was improving at all. It's a very tough sport. It got to a point where I wasn't sure that giving up my whole life for this was doing me any good. I think every athlete in their career goes through a time like that. But being off the ice for 3 months made me realize I loved the sport too much to quit."*

She returned to the ice, and the rest, as they say, is history.

So the next time you're fed up and want to quit, think about Elizabeth Manley and all of the other achievers who just kept at it, and made it pay off.

"Yesterday is a cancelled cheque. Tomorrow is a promissory note. Today is cash. Spend it wisely."
—Anonymous

A Legend In His Lifetime

K. C. Irving

In 1989, I was invited by the Miramichi Regional Development people to help present their First Annual Miramichi Achievers Award to K. C. Irving. I travelled to Newcastle, New Brunswick wondering what it would be like to meet the man who had achieved so much in his lifetime. A man who had become almost larger than life. According to Forbes Magazine, K. C. Irving had become one of the world's fourteen richest men.

It all started in 1924 when at the age of 25 he built his own garage and service station in Buctouche, N.B. and began importing oil and gas from the U.S. He went up against the giants and became one himself. Today he owns thousands of Irving Stations, refineries, radio stations, television stations, newspapers, pulp mills, retail stores. You name it, he's got it. . . or is in the process of acquiring it.

When I met him, at age 90, his handshake was as firm and strong as the will and determination that brought him his success. In presenting his Achiever Award I quoted Dr. Frankel who wrote in his book. . . 'The Doctor and The Soul'. . . *"happiness is doing, doing is achieving"*

If Dr. Frankel is correct, and I believe he is, then K. C. Irving must be one of the happiest men alive.

On a lighter side, two days earlier while driving into St. John to visit Bob Henry, program director of radio station CHSJ (an Irving owned company), I stopped at a corner phone booth to phone Bob for directions. I explained that I was calling from a phone booth near an Irving gas station. Bob chuckled and said, *"Dick, when you're in New Brunswick you're always near an Irving station."*

I told that story during the award presentation. Mr. Irving and the audience laughed.

She Turned Tragedy Into a Crusade

Inge Clausen

On August 21, 1981, a devastating tragedy struck the Clausen family of Duncan, British Columbia. While jogging near her home on a sunny Sunday afternoon, their beautiful fifteen year old daughter Lise was attacked and murdered by a known sex offender released on mandatory supervision.

Lise's mother, Inge Clausen is a very strong willed determined person of Danish descent. As devastated as she and her entire family were, she made it her mission in life to prevent this kind of tragedy from ever happening to another family. She gathered a group of friends and formed "The Citizens United for Safety and Justice." Inge explained how it began...

"I think it actually got started with some friends and relatives sitting around the coffee table talking about what had happened to Lise. None of us really understood the meaning of mandatory supervision, which is what this inmate was out on when he killed her. When we finally understood what it was we decided that something had to be done to change it. We did not want another family to go through what we did."

They began writing letters, lobbying members of parliament, police departments, the corrections department, and parole department, urging stricter parole laws. Word of their efforts caught the media's attention. Inge began hearing from other Canadians who supported her cause. Soon their membership exceeded 3 thousand. In 1986, they successfully pressured the government into introducing Bill C67. A law that controls, to a degree, access to parole for known sex offenders.

Last year, parents of a similar tragedy started a branch of Inge's volunteer organization in eastern Canada.

Inge Clausen turned her family's tragedy into a crusade for the protection of Canadians. She's another Canadian Achiever.

Persistence Paid Off

Ralph Robinson

The broadcasting industry seems to attract the kind of person that falls into the risk taker-achiever category. High profile broadcasters such as Ted Rogers, Alan Waters, Harry Steele, Philippe de Gaspé Beaubien and a number of others come quickly to mind. There are many—called in the industry, mid-market broadcasters—who are among the country's top achievers. One in particular is Ralph Robinson. I single him out because he is proof positive that persistence pays off. And in Canada you can make your dreams come true.

From the time he was a youngster growing up in the Prairies, he wanted to be a radio announcer. It was the '30's, the world was in the middle of a depression, and radio was in its infancy. Ralph was 18. He started knocking, or should I say banging, on radio station doors. One finally opened: CHUB Nanaimo, and Ralph began what became an illustrious career. For many years he worked at CKOK, Penticton, CFJC Kamloops, CKOV & CKIQ Kelowna. In 1972 Ralph decided, enough was enough. He wanted to own his own radio station. He applied to the CRTC for a licence to start an AM station in Penticton. The CRTC turned him down; they said Penticton was too small for another station. Two years later he tried again. Again he was told Penticton was too small. It was obvious the CRTC didn't realize what kind of persistent guy they were dealing with. In 1980 Ralph gathered a group of local investors who believed in Penticton as he did, and off they went to the CRTC once more. This time they won. Ralph's radio station. CIGV-FM would become a reality.

"I just persisted. I didn't stop. I spent eleven years working on those applications. I just kept up until one was accepted."

On October 18, 1981, Ralph and Jean Robinson's 29th wedding anniversary, Ralph's dream came true. CIGV-FM signed on the air. That's the good news. The bad news is it was 1981, the world was in another depression, but that didn't stop him. Today Ralph and Jean are major shareholders in 3 stations. Besides running these stations, Ralph is also a volunteer for local community projects. He carries this same dedication to the broadcast industry. So much so, that his colleagues named him 'Broadcaster of the Year'.

"If someone wants to achieve, they can. But it's important that they want to."

What Ralph says applies not only to broadcasting. It applies to every profession. You have to want it so bad you can taste it—and then be prepared to work for it as Ralph Robinson did. He's another Canadian Achiever.

They Believe in Themselves

Ron & Fran Ridley

When the business community of Williams Lake, B.C. honoured Ron Ridley as "Entrepreneur of the Year" they made an excellent choice. Ron and wife Fran, originally from Windsor, Ontario, moved to Williams Lake in 1976 to buy a car dealership which they have built into a wonderful story of achievement. By industry standards the dealership they bought was quite small. It employed 36 people with sales of 3 million dollars. That was not good enough for Ron & Fran. They kept expanding sales and expanding their premises even during the tough times of the early 80's. As Ron explained. . .

"We had a great determination to survive and grow during that period. We always had faith in the future. We know that tough times never last but tough people do. We made adjustments for the times and we were able to weather the storm."

Weather the storm they did. Today Lake City Ford has 3 locations, employs 96 people, with sales this year of 26 million dollars. And they're doing all of this in an isolated trading area of only 40 thousand people.

They achieved this phenomenal growth through a lot of hard work and a management style they call . . . people, passion and product. Fran believes

with a passion that employees are a company's most important product...
as she explained to me...

"They want an exchange of information. They should be informed of what's happening day to day in the dealership. And they want to know they are part of a winning team."

Most companies believe that it's easier and safer to look outside the company for key people rather than promote from within. Not Fran.

"We believe in promoting from within. We know the people that we are working with. They have come up through the ranks. They want to achieve and should be given the opportunity. We believe it's more beneficial to promote from within."

Ron & Fran Ridley are achieving because they believe in themselves and their people.

Never sell yourself short.

He's 'Atlantic Canada Plus'

Harvey Webber

Harvey Webber is a Nova Scotia retailer whose plan to create jobs in Atlantic Canada (ACP) is working. The 76 year old native of Sydney, Nova Scotia, won't let age or economic downturn dampen his enthusiasm. He studied law at Dalhousie and upon graduation in 1936 he took over the family owned ladies wear store.

Harvey Webber is not a conformist. Over the years his Store "The Smart Shop" in Sydney grew to its present 3 floor location. As a successful retailer, he has every reason to be satisfied and enjoy leisure. Instead, he spends part of every day on community service.

In 1977 he presented to the people of Atlantic Canada, a radical self help plan for job creation. It encourages residents of the 4 eastern provinces to spend their money on goods or services produced in Atlantic Canada. His ACP plan tells people that 1% of their spending re-directed to their own goods and services will create between 5 and 10 thousand jobs. Is it working??... You bet it is.

Due to ACP's success the Atlantic Canada Opportunities Agency selected it as their agent to help regional suppliers access government contracts currently totalling six billion dollars annually. Four regional offices and one in Ottawa were opened to achieve this goal.

ACP has also helped develop a deepening sense of pride and confidence in Atlantic Canada manufacturers, retailers and their customers. As evidence of popular support, readers of a regional magazine voted Harvey "Atlantic Canadian of the Year" in 1981.

Although Harvey had graduated from Law School, he never practiced that profession. Nonetheless in 1985 as recognition for community service the Government of Nova Scotia awarded him the prestigious honor of Queens Counsel (Q.C.). In 1987 the Governor General of Canada, again for a lifetime of community leadership, bestowed upon Harvey the Order of Canada.

In 1990 the Dalhousie Law Alumni Association chose Harvey for the Weldon Award—"For Unselfish Public Service".

In a region of Canada that has always produced Canadian achievers, Harvey Webber stands out.

Fame On The World's Cycling Circuits

Steve Bauer

In 1964 Steve Bauer of Fenwick near St. Catharines, climbed on his first 2-wheel bicycle. He was 5. Twenty years later at the Los Angeles Olympics in 1984 Steve won for Canada the first silver medal in cycling in 76 years.

Steve turned pro after that and in his first race, the World Championship in Barcelona, Spain, he came in third. His career as a World Class Cyclist was set. Since then Steve has consistently been a top money earner racing in Europe where the sport is very big.

The biggest, most prestigious event in professional cycling is the Tour de France. It's a grueling, month long race through France ending in Paris. Each day the leading cyclist wears a yellow sweater to show the world he's leading. In the 1988 Tour de France Steve wore the yellow sweater for 5 days.

The big money in cycling is in Europe, Steve lives there most of the time. However, his recent book on bicycling, simply called "Steve Bauer on Bicycling", plus some nice Canadian endorsement contracts ensure that we'll see a lot more of him here at home. Steve Bauer—another Canadian Achiever.

Steroids don't win gold medals, commitment does.

Canada's Best

Anne Murray

What can possibly be said that hasn't already been said about this wonderful person?

Today she's one of the top entertainers in the world, and a woman who represents the very best in popular music. However, life for Anne Murray wasn't always so good.

Her family sent her to a Catholic College, where she lasted one year. She switched to the University of New Brunswick, and failed her first year. She auditioned for a singing part on TV's "Singalong Jubilee", and was rejected. Two years later, she finally got that part, and also graduated with a degree in physical education.

In those days singing was her way to make a few extra dollars while she worked as a physical education teacher in Prince Edward Island. The big decision came when she had to choose between renewing her teacher's contract, or trying for a career in music. She took the advice of some friends, and began the long road to stardom.

In 1969 when Anne released "Snow Bird", her timing was perfect. A new Canadian singing star appeared on the scene at a time when Canadian radio stations were required to give more attention to Canadian music. The way Anne puts it, *"I had horseshoes coming out of my ears"*. Horseshoes maybe, talent for sure.

Anne Murray, a Canadian like you, had a dream and made it work.

"As far as the future of the Canadian music business is concerned we badly need to get together in the artistic ranks. We should brag about each other. The Americans are great at that."
  —*Bobby Curtola*

Sewing Canvas at Kettle Creek

Mellanie Stephens

It took Mellanie Stephens a while to find herself. She dropped out of high school in St. Thomas, Ontario, before finishing grade 11 and drifted around for seven years. She finally returned home to Port Stanley, Ontario, and got a job sewing women's clothing for a local factory, but kept telling herself there must be a better way to make a living.

A friend agreed to co-sign a note for her and Mellanie borrowed

$15,000.00 to set up the 'Kettle Creek Canvas Company'. She began to sell canvas gear for sailors. Her little business did well but Mellanie had an urge to challenge her skills and creativity ... *"Clothing, I thought. High quality, comfortably designed clothing, made from natural fabrics."*

The next step was to design and make the clothes, move from her workshop to a retail store and see what happened.

The 'Kettle Creek Canvas Company' opened on Main Street in Port Stanley on May 24, 1979—a holiday weekend—and the people came. And they bought. *"Not only were we launched, we were back-ordered. Our problem, if you could call it that, was solved when we got together with women in the community who had a love of sewing and the skills to match."*

A cottage industry was born in the age of high tech!

'Kettle Creek' is a success thanks to high standards of quality fabrics and craftsmanship. And the home sewers continue to be part of the team. From its humble beginnings in a tiny workshop, Mellanie Stephens had expanded 'Kettle Creek Canvas Company' to 60 stores across Canada, employing 225 people.

Unfortunately the current recession coupled with too rapid expansion has created severe financial pressure on Mellanie's company. On March 18/91 creditors approved a reorganization plan that will close 19 of her stores.

Blowing The Lid Off

Ron Foxcroft

Mid way through my speaking engagements I surreptitiously place my hand over my mouth and jar the audience awake with a shrill ear piercing blast on my FOX40 whistle. What's a FOX40 whistle? I'll explain in a moment.

They say if you build a better mousetrap the world will beat a path to your door. Ron Foxcroft designed a better whistle and the world is blowing down his door.

For years Ron Foxcroft was an amateur basketball referee. In real life he is the operator of a successful trucking company in Hamilton, Ontario, called 'Fluke Transport'. Their slogan was "if it's on time, it's a fluke". (So help me, I did not make this up. It's painted on his trucks.)

Ron refereed games where thousands of fans cheering and yelling would drown out his referee's whistle. There had to be a better way. In 1984, he set about designing a new shriller whistle. One that could be heard above any crowd no matter how noisy. It took three years to develop just the right whistle, and in 1987, Ron was ready to market it. He introduced it at the Pan Am Games in Indianapolis. People went nuts. He had people knocking on his hotel room door at two a.m. wanting, demanding, to buy them. It's now being used at every major sports event. South American police ordered several thousand. Referees at the Olympics use this new Canadian phenomenon. In fact, it's now being sold through over 6,000 outlets in 50 countries.

He told me recently... *"We have really made an impact in the world personal security business. We expect the U.S. military will soon announce that our whistle is their official survival whistle. It was to have been announced a while ago but the Persian Gulf Crisis is holding it up.*

"Lifeguards are using our whistle because they have finally found a whistle that will work when wet. Water doesn't affect them."

Recently, Ron introduced a new whistle. *"We call it the 'Mini FOX40'. It's smaller, available in assorted bright colors and has the same high shrill of the other one. It's no different."*

Why, if it's the same as the other one did they bring out a new one in assorted colors, you ask?

"A whistle is no different than any other consumer product. Customers want to have choices. And I believe in giving customers what they want." Not to mention he gets more shelfspace.

The factory in Hamilton, blows out over 10,000 whistles a day. And still can't keep up with demand. Ron's biggest single order came in the Fall of 1990 when Shoppers Drug Mart and Images Magazine ordered 250,000 whistles for a consumer promotion selling the whistle as a personal security warning device. The 'FOX40' is different from regular whistles in that it does not have a pea in it. Rather it is a scientifically designed three chamber configuration with each chamber set to a different pitch. The harder you blow, the shriller the ear piercing sound. Another sound it creates is that of cash registers ringing. Ron expects to sell over one million whistles in 1991. That will generate over 3 million dollars in sales as the world whistles a path to his door.

Ron's company 'Fortron International Inc.' is a family affair. Wife Marie, son Steve, and sister-in-law Elizabeth Grant, have worked with him since day one. In fact, Elizabeth is in charge of Foreign Sales.

Always on the go, Ron is looking to develop other sports related items that he can blow the lid off. Ron Foxcroft, another Canadian Achiever.

Nothing takes the place of persistence.

She Beat the Best

Nancy Green-Raine

It would have been somewhat of a miracle if Nancy Greene had not been a skier. Her mother had been a ski racer and her father helped build one of the country's first chairlifts, near the family home in Rossland, B.C.

She got her first break in 1958 placing second in the Canadian Junior Championships, her first serious competition. Two years later, she raced in her first Olympics where she was inspired by Anne Heggtveit's gold medal victory for Canada. In 1967, Nancy's years of hard work paid off when she won the first World Cup in a dramatic final race. The next year she won a gold medal in Giant Slalom and a silver medal in Slalom in the Grenoble Olympics. She completed the year with a string of victories to win a second World Cup and was named Canadian Athlete of the Year.

Nancy retired from ski racing, and married National Team coach Al Raine the following year. They moved to Whistler and later built the Nancy Greene Lodge. In 1989 they sold the Lodge to concentrate on their personal commitment to developing a new crop of outstanding skiers. In 1991 Nancy and Al were honoured as Whistler's Citizens of the Year in recognition of their work in building and promoting Canada's finest ski resort.

The Avon Lady Who Became President

Christina Gold

Christina Gold is president and chief executive officer of Avon Canada in Montreal. She heads a company with sales this year of 260 million dollars and a sales staff of 45 thousand representatives. When you consider that less than 3% of highest management positions in large Canadian corporations are held by women, Christina's appointment says a lot about her unique ability. How did she react when she learned of her appointment... *"Truthfully, I just went... wow! I was so excited I just couldn't think straight for two or three days."*

It wasn't easy getting to the top, and it won't be easy staying there, it never is. She joined Avon 20 years ago as an accountant. Over the years she worked in every department. Yes, even as an Avon Lady calling door to door. What does she feel are the qualities necessary to achieve as president of a large corporation?... *"That's a hard question to answer because you are who you are... obviously communication skills are very important in terms of in being able to talk to people. Another thing that is very critical is listening. Not only do you have to listen to your employees, you have to listen to your customers and understand where your business is going. So, listening is a skill that one really has to develop. Another is being able to delegate because you can't do it all yourself. And you have to work hard. You have to be willing to take risks. You also have to have faith in your commitments in terms of when you're going to do something, do it. You have to make decisions and get going. Finally you must really have confidence in your people and trust the people who work with you knowing you can rely on them to make the right decisions... it's not a one person team. It's many people working together to make the company successful."*

That's good advice even if you don't want to become president. Following her own advice has made Christina Gold a very successful person. She's also a very nice person, and she's another Canadian Achiever.

Blind Golf Champion

Nick Genovese

The baritone singing voice of Nick Genovese of Dundas, Ontario, became a familiar one to CBC radio listeners of the 1960's. He is still in demand as an entertainer on the club and banquet circuit. What the radio listeners didn't know, but what was obvious to live audiences, was that Nick is blind.

On Friday, March 13, 1946, at the age of 17, Nick lost his sight in a welding accident at Steel Fab Ltd., where he was apprenticing. So, Nick simply decided to redirect his energies and develop what he had been told was a 'good rich voice'.

Being blind was no hindrance to a singing career nor to Nick becoming a success with his own insurance agency. During the years I lived in Hamilton, Nick handled my insurance requirements without a hitch. During my term as Kinsmen Deputy Governor, Nick was president of the Kinsmen Club of Dundas. Using the club's secretary Gary Staley, as his eyes, Nick was the top president in my zone.

But his most inspirational accomplishments have been on the golf course. He has won 18 titles, including the National Blind Golfers Championship. He's played golf with many top celebrities including Bob Hope. How does he do it? According to him it's simple. . . . A sighted coach lines him up on the ball, tells him the direction and distance to the pin, and Nick does the rest. For years Nick's brother Carmen was his coach. In 1975 Carmen passed away. Nick stopped playing golf.

In 1989, Nick sold his insurance agency, picked up his clubs and three coaches... his son John, a 32 year old school teacher; Bob Lemaire and

Cam Holstein... and headed for the links. In fact, as I sit here writing this story on Sunday, January 6, 1991, Nick and Cam are competing in a tournament in Phoenix, Arizona.

Pat, his wife of 35 years, is glad he's back on the links making a point to inspire all handicapped people.

Nick Genovese, a Canadian Achiever who converted a tragedy into opportunity so that blindness is now merely an inconvenience rather than a handicap. Yes, Nick is still using his magnificent rich singing voice at weddings, Christmas pageants and the like. So, if you're playing golf one day and you hear the strains of a basso profundo "fore" bellowing across the fairways, you'll know Nick Genovese is nearby. Go say hello, he'd like that.

Dean of Canadian Painters

A. J. Casson

At 92 years of age, (born May 17, 1898) it would be quite justifiable if our Toronto born "Dean of Canadian Painters"—A. J. Casson just sat back and revelled in his past accomplishments. A master of oils and water colours, his paintings hang in galleries and private collections the world over. Canada has honoured him with every award it can give its artists. But this man of world renown, who paints with such majesty, and who is the last of the famed "Group of Seven" is still going strong.

Presently his "Artist in Residence" is displayed at Toronto's Sunnybrook Hospital, where his wife resides. He has painted the hospital's Christmas Card for several years. He donates the painting to the hospital. They use it as a fund-raiser selling note paper and Christmas Cards.

"It's the least I can do," he told me. *"They are wonderful to my wife and they can sure use the money."*

The money goes for research into Alzheimers disease, the heart-breaking affliction suffered by so many, including his wife. With failing eyesight A. J. Casson has not painted a major work for several years. His 1215 Outdoor sketches, when they do come on the market, sell for upwards of 8 thousand dollars. None of his larger works have come on the market for so long now that he says, *"Lord knows what they would be worth"*.

His paintings are kept as treasured gems by astute collectors. Trivia buffs looking for some Canadiana can use this at their next party. Question: What does A. J. in A. J. Casson stand for? Give up? It stand for Alfred Joseph. But he told me, *"When I was about ten the kids started calling me A. J. (ey Jay) and it stuck. That's all I've ever been called since."*

I proudly call him a Canadian Achiever.

Medical Director of 800 Hospitals

Dr. Ken Williams

At age 18, Ken Williams was working as a logger and then a high rigger in the B.C. forests. It's a dangerous job now. Back then it was treacherous. He was a bright young guy. There was something different about him. Four of the other loggers in the camp noticed it, pooled their money and made a commitment to finance Ken's medical education. They didn't want him to face a life of hardships which was the loggers' fate back then. And still is.

Off Ken went back to school, finally graduating from the University of Manitoba as Dr. Kenneth Williams, M.D. He returned to the B.C. interior to practice and repay his mentors who had shown faith in him and made his new life possible. He told me... *"I was in practice up in the East Kootenays for about eight years, pushing back the frontiers of ignorance. I quit that and went on to different careers from there."*

He enrolled at Yale University and specialized in hospital management. Over the years he was medical director of several hospitals in Canada, including Hamilton's St. Joseph Hospital, where he remained for a number of years. The U.S. beckoned... he went... and within a short while was medical director of 800 Catholic hospitals in the U.S. and Canada. *"I got tired of being the organization man. After five or six years I decided to launch out. I'd read the book 'Jonathon Livingston Seagull' and simply said... to hell with it... my wife said if you don't like it, quit. So I quit, and started up my own consulting firm on an international basis. It just grew and grew."*

His advice for achieving is simple, *"there's no free lunch. You have to get out and bust your tail if you want to do it. The wagon trains west aren't running anymore, but there's still so very much opportunity in Canada and the U.S. but particularly in Canada."*

Dr. Williams is retired and lives with his wife in Victoria. He repaid the loans to the four loggers who saw something in him they were willing to stake their money on. He repaid their cash investment during the first few years following graduation. The dividends they received in personal satisfaction continued a lifetime. Two of his four mentors are still alive. Dr. Williams sees them often.

Achieving runs in the Williams family, Dr. Williams is the very proud father of well-known sportscaster Brian Williams.

Salesman 1: "I made some valuable contacts today."
Salesman 2: "Yeah, I didn't sell anything either."

You Can Do What Ever You Set Your Mind To

Candace Wilson

Candace Wilson is one of the most positive people you will ever meet. She believes you can achieve whatever goal you set for yourself. She's proved she's right.

Years ago, Candace was a wine taster in Europe. A career that gave her the opportunity to travel in style throughout Europe, while earning big money to boot. She had always been fascinated by large helicopters and wondered what it would be like to fly one. She returned to Canada, took an intense three month cram course, passed with flying colors and for the next five years flew large helicopters to construction sites up north.

By 1985, Candace had had enough flying. So she quit flying, returned to Toronto and formed a company called "Emerson & Ross". She began selling custom tailored shirts to executives who pay up to $250.00 per shirt. The first year she sold only a few. The next year a few more. As word spread, her business grew. In 1991, she expects to sell over 2000 shirts.

When I asked Candace how she feels now that she's a successful entrepreneur, she replied with a smile. . . . *"I love it . . . it's just great."*

Candace Wilson had no special gift or training for either of the three careers she's mastered. What she does have is the confidence in her own ability to succeed. And in Canada that's all you need. She's another Canadian Achiever.

Thinking Positive Paid Off

Jim Scharf

I enjoy reminding my audience that in Canada you don't have to come from a big city to think big. The Jim Scharf story really drives that point home.

Jim and wife Bruna farm near Perdue, Saskatchewan. Jim's grandfather and father farmed the area, making Jim a third generation farmer.

Jim's mind is always searching for ways to do things better and simpler. He, along with every other grain farmer was vexed at the thought that everytime they delivered a load of grain to the grain elevator, at least 10 bushels of grain remained caught in the corners of the truck box. Jim invented a simple manually operated unit that reaches into the box and cleans out the trapped grain. He's now sold over 7,000 units. And has just received the U.S. patents.

But that's only part of Jim's story. He also designed a kitchen dispenser for plastic wrap called "E-Zee Wrap 1000". But his real coup came two years ago when, tired of all the bafflegab created when the government announced they were replacing dollar bills with the dreaded 'Loonie', Jim saw a golden opportunity. He reasoned that since the loon is a nesting bird, our new 'Loonie' would require a nest to rest. So he designed a small oak box with a slot in the top, called it a "Loonie Nest' and began taking orders from area gift stores. Word soon spread, Jim's 'Loonie Nest' caught on, keeping up to 10 people working to fill the orders.

Jim told me recently... *"There are now probably about 25 different loonie nests on the market, but we were first. We've sold over 30 thousand, and the orders are still coming in. One company bought 500 for a promotion."* At 20 loonies each, that's a lot of loonies.

The "Loonie Nest" ... "Grain Retriever" ... and "E-Zee Wrap 1000" are only sidelines. Jim and his father together farm 20 quarters of rich Saskatchewan soil. *"We did well this year because we planted over 500 acres of lentils. It brings in top dollar now since its being used by consumers in place of meat."*

The 38 year old dynamo is quick to tell you... *"I'm optimistic about Canada. I have big hopes for farming. I just bought another quarter. People have to eat."*

If this keeps up, Jim and Bruna will have to convert a barn into a giant 'Loonie Nest' to hold all of their loonies.

He Earns You Money

Mike Grenby

Today Mike Grenby is one of Canada's most respected and successful financial planners. Back in the late 60's Mike was writing a regular financial column in the Vancouver Sun. He worked there for 25 years. Then he did what most people would like to do. He quit his job and struck out on his own.

Mike pioneered the idea of a regular syndicated newspaper column offering financial advice. It was a tough idea to sell at first but now his column is carried regularly in more than 50 newspapers coast to coast. He's written five books on personal finances, and travels the country holding group seminars. Mike has become a very successful entrepreneur. But it wasn't easy, it seldom is.

I asked Mike if being self employed is everybody's cup of tea?... *"You have to have the right temperament for it. I got into this by easing into it. I worked for the Sun for 25 years and freelanced on the side. So, when I did go out on my own I had a feeling for working for myself although it was still a shock. It's like having a child. When you have your first one you know it's going to change your life but you have no idea just how much. Going into business is the same sort of thing."*

Does Mike recommend becoming self-employed?... *"No, I don't recommend it for everybody. I think if you have the temperament, you're prepared to work hard, you like to be your own boss, you're fairly independent, lots of ideas, then it could make sense for you. But if you like the 35 to 40 hours work week, not having to worry about not getting paid, and enjoy paid holidays every year, then working on your own is probably not a good thing for you."*

So, before you fall prey to the lure of quitting your job, reflect on Mike's advice. If you decide you still want to do it, then go for it.

The Bathtub Admiral of the World

Frank Ney

You don't have to come from a big city to think big. Frank Ney, a successful real estate developer and former longtime Mayor of Nanaimo, B.C., proved just that in 1967. That's the year he came up with the wild idea of holding a bathtub race from Vancouver Island, across 35 miles of choppy Georgia Strait to Vancouver.

In 1967, Nanaimo had a population of 25 thousand. Frank was Centennial Committee Chairman. He wanted to do something that would reflect Canada's rugged pioneer spirit, and at the same time put Nanaimo on the map.

Like every unusual idea, Frank's ran into unbelievable opposition. Who had ever heard of a bathtub race, using real bathtubs with outboard motors? The more they resisted, the more he persisted. The idea caught on and caught fire. 243 bathtubs entered. Here's how Frank Ney described to me what happened when the cannon was fired July 1st, 1967 in Nanaimo Harbor signalling the start of the world's first Nanaimo to Vancouver Bathtub Race... *"Bathtubs were sinking everywhere. That day 142 bathtubs sunk in the first 12½ minutes. It indeed was as the news media reported... 'A Saga of Raw Courage and True Bathtub Seamanship.' Once again we proved conclusively, and incontrovertibly that Canada leads the way in bathtub technology.*

"And that on holiday occasions Canadians seem to prefer corn to culture. The race was publicized all over the world. In fact, I got a medal from the queen for it."

Every year since, the Annual Bathtub Race attracts thousands of people to Nanaimo. It's become an international event attracting entrants from as far away as Australia. What started as a wild idea has become a major promotion event for Nanaimo. Having generated untold millions of dollars in free publicity and tourist dollars.

As Frank Ney says, *"If you have an idea, try it. It's better to have tried and failed, than to never have tried at all."*

He Enjoys Every Minute

Mel Dancy

I've known Mel Dancy as a friend for over fifteen years. He's a remarkable guy. Mel grew up in Hamilton, Ontario. He got his first construction job at age eleven when he bid on a sewer line project at a new home being built near his home. He worked all day with a pick and shovel like a beaver possessed. By day's end the job was complete and Mel received the magnificent sum of 10 dollars. The construction hook was in his blood forever.

By age 18, he was buying and selling land as well as building houses. Like most young people, Mel was restless. So, he moved to Toronto and tackled the big stuff ... highrises. Before long, he had a string of them in and around Toronto. Never satisfied, and always a challenge seeker, in 1977 he bid on and won a contract with the Egyptian government to build an entire village way out in the middle of the Sahara Desert. Mel was there for four years. The project was a shambles from day one. He lost a bundle and earned the nickname "Mel of the Desert".

Bowed but never broken, Mel returned to Toronto and picked up where he left off. Today, at 51 years of age, Mel owns a number of highrises around Toronto and is always seeking new challenges. Ask him if he thinks there is still the same opportunity to achieve in Canada as there was when he started out and he'll tell you... *"Probably now more than ever. Just their desire would carry them through. There have been downturns before in Canada and there'll be downturns again. But you can succeed in Canada no matter what. Canada is the greatest country. It's a godsend to live here."*

Mel still puts in fourteen hour days. Ask him why he does it and he'll tell you very simply... *"Because I enjoy every minute of it."*

Canada needs more risk takers with the work ethics of Mel Dancy.

"When you are making a success of something, it's not work. It's a way of life. You enjoy yourself because you are making your contribution to the world."

—Andy Granatelli

New Years Resolutions... Think Positively

Broadcast December 29, 1990

Monday is New Year's Eve. Next Tuesday is New Year's Day. The day when most Canadians, probably you included, wake up in the morning and begin making a mental list of all the good things to achieve during the coming year. High on most lists are the standards like; going on a diet, doing exercise, more time with the family. If you're a smoker, quitting smoking will likely be right up there near the top. If you imbibed too much New Year's Eve the promise to swear off will also be right up near the top. These are the annual common resolutions that make us feel good heading into a new year. One resolution you should make, and not break, is to promise yourself you will think positively all year. Make this the year you will achieve goals you've always wanted but for one reason or another, have allowed them to cool on the back burner. Think positively about yourself, your ability, your goals. And for goodness sake please think positively about Canada. Last year at this time we hailed the coming '90's as the decade of opportunity. I firmly believe it is. So do the thousands of Canadians who will start new companies in Canada next year. That's right, thousands of new businesses will be created in Canada next year. That tells you a lot of Canadians are thinking positive about themselves and Canada. So promise yourself that the one resolution you will *not* break is your promise to yourself to think positively. If you do, I promise you'll have a happy New Year all year long.

Several days after this editorial was broadcast a listener in Victoria sent me this practical reminder.

"One of your resolutions should always be to speak softly and sweetly. If your words are soft and sweet, they won't be as hard to swallow, should you have to eat them."

"You make your own success."
—*Dr. Leslie Bell*

Canada's Frozen Food Kings

Harrison & Wallace McCain

Brothers Harrison and Wallace McCain of Florenceville, New Brunswick, are known as "Canada's Frozen Food Kings". But it was a difficult battle for the title.

When they started McCain Foods in 1956, offering their frozen french fries to Canadian food stores, many outlets weren't set up to handle much in the way of frozen products other than ice cream. Not only did they have to convince retailers to buy their goods, they also had to convince them to renovate their stores.

With a guarantee from the Province of New Brunswick, the McCains issued bonds to help set up their first factory.

In 1958 they expanded their product line to include frozen peas. By being able to freeze the crop when prices were low and sell it when prices rose the following year, they finally got the company on the road to success.

They now make a variety of food products that are non-frozen including single strength juices and cheese.

Today, McCain Foods has factories across Canada and in eight other countries worldwide. They employ 12,500 people and produced over 2.4 billion dollars worth of food products in 1990, including chips for the English market.

The McCain Brothers—"Canada's Frozen Food Kings".

It's in the Cards

Kevin Zubek

I first told the Kevin Zubek's story on my radio program two years ago, (1989). At that time Kevin was a 16-year-old high school student from Mississauga, Ontario who was well on his way to becoming a successful entrepreneur in the Sports Card Collectible business.

He began as most collectors do, first he was a fan. Then he began trading and selling. In 1989 Kevin was expecting to gross 100 thousand dollars buying and selling sports cards. Not bad for a 16-year-old high school student. Now two years later, at 18 years of age Kevin is working full time with his father in their Sports Card store in Mississauga.

They carry a stock of about 25 million cards. Kevin is rated one of Canada's best in the business. And believe me it's big business. Some cards sell for up to 7500 dollars.

Kevin travels around North America attending card shows, buying and selling. Always on the look out for that one rare, mint condition card that someone back home is willing to pay any price to acquire. For example the value for a near mint set of 1952 Topps Cards (all 407 in the set) is around 45 thousand dollars!

Proud of Our New Citizens

Margret Osbaldeston

Where would Canada be without new citizens. Every year we welcome thousands to Canada. People who arrive and enrich our country. Most born Canadians take citizenship for granted. We shouldn't. Canadian citizenship is the most prized possession a person can have. Just ask citizenship court judge Margret Osbaldeston of Edmonton, *"We can't really blame us born Canadians, we know no other Life. But we are learning to have a country pride. We are learning to realize just how much we really have, and what we must guard and protect."*

Judge Osbaldeston is herself a remarkable woman. I attended one of her new citizenship swearing in ceremonies. I was impressed by her intense personal commitment and concern for each new citizen she swore in. Later, in her chambers she told me a touching story of a young Vietnamese man who arrived in Canada, was taken in by a church group, found employment as a dishwasher, studied English, became a woodworker apprentice, and within 4 years was appearing before her for his hearing of his application for Canadian citizenship. When she advised him he would be sworn in at her next swearing in ceremony, tears came to his eyes, *"Oh judge, thank you"*, he said, *"May I now sing you a song? It's the most beautiful song in the world."* The judge wondered what he had in mind, but gave her approval anyway. The young Vietnamese pulled himself up to his full 5 feet 2 inches, filled his lungs till she thought he would burst, and sang for her what he believed to be the most beautiful song in the world. He sang, word for word in a loud clear voice, a most touching rendition of "O' Canada".

Tell that to the next person you hear speak critically of Canada. Remind the person that we Canadians are a small minority of only 25 million people in a world population exceeding 5 billion people. Millions of people in other countries would give their very soul to change places with us in a moment. Anyone who doubts me need only ask judge Osbaldeston, or anyone associated with the citizenship court.

"Be Canadian and the future is yours."
—Louis-Honoré Frechette

The Lac La Biche Conglomerate

Duane & Linda Young

Seventeen years ago Duane Young arrived in Lac La Biche, Alberta as a 26 year old linesman for the Alberta Telephone Company. He'd been with them for a few years and was earning good money but, Duane had an inner desire to someday own his own hotel.

The town's seedy York Hotel was for sale. So he bought it, cleaned it up, and over the next few years completely rebuilt it.

I stayed there while on a speaking engagement in Lac La Biche. Frankly, I was really surprised. It is one of the nicest and cleanest hotels in Northern Alberta. Although Duane has had no formal training in hotel management I would stack his business savy up against the biggest and best in Toronto. Today, Duane and wife Linda are close to being a conglomerate.

Besides the hotel, they also own a nearby motel, a large campground and marina, the local newspaper, and a six acre site on the edge of town.

"I want to build another 50-60 room extension on the hotel, and develop the acreage. Then I'll be happy."

All of this did not come easy, nor overnight.

"In the lean years when we first started out I was at the hotel a minimum of 15 hours a day, 7 days a week. I would arrive early in the morning when it was still dark and leave at night when it was dark."

Duane is a high energy guy always on the go. His advice to other would-be entrepreneurs is;

"Don't be afraid to work. Don't be afraid to sacrifice. Because that is what you have to do if you want to achieve."

Knowing what he knows now, would Duane do it all again?

"Oh yes by all means. Don't forget I was 26 years old and had no brains, but a lot of guts."

A lot of guts yes. No brains? Don't you believe it.

Capsule Course in Human Relations
Five most important words: I AM PROUD OF YOU.
Four most important words: WHAT IS YOUR OPINION?
Three most important words: IF YOU PLEASE
Two most important words: THANK YOU
Least Important word: I
—Forbes Magazine

Canada's Mobile Mechanic

Bob Krueger

People who work with 34 year old Bob Krueger will tell you he is the finest mechanic around. He can fix anything and everything.

Growing up in Saskatoon, his school chums were always asking him to fix their bicycles, which he did. As he and his friends grew older, they asked Bob to fix their cars. So, at 19 years of age Bob decided he would go into business for himself, as a mobile mechanic. He formed a company appropriately called "R. J. K. Mobile Mechanics Incorporated". Wasn't he worried going out on his own?

"No I wasn't worried. I saw a gap in the market for my kind of service. I knew what my goals were and went for them."

As a mobile mechanic, Bob and his staff travel all over on special projects. Besides having an office in Saskatoon he also has a major operation in Yellowknife, N.W.T. In fact, that's where he lives because most of his large contracts are in the North including Alaska. *"Our company is now registered in Alaska and we have exported the Canadian trade labor to that market. It is being received faster than we actually wished."* Because of the enormous distance between projects, and the limited passenger airline services, Bob flies his own plane.

At 19 Bob Krueger knew what his goals were and headed straight for them. Along the way he's built a solid business employing 22 people and expects to gross 1.2 million in sales this year. (1991)

He's another Canadian Achiever.

His Hillsides are Beautiful

Gerry Mahoney

Gerry Mahoney is a very interesting Canadian entrepreneur. It's hard to believe he's only 44 years of age. For 14 years he worked as a salesman for Bell Telephone. He lived in Burlington, Ontario and commuted daily to his Toronto office. One day he said, *"Enough of this commuting and working for someone else. I'm going to develop my own ideas"*.

He had an idea to place signs on support posts in high traffic areas and sell the advertising space. Sort of like mini-billboards. So, he resigned from Bell and started his own sign company. He no sooner got going, when along came the recession of 1981 and Gerry's dream company collapsed. He sold it for peanuts to another Canadian Achiever featured in this book, Jim Pattison, the world's largest owner of outdoor signs.

Gerry's idea was right, his financial capacity was wrong. *"My old job at Bell"*, he told me, *"sure looked mighty good"*. But in life there is no turning back so he became a print salesman.

One hot summer day during an Ontario beer strike five years ago, a neighbour called to tell Gerry there was some American beer at the liquor store. They joined the line up to buy it, but it was warm. Gerry figured there must be some inexpensive way to carry cold drinks around. He started work on his kitchen table, designing an insulated carrier bag. First attempts failed. The bag became Gerry's hobby.

He studied physics and learned that the key was to reduce the air space. Eventually he came up with a draw-string plastic bag, insulated, with the kind of bubble liner used in swimming pool covers. Then he studied marketing methods. Three years ago the "Koolbag" was market-tested. Gerry had aimed it at the male beer drinker, but found women were equally interested in it for carrying hot or cold food. In 1988 the "Koolbag" won the prize for best new product at the Canadian Hardware Show. Major supermarkets and milk stores adopted it and the bags went on sale at all Ontario beer stores. They're even sold in the Arctic through Hudson Bay Northern Stores.

The market in Canada is too small and the summers too short, so Gerry has licensed his idea to U.S. manufacturer, "Sealed Air Corporation." They tested it with exciting results in Florida, California and Illinois.

Two years ago Gerry began developing another idea of his. Riders on the Toronto Go-Trains will recognize it immediately. Gerry made a deal with the CNR to lease the use of the dirt banks along the Go-Trains routes. He formed a company called "Hillside Communications", and very simply he leases advertisers space to exhibit their corporate logo in the form of beautifully landscaped gardens which are very pleasant for Go-Train commuters to gaze upon as they travel to or from Toronto.

"It's a unique form of advertising. Companies lease a space for 3-year periods. I have four full-time gardeners maintaining the sites. The environmental people love it because we have cleaned up and beautified what used to be very unattractive sites."

Gerry Mahoney is not looking to make a million dollars. He told me, *"That's not my major motivation. I want to enjoy life, spend time with my kids, and just live comfortably."*

"A hard low shot fired by a small player can be just as dangerous as one by a big fellow."
    —*Henri 'Pocket' Richard*

Achieving in Both Official Languages

Jocelyne Doyle-Rodrigue

For the people of Montreal, bilingualism is not a goal, it's a fact of daily life. And that fact was not lost on Jocelyne Doyle-Rodrigue. At the University of Montreal she specialized in translation. After graduating she joined the Federal Translation Bureau in Ottawa and soon rose to a managerial position in the bureau. At the age of twenty-eight. Jocelyne was well paid, secure and doing something she enjoyed.

But Jocelyne wasn't happy. She really wanted to work for herself. So, with a typewriter in her basement and a few freelance contracts, Jocelyne started "Translex" in the spring of 1980. (The company is now called "Exelcom/Translex".) Her timing was perfect. She entered the private translation field at a time when businesses, government agencies and national associations were looking for high-quality translation services. She also found that many English speaking Canadians were in need of good translation of documents and other materials that were being produced in French.

Today Excelcom/Translex employs 53 translators and 28 support staff in their three offices: Ottawa, Montreal and Toronto. Jocelyne's husband, Nelson, a former translator is Vice President of Operations. And what an operation it is. They expect sales this year of 4.8 million dollars.

Jocelyn Doyle-Rodrigue, a Canadian Achiever in both official languages.

An optimist goes to the window every morning and says, "Good Morning, God." The Pessimist goes to the window and says, "Good God, Morning!"

The Man of Stone

Edward Ratcliffe

It takes nature half a billion years to make sandstone. Edward Ratcliffe does it in 14 hours through a process he invented.

His artificial sandstone is sand from the ground at Cambridge, Ontario put under enormous pressure and baked at tremendous heat, just the way nature does it. But, much much faster. It is stronger than the natural product and comes in any colour you want. It's often used to match additions to old sandstone buildings, as well as impressive new structures.

Born in Hamilton, Ontario in 1919, Ed Ratcliffe has led the kind of interesting life that would fill a book. He graduated from Toronto University in

1941 as a chemical engineer, then joined Dupont at Kingston, Ontario where he helped pioneer the production of Nylon in Canada. He left to join C.I.L. and produced explosives. In 1946 Ed returned to Hamilton and joined his father's construction company. After the war it was difficult acquiring building supplies so he created "angelstone" concrete block which looks like stone.

The process Ed uses to create his new sandstone blocks is much more sophisticated. It stimulates the physical make-up of natural stone so that it strengthens with age. Edward's company called "Arriscraft", located in Cambridge, Ontario supplies new sandstone, as well as very old stone, which he quarries from the Niagara Escarpment to construction sites throughout North America. The continuing reconstruction of the Hartwell Locks along the Rideau Canal in Ottawa is just one place you'll find his new sandstone blocks being used. The stone being replaced there was originally installed 140 years ago by the Royal Engineers. This new stone should last even longer.

You will also find his products at the Canadian Embassy in Washington, D.C. Another Washington location, "The Law Enforcement Officer's Memorial" now under construction, is being built using many tons of Ed's Cambridge product.

You'll notice that many architects are now moving away from the razzle dazzle of steel and glass in favour of the warmth and solid dignity of stone. Much of that movement can be credited to the amazing sandstone invention of Canadian Achiever Edward Ratcliffe.

Why People Quit Their Jobs

According to a survey developed by Robert Half International, these are the reasons employees say they quit their last place of employment...

... feeling that opportunity for advancement was limited	47%
... lack of recognition	26%
... unhappiness with management	15%
... inadequate salary or benefits	6%
... bored with the job	6%
	100%

"Nobody has asked me but if I were to choose a national bird for Canada it would be the starling. He struts self-reliantly, asks no favors of anyone, and never puts out his claw for relief."

—Gordon Sinclair

A Farmer's Best Friend

Leon Malinowski

Leon Malinowski never minded getting his hands dirty, or working twelve hours a day. Maybe that's why he's now Owner/President of "Leon-Ram Enterprises", a 15 million dollar a year operation that employs up to 150 people.

Thirty-eight years ago Leon was a journeyman welder repairing farm equipment in Bankend, Saskatchewan. In slow seasons he designed and made equipment, such as the "Leon Doer Blade" for clearing and digging. Patented, the Leon Blade was a humdinger of a success, and as time went by so was Leon's inventiveness.

In 1967 Leon made significant changes. He moved to Yorkton, gave up repairing equipment so he could concentrate on new products and research development. To help guide the company's finances he brought in his brother, Ray. At that time they worked in 8,000 square feet. Currently "Leon-Ram Enterprises" occupies 200,000 square feet, and has four divisions producing trend setting equipment that's sold the world over.

"We are now beginning to diversify," he told me. *"We are doing more contracting and non-agricultural business. We had to because the ag-business is so uncertain right now."*

Is Leon optimistic about the future?

"Oh yes! I feel very optimistic. In fact, we've just bought a lot of equipment for expansion.

"One piece, a 350 ton Press Brake used to bend metal, costs us 150 thousand dollars. We bought several big pieces like that." Then he added, *"By the way, that Press Brake was made right here in Canada, Richmond, B.C."*

Leon is looking to expand his export business. Currently 25% of his sales are to the U.S., Australia and other countries. He hopes to increase this. His staff will tell you that like most self-made entrepreneurs, Leon is the hardest working person in the company. A trait that has made him a very successful Canadian Achiever.

From small beginnings come big achievements.

—D.D.

He Believed in Co-operative Family Games

Jim Deacove

A quiet country setting 12 miles from Perth, Ontario, is not exactly where you would expect to find the hub of a burgeoning toy and game empire, but by the same token, Jim Deacove never expected, or really wanted it to happen. . . it just happened.

Back 20 years ago, Jim and Ruth's two young daughters, Tanya and Christa, were growing up. Jim was perplexed by the lack of educational toys and games he could buy for the girls. The games on the market then were all competitive. He wanted his children to have 'co-operative' games. Games they could play with together in a 'co-operative' rather than competitive manner. Jim, a very quite, patient high school teacher, set out to design a few games for them.

He first made a few co-op games as a hobby for his friends and family to enjoy. Jim's family is much like every other Canadian family. . . sharing, helping and being kind to one another. Friends suggested they make their games in quantity and sell them. So, in 1972, Jim and wife Ruth and daughters Tanya and Christa, turned a hobby into a small business called "Family Pastimes", working out of their home. *"When I started I knew nothing about business whatsoever. I was a high school teacher who had an idea."*

The business grew, they moved their cottage industry out of their home and into a cottage of its own. The games and books were made in small quantities and sold to local craft shops. Soon orders began coming in from across Canada. Then the U.S., then Australia, England, the Netherlands, Sweden, Germany, Spain and Israel. Jim saw what was happening and registered the name 'A Co-operative Game' worldwide.

The Deacoves had difficulty filling the orders. The most they could produce was 40 thousand units and that was not near enough to meet demand. In 1989, the huge toy manufacturer, 'Playtoy Industries' began producing Jim's toys under a licence fee agreement. Now you'll find 'Co-operative Games' in Eatons, Canadian Tire, Sears and other major retail locations. *"I never thought"*, Jim told me, *"that I would ever see my games and books in these locations. We worked for 20 years to arrive at this. The first ten years were mighty lonely."*

What started as a few games to involve children aged 3 to 7 has grown to 69 games and 4 books to involve children and adults as well.

What did he do different? *"What I did different I guess was to have an idea that I strongly believed in. That's the key. It's to have something that you personally feel very worthwhile accomplishing. You also must have plenty of physical and emotional stamina to carry it through."*

The Deacove family, Jim, Ruth, Tanya and Christa, turned their cottage industry into a major industry. Another example of Canadian Achievement.

He Made His Dream Happen

Ted Grant

When you hear what 40 year old Ted Grant is doing now, and you hear what his background was, you'll wonder how Ted's achieved what he has.

Ted grew up on a farm near Portage La Prairie, Manitoba, joined the RCMP and settled in for what should have been a long secure career. But Ted risked it all to become an entrepreneur. *"I started flying,"* he told me, *"in 1972, in conjunction with my RCMP career, I wanted to have something to fall back on when I retired. I'd always wanted to own a fishing lodge. It was a challenge that I wanted to follow since I was a little boy. I knew I'd have to be able to fly a plane."*

Little boy's dreams are made to become men's achievements. Ted started an air charter service in Fort Simpson, N.W.T. His little boy dreams became a reality when he bought a lodge. He didn't stop there. He then bought a hotel, then an airline... 'Simpson Air', which now has 8 planes.

Today, at 42 years of age, the combined sales of his companies exceeds 5 million per year.

Does Ted recommend becoming an entrepreneur... *"If you're a gambler, yes go for it. Just make up your mind you're going to do it, and do it! The first few years in any type of business are tough. You often wonder if it's worth it. But you just have to stick with it."*

Ted Grant, as a boy he dreamed a dream. As a man he made it happen.

Most people don't recognize opportunity because it comes disguised as work.

She Builds Truck Bodies

Suzanne LeClair

When Suzanne LeClair was a little girl growing up in Montreal she decided she would do something different one day. Something Quebec women didn't do. But that had to wait. She married Jacque, an accountant and spent ten years at home raising two sons, Mark and Louis.

Then she chose a new career as a manufacturer. She'd go into the tough male business of building truck bodies. To learn it, she took jobs as a sales rep for two different manufacturers, asked questions and learned the tricks of the trade. Her male employers were happy to tell her because they did not believe a woman could become a competitor. Did they ever have a surprise coming!

In 1978 Suzanne, at age 30, launched her own company "Les Fourgons Transit" with 75 thousand dollars of capital. Most of it raised from a second mortgage on the family home. Now, her company is the giant of the truck body business. In fact, 3 years ago she bought out "Les Boix Campions", one of the companies she had originally worked for.

Suzanne's company produces 2500 truck bodies yearly, creating annual sales of 10 million dollars. In 1986 she took the company on a major expansion program. First she went public on the Montreal Stock Exchange. Then, used the capital to build a modern 125 thousand square foot plant. In 1986 she added on another 25 thousand square feet. But, having shareholders was not to her liking, *"It was too restrictive,"* she told me. *"So I bought back all the shares and privatized the company."*

She runs a very tight ship. Her staff consists of 60 employees including Suzanne as President, Jacque as Comptroller, Mark as plant manager and Louis as sales manager. You can't make it much tighter than that can you?

Suzanne is highly respected in the business community and serves on the Board of Directors of two major corporations: "Sidbec-Dosco" and the "National Bank of Canada".

Suzanne LeClair set out to do something different, and did. She proved the point that a woman can win in any game. Who ever said that building truck bodies was a "man's business" is now busy eating those words.

"America, like Canada, is a land of opportunity."
    —*Louis B. Mayer* (Canadian-born founder of MGM Hollywood)

It's Not What You're Born With...

Harry Tamarin

A good friend of mine in St. Catherines, Bill Watson, told me about a local St. Catherine's Achiever whose story deserved to be told on my program. Bill said this person was an inspiration and example to every Canadian. The more Bill told me about him the more I agreed. If anyone is a "Canadian Achiever" Harry Tamarin is.

Harry was ten years old when he arrived in Canada with his parents from Russia, March 22, 1926. As a teenager he worked with his father collecting and selling scrap metal. When he was old enough Harry started driving a truck which he did until 1949 when he started his own small scrap and new steel company, "Niagara Structural Steel". Over the years his company helped build Toronto skyscrapers, Hamilton City Hall, and in a genuine case of local boy makes good, the "Garden City Skyway Bridge" in his hometown. Then, about seven years ago came Harry's great leap forward to worldwide recognition.

Together with his son Seymour, who had patented a new sport surfacing system, Harry started producing "Omni" artificial playing surfaces for the sports industry. With its proven ability to reduce injuries by 76%, Omni Turf is specified by most U.S. colleges and pro-playing fields. Court #12 at Wimbledon boasts Harry's turf.

The company was expanding so rapidly that three years ago Harry sold off "Niagara Structural Steel". He formed a new company "Tecsyn International Inc.", a holding company listed on the Toronto Stock Exchange. "Tecysn" includes four Canadian and six U.S. companies employing 1000 people. Harry expects 1991 sales of, *"Somewhere around 130 million dollars. With this economy, it's hard to say."*

Harry, now 75, has not only developed an outstanding reputation as a successful businessman, he's also established himself as a caring community citizen. Serving on the Boards of Brock University and the Shaw Festival, he's very proud of the fact that the Shaw Festival people made him an Honourary Life Member. He won't admit it, but I suspect a lot of the steel in the beautiful Shaw Festival Theatre came compliments of his generosity.

The last time I spoke with Harry was January 25, 1991. He was recovering from a surprise 75th Birthday party organized by his sons Larry and Seymour at Buffalo's famous Como's Restaurant. I asked Harry when he was planning to retire? He replied:

"No way, never. What do you want to retire for? I go to Florida and get bored stiff after ten days."

I'm indebted to Bill Watson for telling me about Harry Tamarin. His story does indeed offer inspiration to everyone. It reminds us that Canada is indeed the land of opportunity. And further reminds us that it's not what you're born with that matters, it's what you do with what you're born with.

Her Buttertarts are the Best

Norma & Norm Beer

Norma and Norm Beer of Chilliwack, B.C., are a real Canadian success story. Norm owned his own company delivering to local food stores. Eight years ago Norm suggested to Norma that it would be a good idea to add buttertarts to his line of products. Norma was a wonderful cook but, she had never baked buttertarts before. She decided to give it a try. The first day she gave Norm 14 buttertarts to take on his rounds. Each one individually and lovingly wrapped in clear cellophane. He sold them and asked Norma for more. The second day she made more. . . He sold out and asked for more. Soon, demand for Norma's buttertarts was so great that she was working round the clock in her kitchen and basement. The more she made. . . the more Norm sold.

She rented an empty store, set up baking ovens, and hired staff. Still she could not keep up with demand. Norm's customers kept asking for more of 'Norma's Buttertarts'. Demand became so great that Norm sold his distributorship to work full time with Norma. It's the perfect example of what can happen in Canada if you have the right product and are willing to work at it.

'Norma's Buttertarts' are now being sold throughout western Canada. She produces 550 dozen each day from her modern bakery. Each one individually and lovingly wrapped in clear cellophane. *"We made things more efficient,"* she told me, *"by adding some automatic equipment."* Norm says, *"the biggest gratification for us is the fact that we are now able to provide employment for our staff of 16 people."*

Norma is still unfazed by all of this success. Phone the bakery and she answers the phone which is right near the mixing vats. Norma built her reputation on quality and she won't let anything interfere with that. What is her secret to success. . . . ?

"Give a quality product and good service. That's the main thing. If you're going to change your product, make it better."

"Of those to whom much is given, much is expected."
—Unknown

Beauty and Brains Means Business

Deborah Goodwin

The cosmetic industry in Canada is an enormous industry. It's in the billions of dollars and employs thousands of people. A large portion of the industry is cornered by beauty consultants who arrange private parties in friend's homes. There are over 5,000 such beauty consultants in Canada... each can earn up to 200.00 per week working part time one or two nights a week.

One of Canada's most successful is 33 year old Deborah Goodwin of Winona, Ontario. She started selling part time eleven years ago. At the time she was a 22 year old loans officer working in a bank. *"I was invited to an Aloette Cosmetic Party. The girl putting on the show worked with me at the bank. She explained how she was making an extra hundred dollars a week working two evenings. So, I decided to try it myself."*

She took to selling cosmetics like the proverbial duck to water. Soon she quit her job at the bank to devote full time to her new career. Today, Deborah's company 'Aloette Cosmetics of Oakville' has over 200 beauty consultants and 15 managers plus 5 full time office staff creating sales of 3 million dollars a year.

"The top income earner this year for Aloette International is one of my consultants. She earned over 100 thousand dollars. In fact," Deborah told me, *"most of my managers earned over 50 thousand."*

Deborah's company is a family affair... husband Alan *"directs the franchise, looks after all of our business affairs and leaves me free to concentrate on sales development and training."*

Her mother and brother Brad are also deeply involved in making the company operate so smoothly.

Deborah offers this advice to women looking for a new challenge... *"First off they should look beyond and realize that in this day and age they will probably work in some capacity for the rest of their life. So why not do something they enjoy and get well paid for. Rather than just doing something to get paid for the time being."*

The cosmetics industry is huge... and just keeps getting bigger. So if you're looking for an opportunity to earn money on a part time basis... with the chance of someday becoming self-employed, you might look into becoming a beauty consultant... as Deborah Goodwin says, "the field is wide open."

"If you don't care who gets the credit, you can accomplish anything."
    —*Harry 'Red" Foster*

They Work Together

Jack & Joan Donald

Jack and Joan Donald, through Parkland Industries own 141 gas stations in three Provinces, and an oil refinery near Red Deer, Alberta. They are millionaires living on a ranch outside of Red Deer, where they could live the lives of the rich and famous. But, in fact there is nothing pretentious about them. They're as down-to-earth as you can get.

Only a formal affair, like a shareholder's meeting will get Jack into a suit and tie. Most days he's comfortable in an open-necked shirt, casual pants and cowboy boots.

Born in Edmonton, Jack got his first feel for the gas business as a youngster pumping the stuff at a local station.

"I've tried other things from time to time, but I like the gas industry. It's a people business. I enjoy going to work every day. It's a real challenge."

Running the 10th largest integrated oil company in Canada and being involved in many community ventures, how does he manage to keep everything under control?

"In my office you will see a row of briefcases, each representing a company in which I'm involved. At a moment's notice I can pick up a briefcase and be ready to go. It's organization and having a wife leading and pushing me in the right direction, and on time, is what's important in our operation."

Leading and pushing, Joan Donald is very much involved in their "Fas Gas", "Bi-Lo" and "Gasex" stations located mostly in small towns in Alberta, Saskatchewan and British Columbia. She is Assistant Corporate Secretary of Parkland Industries, the Red Deer based company whose gross earnings were projected to be $175 million in 1991.

That's a far cry from 26 years ago when the Donalds bought their first Texaco outlet in Red Deer for $5,000. Joan was right in from the beginning:

"I was kind of thrown into it. I didn't have the background that Jack did. He went off to get his mechanic's license at the Southern Alberta Institute of Technology and I was left to run the station. So I learned very quickly."

Working together is important:

"We work well together. We each have our strengths and weaknesses. When one has a workload that is almost impossible, the other one will come in and pick up the pieces. We do this back and forth. We enjoy life and every day is fun."

Joan somehow found time to have two children and the Donalds now have five grandchildren. But being grandparents hasn't slowed them down a bit.

Parkland Industries directly employed 132 people in 1990 and approximately 850 more employed through the service station chain. Its assets include a former Shell Oil refinery; oil production of 575 barrels a day, a fleet of 19 trucks, a service station supply company and many other affiliated firms serving the petroleum industry.

Despite some inconveniences, the Donalds had no plans to move from Red Deer. Jack, a former alderman, was Chairman in 1990 of Alberta Opportunity Company whose object is to finance qualified small businesses on behalf of the Province of Alberta. Jack is Director and Chairman of the Board of the Canadian Western Bank and has been on the Board of Red Deer College and many other community organizations.

Joan is equally busy on the home scene: she is a Director of the Red Deer Westerner Exposition Association, a member of the College board and an avid supporter of equestrian events. Yet the couple manages to spend time together on and off the job. It means sharing and trusting.

"It helps when you work together. Joan knows what I do for a living and she doesn't get upset if I'm late for supper, or if I don't get home for supper at all. She's a very intense person and when she worries about some activity she's involved in, I understand what she's going through as well. We've learned to live through the crises together and I feel it has strengthened our marriage."

When I asked them what advice they have for young people going into business for the first time they replied:

JOAN: *"I would say they should have a well-thought-out plan and know the business they're going into. Work in that particular field prior to entering the market."*

JACK: *In every instance, the rules of good business apply. You seek out an opportunity and analyze it. My Dad told me you'll never go broke making a profit, just as long as you are not too greedy in the process. I'm a firm believer that there are many opportunities for young people in business today, different kinds of opportunities than there were 26 years ago. Canada is a young country and it's growing. It requires people to find out what its needs are, then go out and fill those needs."*

Despite all their success Jack still keeps his mechanic's license up-to-date, *"Just in case"*, and meantime the Donald's homespun style has filtered down to the firm's executives who all drive pickup trucks so they can deliver a load of motor oil if necessary. Although he owns a Mercedes, Jack usually travels to work in a pickup truck himself.

Parkland Industries is booming in a world of oil adventure. The Company expects to add many more outlets, perhaps as many as 10 a year. Recently they acquired the Western Canadian right for the U.S. convenience chain AM/PM. And it all began with one leased station and the belief that hard work and working together can be fun. Jack and Joan Donald—Canadian Achievers.

Small Business...
The Real Canadian Achievers

Broadcast October 15, 1990

Small Business Week is celebrated in Canada every October with much fan fare and so it should. Because the real force that drives this country are small businesses employing up to 20 people. Small business week is proclaimed annually to recognize and pay tribute to the contribution independent small business makes to Canada's economy. In case you're wondering how important that is, here is information that may surprise you. A Stats Canada Survey showed that 44% of all working Canadians are employed in companies small enough to be owned and managed by the employer. When the survey was conducted in November, 1986, it showed that 40% of the companies had been established in the previous 5 years. Think of the opportunity that has created for Canadian Achievers.

An article in the Financial Post stated that from 1978 to 1986, businesses with less than 20 employees created 85% of the total net new job growth in Canada. Or 1.2 million out of 1.4 million jobs. Times are changing. There's opportunity for everyone.

This Canadian Achiever salute and tribute is directed to every small business in Canada. Without you we'd be in tough shape.

They Produce a Lot of Jack

Bill Smith & Gerry Smith

In the mid 1970's Bill Smith of Toronto and Gerry Smith of Brantford, started working at Seeburn Metal Products in Orillia, Ontario. They aren't related. At the time they didn't even know each other but, that's all changed.

By 1985 they owned the company. What do they produce? They produce new car jacks. In fact, they produce over 4.5 million car jacks every year. That's about 50% of the North American car industry.

They produce their jacks at plants in Totteham and Beaverton, Ontario. They ship them to new car plants in Canada, the U.S. and here's a switch, to Toyota in Japan. The only other major competitor in the new car jack industry is the Universal Tool Company in Butler, Indiana. Between them they share over 80% of the North American new car industry.

47 year old Bill Smith is President, 41 year old Gerry Smith is Executive Vice President. They are very proud of their achievements. So are their 550

employees. Sales this year should top 50 million dollars! The company has a value of, according to Bill Smith, *"Somewhere between 16 to 20 million dollars. Jerry and I each own 50% of the company"*.

That's a lot of jack, no matter how you count it. Bill Smith and Gerry Smith, two Canadian Achievers.

Their Key to Success is Their People

Ketty & Mariano Alzetta

"You must like people. We love our people. They are everything to us. Without them we are nothing."

That's what Ketty Alzetta said when I asked her what was the secret to their success and their excellent Montreal restaurant, "La Capannina". The people she refers to are their customers and staff.

Ketty emigrated to Canada from Egypt 26 years ago. She met Mariano at the hotel where they both worked. 19 years ago they started a restaurant, they had partners, it failed. Six years ago, and much wiser, they tried again. Only this time, no partners, and it worked. Their restaurant has 13 staff, 110 seats, and is always busy. The menu is Italian with the key ingredients being the personal warmth and meticulous attention to detail of this caring couple.

Although their restaurant does not open until noon: *"We're here at eight in the morning. We must see that everything is okay. Then we wait to receive our people"*. Ketty and Mariano are still there at closing time around midnight to say good-night to their people and invite them back again and again.

In a world that's become increasingly more complicated, Ketty and Mariano Alzetta have built their successful business around the uncomplicated philosophy of service. They know that every restaurant sells food. The successful ones surround the food with service and ambience.

Believe It Or Not

Jimmy Pattison

Born in Luceland, Saskatchewan, raised in Vancouver, Jimmy Pattison is a legend in the financial world. A certified self-made billionaire. Everything he has now, he's earned.

In 1952 he started selling used cars. People who were in the business then say he was the best. In 1961 at age 32, he mortgaged his home to buy a General Motors dealership and the rest, as they say, is history.

His group of over fifty companies has combined annual sales exceeding 2 billion dollars. In a 1989 interview I asked him what he'd done different from anyone else? He replied, *"Maybe I took a few more risks."*

Jimmy is respected around the world as an astute entrepreneur with an uncanny knack to select the right people and spot business opportunities in unusual circumstances. Including show business success, like buying John Lennon's car at an auction then later donating it to the B.C. Government where it now rests on display in their Transportation Museum in Cloverdale, B.C.

He raised more than a few eyebrows a few years ago when he acquired "Ripley's Believe It or Not". He owns the comic strip, TV series, and all of their museums containing a priceless collection of unusual items. Believe it or not, Jimmy Pattison's "Believe It or Not" museums own the world's largest collection of shrunken heads. Whether it's shrunken heads for his museums, or companies with shrunken profits, Jimmy Pattison turns whatever he tackles into a profitable experience.

Shortcuts to Achieving...
There Aren't Any

Broadcast November 21/90

Fortunes are being made today by some less than honest people offering to fast track you into becoming an overnight success, or better still, overnight millionaire. Newspapers and magazines carry ads offering shortcuts to unbelievable riches. All you have to do is invest some of your money, a bit of your time, then sit back and watch the money roll in. It worries me when I read the claims some business opportunity ads make. Recently while doing research for this program I answered an ad that asked, "Are you ever going to earn 30 thousand dollars a month doing what you're doing now? If not, call this number." I called and got a recorded message from a high energy pitchman telling me that I could quickly join other Canadians who are making fortunes by investing in a new and dynamic innovation. I hung up before learning what it was. I wonder how many people answered the ad and didn't hang up and fell victim to the pitch? I'm not saying that all business opportunity ads are shady. What I am saying is there are no shortcuts to achieving. In the six years I've been doing research for this series, talking to hundreds of genuine achievers, I can't recall one achiever ever telling me he or she found a shortcut. There's an old saying, *"hitch your wagon to a star, but keep your feet on the ground."* Anything worth having is worth working for. Don't develop an itch that you're not prepared to scratch for.

They Bought the Company

Mel Steinke

"There is tremendous opportunity in Canada. The kind of opportunity that presented itself to us is out there in business today. The first thing that a person must do is identify the opportunity. Keep your eyes open. Look for opportunity. When you see it, decide whether or not you as an individual can believe in it and can establish your own personal belief in the achievement. If you can attain that belief, you can do it. There is no limitation whatsoever to your ability to be successful in business in Canada. If you have a good business strategy and believe in yourself. . . you can do it."

That's what Mel Steinke told me while we were discussing his own amazing career and the successful acquisition by him and fellow employees of the company they worked for.

First let me tell you a bit about 37 year old Mel. He was born and raised in the small northern Ontario town of Massey. His high school teacher, a real computer enthusiast, introduced Mel to computers and Mel was hooked. At 16 years of age, he formed a small company to provide computer services to the provincial government. He moved to Toronto and got a job at Datacrown which eventually became Polaris Consulting Services. He quickly rose up the management ladder.

In 1987 Mel learned that Polaris was being sold. He quickly gathered his fellow managers together and they decided they would buy Polaris. But talk is cheap. Polaris was a big company. The asking price was around 5 million dollars. It meant they would really have to go to the well to get financing. Which they did. And were successful in their bid. How did they feel going through it? *"There is no question that throughout this exercise we experienced virtually every emotion that is known to human kind. The first feeling you have when you know that the company you've been building is up for sale is that of disappointment. And second to that is uncertainty. What is going to happen? The third set of emotions that came into play were that of. . . can we potentially do this? And then an element of optimism and enthusiasm that said. . . yes we can. We can take on this organization and make it even more successful! From that point on it was a roller coaster ride of emotions. The excitement and the potential of owning your own business. The anxiety of being out on your own without a large organization supporting you. And the realization that you have your own large personal stake at risk in doing it."*

Well, not only did they do it, they turned an already successful company into a phenomenally successful company. Revenue increased in two years from 10 million dollars to 25 million dollars.

Last summer (1990) the partners accepted an offer and sold Polaris to the giant accounting firm of Deloitte & Touche, one of the world's largest accounting and management consulting companies.

"We have maintained Polaris as a separate company with the opportunity to build and become one of the largest computer services companies in Canada."

Ask Mel what the secret is to success and he'll tell you... *"The first step in taking on any challenge is to create a vision, a dream. The second step is to get your dream shared by others."*

Mel is quick to point out that the success of Polaris, and the success of any project is based on having a strong management team. *"Surround yourself with good people."*

Help or Hindrance?

Family Businesses

Broadcast August 28, 1990

There's an old saying about family businesses: *"It's three generations from shirt sleeves to shirt sleeves."* Meaning the first generation starts the company by rolling up their shirt sleeves to get the business off the ground. The second generation comes in wearing a suit and expands the company into a well-run, successful corporation. The third generation takes over and runs the corporation into the ground, leaving everyone in their shirt sleeves having to start all over.

The second generation is called *"The Sandwich Generation"*. They're sandwiched between the usually tough, gruff Founder parent, who questions their every decision, and they're sandwiched between their own children who seldom desire to achieve in the family business.

The second generation usually has more pressure on them than any of their employees.

So, is being in the family business a help or hindrance? You decide.

Achieving is getting up just one time more than you fall down.

They Wanted a Piece of the Action

Pat Thody

"Well I guess the feeling was . . . we finally did it. We knew what we were getting into. We knew that we were going to have to scrape all of our money together and that it would be tough for us all."

That's how Pat Thody described the feeling he and eleven other managers of Simmons, Canada's largest mattress company, felt when they finally acquired the company from the U.S. parent.

Two years earlier, Pat, who was president, and eleven other employees, including head office executives and the managers of the six bedding plants located across Canada, approached the U.S. head office with an offer to buy the Canadian operation. At first Simmons head office in Atlanta, Georgia, said 'no'. Pat persisted, they started to warm, finally they agreed to sell them the Canadian operation. It was a huge undertaking, Simmons is Canada's largest mattress manufacturing company with over 600 employees.

Those magic words, "piece of the action". Where would Canada be if it wasn't for achievers willing to risk it all for a piece of the action? Pat Thody and his group have a king-size challenge ahead now that it's their own money and future that's on the line. We wish them nothing but good luck.

"Well Canada has 26 million people and they all sleep. The average home has 2½ beds. It's a huge market."

Negotiations were friendly from day one yet it took nearly two years to close the deal (June 29, 1990).

Now that it's over, what advice does he have for anyone thinking of acquiring an existing successful company? *"The first thing I would advise is to find credible mergers and acquisitions people with a good background, and depend heavily on them. It's a very complex business deal when you acquire a company. Unless you have a lot of experience yourself you should get professional help. You'll never regret it."*

They say there are two things you should never buy: cheap shoes or cheap legal advice. If you're thinking of buying an existing company or forming a new company follow Pat Thody's suggestion. . . *"Get good advice . . . it could be your best investment."* Never rush into anything. Remember, if it's worth having, it's worth waiting for.

*Joining Pat in the bid were Brian Anderson, Jack Dudley, Peter Ingram, Ted Jackson, Terry Pace, Dave Puttock, Ron Meadley, Michel Arbic, John Main, Russ Westman, and Alan MacLean.

She Makes Everyone Feel Welcome

Pauline Hill

I first met this feisty lady while attending a Rotary meeting in Toronto as a guest of my good friend and fellow-broadcaster John Spragge. In place of the usual tired old 'welcoming committee' one meets at most service club meetings, I was surprised to be 'welcomed' by this dynamic little bit of a woman with a firm handshake, sparkling eyes, and a *"welcome"* that sounded genuinely sincere. *"We are really pleased to have you attend our meeting,"* she said, and then with a mischievous smile added, *"but your choice of friends could stand some serious improving."* She then joked with John for a few moments and turned to 'welcome' the next guest.

Once inside, I mentioned to John that she was the best person I had ever been 'welcomed' by at any meeting I've attended. John laughed and said, *"Are you surprised? . . . That's Pauline Hill, Chairman of the Board of Welcome Wagon."*

Following the meeting we chatted with her. Once I found out how she had become chairman and how she and two other ladies had rescued the company from the hands of U.S. investors, I told her, *"Pauline, I must share your story with my radio listeners."* And here it is. . .

Pauline was born and raised in Edmonton. It was while living in Regina in 1953 that she became a Welcome Wagon hostess and began a career that would take her to the top.

Along the way she's had many firsts. First woman member of the Toronto Ad and Sales Club. And its first woman president. First woman member of Toronto's Downtown Rotary Club. First woman chairman of the Canadian Council of Better Business Bureaus. And one of only 19 women in the world to receive a special citation from the world's "Who's Who of Women". The citation read. . . 'for an outstanding contribution to women's entry into a man's world.' Pauline Hill is an achiever. Her greatest business achievement came in 1979 when she headed a group to acquire ownership of 'Welcome Wagon' from the giant Gillette Corporation in the U.S. It was not a friendly take over, but Pauline's group won and 'Welcome Wagon' became a Canadian company. Two other people who figured prominently with Pauline in the acquisition bid were Joan MacKeller who is now President and Chief Executive Officer, and Ursula Van Heel who served as Chief Executive Officer 1988 and 1989. Here's how it happened ... *"We got word that the company was being sold by its owners, Gillette of Boston, to a group of 300 American managers of 'Welcome Wagon.' Among the five of us Canadians who wanted to buy the company, we had something like 180 years experience. We were rather hurt that we were not part of that 300 group. So, we got our dander up, put in our offer to purchase, and went to the then foreign review agency. It took almost a year, but the U.S. offer to purchase the Canadian company was rejected by F.I.R.A. and our offer was accepted."*

They immediately ran into the crushing interest rates of the early 80's that soared to 23%. But they hung in. Arranged deferred payments and pressed on. One of the biggest things they had going for them was... *"the enthusiasm of our people. Our hostesses were proud of the fact that our company was now a Canadian company. That first year our top line went up 22%."* And it's been going up every year. *"We've done much better than the American company... we're into about five programs that the original founder wasn't in to."*

One of these programs was started when they recognized there was a growing need by convention and conference organizers to have professional help in acquiring items for 'Booty Bags', that are an expected must by most delegates. 'Welcome Wagon' has now created a separate division that does just that.

It's the old law of marketing 101... *"Find a need and fill it... that's what we're doing. And we are filling it with products from 'Welcome Wagon'."*

As busy as she is criss-crossing the country keeping in touch with her 1300 'Welcome Wagon' hostesses, Pauline still has her own territory in Toronto that she works as a 'Welcome Wagon' Hostess. *"I enjoy welcoming people."*

He Thinks Big!

Bill Pardy

If you've never heard of Pasadena, Newfoundland, well you have now. It was a farming community then a dormitory for Cornerbrook where Bill Pardy was born 42 years ago.

Thirteen years ago Bill was elected Mayor of Pasadena and was determined to put the town on the map. He discovered the concept of an "industrial incubator", a low-rental centre for people who wanted to get into small business. He persuaded the Federal Government to put money into it. He brought business people in from Western Canada to advise local entrepreneurs and sent some Pasadena people out West to see how things were done.

In 1986 his Venture Centre finally opened. *"We're taking it slowly"*, he said, *"But we created over 300 new jobs which is a boost for a town of 3500 in an area like ours."*

Bill produced a video series called "Small Business—An Awareness Program". It was an immediate success. Copies were placed in schools and post-secondary institutions in Newfoundland and across Canada. Some went as far East and West as China and Italy.

Bill recognized the advantage of linking up via satellite with communities in countries facing the same difficulties as Newfoundland. After months of negotiations, a six hour satellite hook-up with Belfast Northern Ireland took place December 2, 1990.

"I really believe", he told me, *"that satellite transmission is the way to go. Linking up via satellite provides each area with the opportunity to share experiences, ideas and theories."*

Bill was the driving force behind the outstanding success of Junior Achievement of Canada in Pasadena and Cornerbrook. Both 1990 winners of the annual Junior Achievement Major Awards were Junior Achievement companies from Pasadena. The companies were "Note-it-All" managed by 21 teenaged entrepreneurs from Cornerbrook and "Tray-Gourmet" managed by 12 teenagers from Pasadena.

When you consider that there were over 8100 junior achievers operating 480 Junior Achievement companies across Canada that tells you a lot about Bill Pardy.

In January 1991 Bill accepted a larger challenge on the Mainland. He is now working his imaginative magic with the "Atlantic Canada Opportunities Agency".

Bill's accomplishments reinforce what I say so often on my program and in every address. "In Canada you don't have to come from a big city to think big!"

Entrepreneur Awards...
Good for your Community

Broadcast January 14, 1991

A side benefit of hosting "The Canadian Achievers" is the invitations I receive to attend and participate in awards presentations. 'Entrepreneur of the Year', 'Citizen of the Year', 'Achiever of the Year'. There are many different names, but they all have the same positive effect. It's wonderful to see how more and more communities are selecting, honouring and presenting a well earned award to the individual or company that has shown growth and community concern during the year. I'm all for it. Every community should select and pay tribute to a local person or company each year. It's good for them to receive recognition. These positive vibes are there in every community in Canada. You can probably name half a dozen people in your own circle of friends who quality for an award. Canada is bursting at the seams with achievers. They're building this country, they deserve recognition.

He Got Started When He Quit

Harry Steele

When Harry Steele grew up in the tiny Newfoundland outport of Musgrave Harbour, there were no roads, no electricity and the nearest rail connection 60 miles away was cut off six months of the year.

"If you went outside you had to do it by horse, dogteam or on foot. You weren't really part of the outside world. I think that makes you self-sufficient."

If self-sufficiency is what it takes to become one of Canada's major industrialists, Harry Steele has it in spades. Nowadays his name rings like a bell-buoy across the waters of Atlantic business.

After serving in the Royal Canadian Navy for 24 years, he retired in 1974 as Base Commander at Canadian Forces Base in Gander. That is when many men sit back and let their arteries harden but for Harry it was really just the beginning:

"I was glad I got out of the navy when I was still young enough to tackle something else. I think the military gives you very good training and I consider that joining the navy when I was young was a good idea, but many men make a mistake by staying in over 20 years. Your initiative becomes stifled; it makes you too conservative. That didn't happen to me."

It certainly didn't! In the late 70's Harry spearheaded the development of Eastern Provincial Airways which he sold to Canadian Pacific, (now Canadian Airlines International) in 1984. Four years earlier he had established Newfoundland Capital Corporation Limited, (NCC) a holding company with interest in transportation, communications and hotels. At 61 years old, (1991) Harry is young and vigorous, and bursting with energy. It was difficult holding him long enough to tape our interview. He has strong opinions on the free enterprise system and has been compared with Ayn Rand (The Fountainhead, Atlas Shrugged, etc.), business tycoon Conrad Black, and Lord Beaverbrook (the former Max Aitken, a fellow Maritimer who owned British newspapers and became Lord Beaverbrook).

He had quit Eastern Provincial Airways as Vice President of Marketing because he disagreed with the way the airline was being run. It was losing money and Harry didn't approve. He returned little more than a year later, bought it, and turned it around making profits as high as $4.4 million. He had a similar experience with Clarke Inc. which NCC bought in 1981. The return on investment went from a negative 9% in 1982 to a positive 46% in 1986.

Harry's communications division publishes 41 newspapers and specialty magazines, and operates 15 radio stations across Canada. He thinks the opportunity for young people to get ahead is better today than ever before.

"There's great opportunities now because times are tough and when times are tough opportunity is born."

He doesn't think it is necessary to have a financial pillow to get a leg up.

"It certainly wasn't there in my place. My mother and father never had a bank account up until the day they died."

His best advice for young people heading out into the business world or launching a career in any profession?

"It may be trite to say it, but the first thing to do is to look after yourself physically. Stay away from drugs and alcohol. That's the best piece of advice I can think of to give any young person."

A graduate of Memorial University, Harry was given an Honourary Doctorate degree from Saint Mary's University in 1983.

Altogether, not bad for a boy from the outports who rose to become one of the biggest movers and shakers in Canadian communications. He has no regrets about his life and would do it all over, except maybe getting out of the navy sooner.

"It was a stroke of fate that Paul Hellyer helped me make that decision. He advocated unification of the Forces and I was dead set against it. I guess I can thank Paul Hellyer for helping me get started in my career!"

Another Canadian Achiever who got mad and quit one career and made a bigger success in another.

Canada... The Land of Opportunity

Broadcast January 25, 1991

Canada is, without doubt, the land of opportunity. Even when our economy is soft you'll still be hard-pressed to find a country that offers as much raw opportunity. News reports often carry a string of lay offs, cut backs, and bankruptcies. What they fail to report is the ground-swell of small businesses starting up in record numbers. You can become a millionaire in Canada faster through honest effort than anywhere else. In Canada you can start a business on a shoe-string, work hard, build it up, and create personal wealth. Believe me, I see it happening every day. A recent study by the accounting firm of Ernst-Young indicated that over 425 thousand Canadian households had a net worth exceeding one million dollars. On a per capita basis there are more millionaires in Canada than in any other western industrial nation. I wish newspapers would spend more time reporting that fact and less time running around reporting the sky is falling. You can talk yourself into whatever frame of mind you want. If you're an achiever you'll look for the positive indicators. Believe me they are there. They may be a little harder to find these days, but they're out there. They always have been, and always will.

King of the Carvers

Paul Burdette

When he was a very successful construction superintendent for the Otis Elevator Company eleven years ago (1980), Paul Burdette suddenly chucked it all and went to work as a full-time carver of wildlife. Today he is rated one of the ten world Masters of the International Wildlife Carvers Guild. His works sell for up to $45,000 each and are displayed in galleries worldwide including the Smithsonian Institute.

It all started back when he whittled for badges in competitions in Cubs, Scouts and Venturers.

"Carving was always something I wanted to do. But it took a lot of guts to quit a good job and move away from my hometown of Toronto to the country where we opened "Gallery in the Country" at Orton, Ontario near Orangeville. I finally won enough prizes and gained enough confidence that I knew I could make the break."

Paul won the world championship in decoy carving in 1974 and finished second in the world championship in decorative lifesize wildfowl in 1976.

"Decoy carving of ducks is the roots for wildlife carving as it is known to-day. The old antique decoys were the functional decoys: the utilitarian tool which is now collectible. In the beginning that was what got me going. Now, people like myself have just expanded on that old art and brought it up to the real bird."

The decoys entered in carving competitions are placed in a tank of water to be judged, just like the bird in water. His really look like the real thing, but . . .

"I've gone far beyond decoy carving. I do many full-bodied birds flying and perching and preening. I go beyond even calling myself a carver. I use wood but I don't use as many sharp-edged tools anymore; I use lots of types of grinders, stones and cutters. There's a lot of electrical equipment for do-ing my work these days."

A piece can take up to eight months to complete and although it may sell for $45.000 or more, Paul figures that is underpriced.

"When you consider the amount of work that goes into a single piece and compare it with painting, it is very underpriced. The painter on the other hand, who paints two-dimensional work, might do eight to ten pieces in eight months and sell them for $10,000 or $15,000 each. There is of course, the satisfaction of knowing that when you are creating something there is somebody out there who will pay $45,000 for it. Anytime you do what you love to do, and to create and have the piece come out so it pleases you, it is very satisfying."

Is there a reluctance then to sell it to some stranger who will take it away forever?

"All the people I've had who've gravitated towards my work have all had the same feelings towards art and wildlife. So when something goes away it is going to a good home. It's like raising show dogs and everybody wanting one of their pups. They want them to go into good homes. With some people you can go to the extent of screening them and going into their homes. I have done that but of course I can't screen buyer's homes when they come to me from the U.S., England and Germany."

Opening the gallery in Orton has been a mixed blessing. While it has given work and a good living to his wife Dolly and sons Glen and Mark, it has its disadvantages too. But that was not apparent when he first made the move to the country.

"When I started off with the gallery business, which evolved because I wanted to expand upon having a studio to show my own work, I created a tail that wags the dog. I ended up having less time to carve than I thought I would. Whereas I thought I would have more time for my sculpture, I ended up having less time than when I was working for Otis."

It's a classic example of nothing succeeds like success and everything has its price. But Paul is not complaining. He's a success on two fields now.

"Right from the day we opened it was like a fairytale come true. It was beyond my expectations and my wife's expectations. I just never expected we'd get that kind of response. We knew that it was fitting to have a gallery in the country because we knew we're going to be dealing with a lot of wildlife and floral scenes and the country was a fitting setting for them."

Word of the gallery's success soon spread and others began to emulate the Burdettes.

"It's a compliment too. We've had people call from the United States and who've come up to see why it worked for us and to see if it would work for them. They would all love to be out where we are. I guess a lot of them never wanted to take the risk—to make the move."

Paul's gallery has expanded to include original paintings by many of the world's most noted naturalist artists.

I asked Paul what his advice is for anyone wishing to start a business?

"You have to have honesty and integrity in everything you do. With the people you deal with; with the general public. People look to me to guide them, especially in our business. They rely on me to tell them if it is good work or not good work.

We have a basic philosophy, my wife and sons and myself, which I have tried to instill: we will never sell anything in the gallery that we wouldn't be proud to have in our own home. Another thing a person going into business has to realize is you have to work hard. Your days are not going to be 9 to 5.

It is more like 14 hour days, sometimes longer than that.

"The job is there to be done and you can't say tomorrow is another day and I'll get to it then. The people who get ahead are always the doers who put that extra into it."

Paul Burdette took the risk: he left the safety of a good paying job and found success as a Master Carver and a gallery owner. He's another Canadian Achiever.

Don't ever be afraid to admit you were wrong. It's saying you're wiser today than you were yesterday.

She Came Back to Haunt Them

Dawn Morris

The farm implement business is thought of primarily as a male domain. Not so, says Dawn Morris of Dawn Morris Productions. Dawn proves it every February when she organizes, stages and runs the largest indoor Farm Implement Trade Show in all of North America.

It's called the "Canadian International Farm Equipment Show", held at the Toronto International Centre. It attracts over 60 thousand farmers and manufacturing reps from around the world.

This 63 year old dynamo has been in the industrial trade show business for many years. She went out on her own in 1986 when her long time employer, Maclean Hunter; trade show division, suggested she had served the trade show industry long enough and well enough. New management suggested to Dawn that maybe now was the time for her to strap on their generous golden parachute and bail out... retire. She was 58. Maclean Hunter made the same offer to another long time employee, Bob Gowdy.

Dawn and Bob accepted joyfully, took their money and formed Gowdy-Morris Productions in direct competition with their former employer.

Using their knowledge and contacts, they were an immediate success. In September 1987 Bob decided he really did want to retire. Dawn bought him out and moved the company head office from Toronto to Peterborough, Ontario, where she and husband Howard lived.

Her staff of three moved to Peterborough with her. Part of that staff includes daughters Jane Hickman, the company's show co-ordinator; Lesley Nicholson, sales manager and her neice Barbara Johnson serves as Dawn's 'right hand'. Dawn's husband Howard, a retired building contractor, is happy to let Dawn do her own thing while he rebuilds and restores old cars as a profitable hobby.

Doing her own thing is proving very profitable for Dawn Morris Productions. The farm equipment show and her other big show, 'The International Lawn, Garden and Outdoor Power Equipment Trade Show', will generate 1991 sales of over 1.3 million dollars.

Her latest venture, a "Collectibles Show', is slated for June 1992. Dawn Morris is typical of the quality people large companies are releasing into the market. Every once in a while you hear of one becoming their former employers biggest competitor who comes back to haunt them.

I hope her story makes you smile, and say, as I did... "good for you Dawn, they had it coming."

I first met Dawn at a conference of the Canadian Farm and Industrial Equipment Institute (CFIEI) in Manaki Lodge, Ontario, where I was speaking. The president of CFIEI, Brent Hamre, pointed her out to me and told me her story. I told Brent "introduce us, I must meet her. She is the very essence and proof that Canada is such a great land of opportunity."

Later Dawn told me, *"I had confidence in myself. I wasn't ready to retire. New management came in, offered me early retirement, and I took it. I felt quite confident that I could do well on my own in the trade show business."*

Let Dawn's story of achievement serve as a warning to all 'new management' who believe that a few grey hairs is a sign that a person is slowing down and becoming too old. Because, as Dawn Morris says and proved... "you're never too old."

He Lit His Own Fire

Paul Campbell

Paul Campbell felt he was entitled to become President of the Canadian subsidiary of Wilson & Cousins because he had been named *"Manager of the Year"* twice from among several hundred branch managers in that international company. The company thought otherwise and brought in their own man from the U.S. Paul was miffed. He went home and told his wife Elizabeth he was quitting to form his own company. He made the right move.

"In 1991 we'll do $4.5 million in our product alone."

Eighteen years ago his Georgetown, Ontario-based *"United Fire Safety Company Ltd."* started its first year with sales under $100,000.

"But we were heading in the right direction and we had good bankers on both sides of the border."

So what does the company sell? Fire safety equipment, including Paul's personally-designed nozzle and hose caps, break caps and hydrant wrenches. You'll find their products in nearly every hotel and motel. Since meeting Paul and doing his story I now check hotels where I stay. Usually I find the hotel is equipped with his products.

"The key to the whole operation was the nozzle. We have a patent on both design and invention. The difference between our nozzle and the conventional type is that first of all it's a constant gallonage nozzle, which is a firefighting term: it just means the pumps don't have to fluctuate as the stream changes from wide angle to the straight stream.

"To have this in an industrial firefighting nozzle was a first back in 1975. Beyond that, it was simply designed around a molding principle because it was of polycarbonate rather than brass. Polycarbonate is a space-age material which lends itself to our industry because it will not support combustion and it is so strong. It is used on nose cones on rockets. We have tested these nozzles to 1,000 pounds p.s.i. (per square inch), and you still can't break them."

A very good product indeed. And one that sells in 52 countries around the world!

I never expected we'd do so well. I thought if we promoted it and sold it, our product would maybe make us a living. Now it's more than that."

It's not a big firm for providing jobs:

"Four in Canada and six in the U.S., but these people just assemble and test the products because the parts are molded for us outside. But I can assure you that we employ a lot of people in the process of putting that product where it is."

And 'where it is' even surprises Paul Campbell.

I was sailing in the Virgin Islands and I remember sitting down in one of their little chase boats that they use in the event that your sailboat is five miles away and has some problem. Every one of those chase boats had our hose and nozzle on a rack in the back. It made us feel just great knowing our products were in use in the Virgin Islands!"

What advice does designer-inventor Paul Campbell of Dundas, Ontario have for other hopeful Canadian Achievers?

"If you have a dream and you have a design for some product, and you're honest with the people who are going to work with you, and with your bankers, go ahead and fulfill your dream. Do it because you can have a lot of fun and it's very satisfying when you see everything up and running.

"If you have covered all those bases and you have a good product to provide to a needing market, do it! It'll fly!"

It certainly has flown for Paul Campbell. He's happy now because he was denied the promotion he felt he deserved. So he got mad and quit, and hasn't looked back. He's another Canadian Achiever.

Like Hell We'll Sell!

Sherry Rutech

When the head of the family business suddenly dies and you find yourself with a multi-million dollar business to run, what do you do? Run it yourself—or take everybody's advice and sell it?

Sherry Rutech, a 21-year-old University of Calgary student at the time, faced a dilemma. Her mother and sister wanted to sell. Sherry had no business experience.

"But no way was I going to allow anybody to sell the business my Dad spent 16 years building up. To heck with that. Dad worked too hard to build up the company."

Trans-Mutual Truck Lines of Calgary had 35 employees and was doing $3 million in sales in 1983 when founder John Rutech died suddenly of a heart attack. As determined as she was, this was not going to be an easy job for the new lady boss. The employees did not cotton to the idea of a young, inexperienced woman taking over.

"I was terrified. Meeting with the staff the first time was one of the worst days of my life. But I got through that crisis and after that, although they still didn't like me, they tolerated me. It took time to earn their respect."

It wasn't just the employee's respect she had to earn. Cominco, the huge mining and smelting company, was Trans-Mutual's best customer. Tough customers too.

"I met 16 of them in their boardroom. I thought I'd die. They asked me so many tough questions. I knew that if I failed the truck line would fail too because without Cominco we couldn't survive."

Sherry must have impressed the Cominco bosses because they stayed with Trans-Mutual. In fact, Trans-Mutual maintained the $3 million a year in total sales established by her father, and Sherri cut $150,000 a year in operating costs. She made other changes, the most important of which was the installation of a computer.

"It's made a phenomenal difference."

But the real success for Sherry was the people she works with.

"You have to hold on to the people who support you, the people who believe in you. Without them, I would never have made it."

What would she do differently if she took over today knowing what she knows now?

"I would be more patient. Take more time making decisions, not making decisions just for the sake of making decisions." She also believes after seven years in the driver's seat of the company, that keeping customers happy is absolutely essential.

"It's been tough at times, but we've managed to do it."

The only female president of a trucking company in Alberta, Sherry at the ripe old age of 28 in 1991, does not know how to drive a truck. Although she told me she did try once and decided she was an administrator.

What does she think about women's chances in the trucking industry?

"It's more difficult to manage a home if you are a driver. It means missing the school concert. Sometimes you don't see your family for days or weeks at a time. It takes a pretty special woman to be able to do it for a living.

"There are lots of tough women out there right now driving the big rigs, but it takes more than strength to exist in that male world. There is still a lot of male resentment against women drivers."

Sherry feels that the times are changing, just as attitudes are changing in other areas of the trucking industry. Towards the environment, for example.

"There are more and more concerns being expressed about pollution and keeping the environment safe. The government guidelines are getting stricter and drivers are too becoming aware of cleaner fuels and about the hauling of hazardous materials. I think things are getting better."

Sherry Rutech went from a 21-year-old university student with no business savvy to President of a large trucking company. She learned the business as she went along. She admits she made mistakes but she figures she learned from them. If she had it to do over, would she?

"You bet!"

She's another Canadian Achiever.

Winning Against the Odds

Tim Phillips, Gerry Watier & Tom Yu

It's still quite difficult to sell Canadian manufactured products to companies in the Pacific Rim countries. They have certain advantages over us: closeness to market, lower interest rates and lower wages, to name just a few. So you can imagine how Tim Phillips, Gerry Watier and Tom Yu felt three years ago when the company they work for in London, Ontario, *"Unifin International"*, an operating unit of *"Intercity Products"*, (formerly I.C.G.—Keepright) was asked to bid on a contract to supply coolers for direct current motors to a Japanese manufacturer.

What made it tougher was the fact that the Japanese manufacturer owned a company in Japan that made that very item. In effect, Tim, Gerry and Tom were competing against the manufacturer's own company. Not quite a level playing field. Well, their Canadian ingenuity won out and they got the order. Then, they were asked to bid on a project in India. They won out again. They won out on a third major contract back in Japan. Unifin began doing so much business in the Pacific Rim that they opened an office in Tokyo to service and sell their Pacific Rim customers.

It is said that influence flows from the top down. That is certainly true in the case of this company. Its founder, Bob Graham, started the company in 1956 when he was a 25-year-old stockbroker sent out to Winnipeg from Montreal to "look into" this new commodity called *"natural gas"*. That was the beginning of I.C.G. which over the years has become one of Canada's most successful conglomerate companies.

When you talk with Bob and the people he surrounds himself with you quickly understand the success of "Unifin" and the company's other divisions. Bob and his people help prove that Canadian-made products and Canadian-fueled sales and marketing ingenuity can win markets anywhere, against any competitor.

Business Opportunity Ads...
Fact or Fiction

Broadcast December 13, 1990

It seems we're all in a hurry to get ahead these days. Our cars must accelerate faster, planes must jet us there faster, parcels have to be delivered across Canada overnight. Everything seems to be speeded up. Or as they now say, fast tracked! Even achieving has to be fast tracked. There is a whole industry feeding on our hyped-up need to achieve. It's the business opportunities columns in newspapers and magazines. I swear, the most creative writers in the world are now writing the enticing prose featured in some business opportunity ads. Ads that offer you untold opportunity to achieve enormous income almost overnight. The ads for some franchises are so enticing I often ask myself... *"if it's such a good deal, how come their brother-in-law doesn't take it?"* I'm not saying that all business opportunity ads are shady or misleading. I am saying you should be careful and selective in following up any opportunity that sounds too good to be true. Because, if it sounds too good to be true, it usually is. Too many people, in their hurry to achieve let their backbone become their wishbone. It's an easy trap to fall into. Are business opportunity ads fact or fiction? The answer is yes and no. The best advice is investigate before you invest.

"The best insurance against disease is health. Only God can give you insurance against illness."
—*Maurice Duplessis*

Your Money and How to Keep It

Brian Costello

As a young man growing up in Hamilton, Brian Costello had a choice of two career paths he could follow. He could have become a radio announcer which he wanted, or he could become a stock broker/money manager which he also wanted. He chose the path that led to the bank vault. . . money management. That was 25 years ago. Judging by his success compared to some radio announcers I know, Brian took the right path.

Today he is one of Canada's most successful and best known money management experts. His book, "Your Money and How to Keep It" is the largest selling book of its kind in Canada. Brian has worked hard to get where he is. I know, I've followed his career for the past 25 years. His first book and the two others he's written have helped average people like you and me step gingerly through the minefield called 'Financial Planning'.

Always on the leading edge of technology, Brian has developed a microcomputer software program called "Home Tax Plus". It's designed to assist you in the preparation of your annual tax returns plus, according to Brian, much, much more.

And now with the GST adding more confusion to our financial plans, Brian Costello is smiling all the way to the vault.

Late to bed
Early to rise
Work like Hell
And advertise
—*D.D.*

Blind Auto Mechanic

Eric Davidson

On December 6, 1917 a terrible explosion occurred in Halifax Harbour levelling many parts of the city. Two-year-old Eric Davidson was one of its casualities. He was blinded by flying glass.

As Eric grew up he attended the Halifax School For The Blind and developed a fascination for cars. He loved cars and he learned everything he could about them. He liked to putter, take things apart and put them back together, including car engines. As I said, he was fascinated by cars.

In 1944, because of World War Two, there was a serious shortage of mechanics so Citadel Motors in Halifax decided to give 29-year-old Eric a chance to try out as an apprentice mechanic. Using memory retention, Eric was able to get the job and later get his mechanic's papers specializing in ignitions, carburetors and pistons. He moved to Ontario, then returned to Halifax and spent 25 years as a mechanic with the City of Halifax.

Now 75, and retired, he still loves to tinker on cars. In fact, 10 years ago Eric bought a seven passenger 1922 Reo Touring car that he has completely restored. He enjoys it when his son Andrew starts up the Reo and takes Eric and his wife of 41 years, Mary Ellen, out for a Sunday drive.

"We have to stay off the main highways", he chuckles, *"because it just can't keep up with the newer cars."*

The Red Reo is a familiar attraction in local parades as well. You can bet your last dollar it runs like a top. Eric Davidson is another Achiever who simply would not allow blindness to become a roadblock.

It's Never Too Late To Start Over

Suzanne Hillier

Suzanne Hillier, now of Brampton, Ontario but originally from St. John's, Newfoundland is one of the busiest family law specialists. And well might she be, tempered as she was by many a trial and tribulation.

Her original career was teaching. Then came the personal traumas that changed everything. First there was the death of a five year old daughter, the pain of which brought on a marriage break-up. She moved to Florida, where she spent a year supporting three children by freelance writing for Esquire and New Yorker, no mean feat in itself. Emotionally stabilized by this independent lifestyle, she rejoined her husband only to spend the next 5 years watching him succumb to cancer. Seeking diversion from those pressures and inspired by her father's 22 year career as Attorney General of Newfoundland, she took up law.

Here she was widowed and raising three teenagers, when she wrote the difficult bar exams. Today she is the senior partner in the law firm of Hillier and Hillier. The other Hillier is her daughter, Ava.

Suzanne Hillier, indeed advises from experience, and proves a shining example to all that 'it's never too late to start again'. She's another Canadian Achiever.

"I know there are some who feel a sense of embarrassment in expressing pride in their nation perhaps because of the fear that they might be considered old-fashioned or parochial."

—*The Rt. Hon. John G. Diefenbaker*

He's the Center of Centreville

Burney MacDougal

This is the story of a New Brunswick conglomerate that started and stayed in a small community.

In 1960 when Burney MacDougal opened his machine shop in Centreville, New Brunswick little did he ever imagine that his small shop with one employee would grow over the next 28 years into a conglomerate group of companies employing 75 people, and doing 15 million dollars a year in sales. It wasn't easy, it took a lot of hard work and risk, but that's what happened and it hasn't stopped yet.

Burney started out by repairing farm equipment, then building custom truck bodies for the logging industry. Then they branched into highway snow and ice control equipment. Today 40% of his production in one company, *"BWS Manufacturing"* in Centreville is sold in the United States, Africa and South America.

Believing that you must always keep expanding, Burney MacDougal's group of companies includes a tractor dealership, a truck dealership, a leasing company and an investment company. Not bad for what started as a small operation in a very small community. Proof, once again, that in Canada you don't have to be in a big city to do big things.

Burney MacDougal of Centreville, New Brunswick, population 600. Another Canadian Achiever.

She Brought Cats & Phantom to Canada

Tina VanderHeyden

Hard work, some luck and knowing from an early age that she wanted to be in show business is the secret behind Tina VanderHeyden's success.

For over 18 years Tina VanderHeyden has been promoting and marketing live entertainment in Canada. It's a very competitive world and promoters come and go in rapid order. It takes a special kind of tenaciousness to last.

She moved from Vancouver to Toronto to work for the National Ballet. Restless working with others, she decided to move out on her own forming a company, Tina VanderHeyden & Associates. Her clientele included Bill Cosby, Frank Sinatra, Richard Burton, Don Rickels, Liza Minelli, Vanessa Redgrave and many other illustrious stars.

But her own star really moved up when she risked everything to coproduce the Canadian cast version of CATS—the Andrew Lloyd-Weber stage musical based on the work by T. S. Eliot.

"CATS set the precedent for me and my career. I had always been interested in producing shows using mainly Canadian talent. My only worry when I got the contract was whether I could find the talent pool."

She needn't have worried. The flood of aspiring dancers, singers and actors never stopped and the Canadian production, which ran for two years in Toronto before taking to the road, was judged by some critics as better than the New York and London West End versions.

Tina's next big break came two years later when she got the contract to co-produce with Cineplex's Garth Drabinsky, the six million dollar version of *"The Phantom of the Opera"*. The story of The Phantom was written in 1911 but, the musical version as it is now staged is relatively new. It is also one of the most challenging of all operatic-based works to mount. Versions are now playing to sold-out audiences in nine countries.

The Phantom of the Opera opened in Toronto in September 1989 in the magnificently renovated Pantages Theatre, built in 1920. It's expected to run there at least three years. It was sold out for the first two years after opening.

Tina is very happy with the success of both CATS and The Phantom, but it has been hard work.

"For theatre to be a success in Canada you really have to get out there and sell, and promote. Even if it means you get arrested in the rain in Saskatoon!"

The reference is to the fact that Tina was caught putting up posters in violation of a bylaw against it in the Prairie city.

Although she enjoys being in a very glamorous business, it is a 24-hour-a-day job and you have to be prepared to make some sacrifices.

"I am extremely fortunate having a fabulous husband who makes it possible. But there are negative sides. Not being there when your baby takes his first steps. I really miss that. They say that women can have it all. It simply isn't true."

However, it's been a lot of fun.

"Anyone thinking of getting into production and management in theatre should be well-prepared to work hard, know your business and look for the breaks. Nothing comes easy. Show business is half show and half business. And the business part is really important."

Don't be afraid to go out on a limb. That's where the fruit is.

Home Based Businesses

... [broadcast Friday, February 15, 1991]

It's estimated that by the year 2000—40% of the labour force in North America will be working from their homes. We tend to think that home based businesses, people operating an office in their home or as I prefer to call them, "cottage capitalists", are a new phenomenon. Actually they're not. There was a time when most businesses in Canada were home based. Farmers, tradesmen and shopkeepers worked and lived in the same space. Industrialization changed all of that. But now thanks to computers, fax machines, cellular phones, call forwarding, and photocopiers the pendulum is swinging back. It's quite easy to convert a small area of your home into a fully operational business office. That's what I did, and that's what Canadians are doing in record numbers! So, if you're going to start your own business plan to work from your home. Over 50% of Canadian businesses started out in the home. But a word of caution, setting up a business in your home can present problems. I suggest you do your research first. A book you should read is called "Home Inc." written by Canadians Diana and Douglas Gray. Starting your own business and going on your own can be intimidating but don't let it worry you. Just remember, many of today's large well established companies were started on a shoe-string by dreamers who made their dreams come true. If they did it—so can you!

She Worked Her Way to the Top

Audrey MacLean

The TORONTO STAR is Canada's largest newspaper with a daily delivery of about 550,000 and a Saturday edition of 850,000 copies. It employs 2,600 not including delivery people.

TORSTAR'S gross revenue for 1989 was just under $1 billion. It's a big company and quite intimidating to a shy, 17-year-old girl from Yarmouth, Nova Scotia who started there as a junior file clerk in 1959. Today that shy, young girl, Audrey MacLean is Director of Operations, Planning and Control.

"I'm basically responsible for putting the paper together, deciding how big it's going to be, where the section breaks are, where the ads go, and ultimately getting the paper out.

"I have been credited with helping save the company millions of dollars but it was not through an idea I had, but basically an on-going effort. For

example, when the paper is put together there has to be consideration for how many pages it will contain. To put this into perspective, one page using both sides costs THE STAR almost $5,000 in newsprint. So if I can create the newspaper and satisfy all the different departments: news, advertising, the advertisers and the readers, and save a page or two, or three or four, I certainly can save the company a lot of money. Which is what I have been able to do."

Audrey says it is a daily effort and you have to be prepared for it. Planning ahead is the key:

"We seriously start to make up the Sunday edition on Thursday. For Wednesday's paper we start Monday morning and develop until about 3 p.m. Tuesday afternoon. Then it's closed as far as getting the information to the news department and the composing room, where the ads go, where there's colour to be used and how big it's going to be."

Audrey has a big job, eight people report directly to her.

"But in many ways more do. Because I coordinate the efforts of all the different departments. One big concern at any newspaper is the jockeying for position by the various departments and freelance contributors. Trying to put the ads where the advertisers want them to be. That's the biggest challenge: trying to satisfy everyone when you only have X number of pages. And, of course the news-people want all the front pages. It's a daily effort trying to make everybody happy."

When Audrey started out in the newspaper business 33 years ago, there were a few women reporters but women were mostly employed in clerical positions and selling advertising. That has all changed now and there are women in every department. But there are not many in key management positions like her's. What did she do differently that got her to the top?

"I was lucky to have some ambitions given to me by God. And probably the most important thing is that I care. I care about people and I care about doing things right. I had to work hard and that hasn't stopped. Now that I have made it to this level at THE STAR there are other women who have similar ambitions. There are a lot of ambitious women in every company today. So I do a lot of mentoring. Not just to women, but largely to women.

"Sometimes they need help and they look at me and say: she made it. So can I.

"My door isn't always open because my job is very hectic at times, but I always try to find time if someone wants to talk."

With such a busy schedule and always deadlines to meet, does she have any time for herself?

"I try not to add up the hours I work in a week! I guess it's 60 or 70. At home I get a lot of phone call interruptions, but I tend to stay away from THE STAR building on weekends if I can. And when things are slow I goof off. I take my holidays and go to warm climates in the winter and try to get

away from it all. I'm not the sort of person who takes work home mentally. It doesn't eat at me inside. I probably couldn't do what I do if that were the case."

What's Audrey's advice for anyone working for a company who wants to reach the top?

"I'm not sure they would take my advice. Most young people I talk to today have a different attitude towards work than what I had when I was starting out. Maybe even from what I have now. I would advise them not to just do their own job but to be looking for ways to help the person next to them. Reach out. Do a little more than you are actually required to do. Take criticism.

"Take every opportunity you can to learn something that isn't part of your job. Because you'll be recognized for it; I certainly was. I had only a grade 12 education when I started but I supplemented my education with many courses, mostly in learning to work with and manage people."

Does she have any regrets for all the hard work and time she has put in to get where she is?

"I wish sometimes I had had more time to spend with my children. I was widowed when they were two and four. But, when I did see them it was quality time. However, I do sometimes think maybe I should have slowed down a little bit then."

This is a common statement I hear from most Achievers.

Audrey MacLean is an enthusiastic person with a positive attitude that has taken her to the top in her profession. She believes in team work and in taking advice from the people who work with her.

"I don't believe in taking the attitude that I am the boss and they are going to take direction. Maybe my way is their way because their way is better then mine."

Good advice from a woman who started at the TORONTO STAR as a file clerk and rose to become the Director of Operations. If you take her advice, you can make it work for you too.

She's another Canadian Achiever.

Education will never become as expensive as ignorance.

The Little Town That Did

Karl Schutz

I mentioned in the foreword of this book that in 1979 I bought radio station CKAY in Duncan on Vancouver Island. We sold our home in Burlington, Ontario and moved West to enjoy life in this most beautiful part of Lotus Land. Duncan is adjacent to the town of Chemainus.

At that time Chemainus boasted a MacMillan Bloedel sawmill employing 650 people which in turn provided employment directly or indirectly to several thousand throughout the community. Imagine the impact on this small community when, shortly after we arrived, the news broke that MacMillan Bloedel was closing the mill. Not just cutting back, closing and tearing down the mill. *"Good-bye Folks, we're going"*, was their brutal message.

When this happens in a small community everyone panics and shock sets in. Long soup lines, boarded up store fronts and deserted streets are the predictions of most people. But not Chemainus businessman Karl Schutz. When this happened he came up with the goldarndest, craziest idea that nearly had him laughed out of town.

Keep in mind that Karl is a visionary. He and wife Betty immigrated from Germany in 1951. An excellent cabinet maker, Karl built a nice life and business in Chemainus. By 1979 he'd sold the business and was in semi-retirement. Karl recalled having visited Romania and seeing old towns that had 300-year-old religious frescoes painted on outside walls of buildings. He said, *"Let's do that here in Chemainus, let's spruce up the downtown, and let's become a tourist attraction."*

It was a crazy idea. Imagine spending taxpayer's money on wall murals while the town's major employer is making plans to split town leaving the city coffers empty. But Karl Schutz is a forceful, determined and persistent person. He drew up a five-year plan. Convinced town council and the B.C. Government to fund part of it. The rest came from local businesses and concerned people. *"The Little Town That Did"* began to become a reality. I would be lying if I told you he had an easy time convincing people. He didn't. It was tough slugging all the way.

In 1983 at a gala celebration Karl's vision came to be when we unveiled the first of what is now 32 beautiful wall murals and town square.

"It was a lot of excitement, a lot of fun. Some hardship but then there is nothing worthwhile without hardship. The wonderful things that happened, the friendships we have made around the world and the success of Chemainus has made it all worthwhile."

Karl's fame spread internationally. He was invited to Australia, the U.S. and many Canadian towns to help them overcome similar problems.

Five years ago Karl had another vision. He envisioned a community where art is not just an exhibit but an activity. His new dream is a Pacific Rim Artisan Village, on a 50-acre site adjacent to Chemainus complete with a 120-room lodge and 250-seat outdoor theatre. When he began telling friends about it we were skeptical. But this time we have the benefit of twelve years of hindsight. We know what Karl can do. We know that if Karl wants to achieve something, he will.

That Five Letter Word ... Pride

Broadcast March 21, 1991

There is a powerful word in the English language that describes one of the most important ingredients you must have to achieve any degree of success. That five letter word is ... pride. The Penguin Canadian Dictionary describes pride as ... *"a sense of one's own worth."*

I can't imagine anyone achieving anything of note without having pride. Pride in yourself, pride in your family, pride in your friends, pride in your work and your colleagues at work. Pride in your community is also very important. After all, how can a community possibly be strong unless the people within that community have pride in it. And of course, pride in Canada. It seems so often these days we hear fellow Canadians make disparaging remarks about this great country and its future as a country. It offends me to hear anyone say anything unkind about Canada or Canadians. Because I know for a fact that we are the greatest nation and people in the world. A great Canadian, former Prime Minister, John Diefenbaker, once said and I quote ... *"I know there are some who feel a sense of embarrassment in expressing pride in their nation perhaps because of the fear that they might be considered old fashioned or parochial ..."* Have pride in yourself and for goodness sake have pride in Canada.

You get people to do what you want not by bullying them or tricking them, but by understanding them.

She Shocked Male Chauvinists

Claudette Mackay-Lassonde

In 1986 the engineering profession, and male chauvinism in general, received a severe shock. A *woman* became President of the 50 thousand member Professional Engineers of Ontario.

For Claudette MacKay-Lassonde it completed a process that started more than 20 years earlier when she decided to become an engineer. In those days engineering was a "man's profession". But Claudette's father, a mechanic with CanRon, a Montreal company that produced electric motors, was very supportive. As far as Claudette was concerned that was good enough for her.

She remembers being told by a male student at the University of Montreal, *"Don't do well. We hate women that do well in engineering"*.

Claudette did well, in fact, she finished at the top of her class and went on to obtain a degree in chemical engineering. She took two additional giant steps by obtaining a master's degree in nuclear engineering in Utah, and a master's in business administration in Toronto. She did very well in University—that's where she met her future husband, Pierre.

He's an achiever as well. Also a graduate engineer, he now is Senior Vice President with the Toronto investment firm of Beutel-Goodman, and President of "Franco Nevada", a mining company. Pierre has been published by the Financial Times.

In 1976 Claudette joined Ontario Hydro as a nuclear safety engineer and rose through the ranks to become Head of the Load Forecasts Department, and was acknowledged as an expert on nuclear power generation. In 1988 she left Ontario Hydro to join Northern Telecom where she is now Director of Premier Accounts in their marketing department.

Claudette MacKay-Lassonde has made a lasting mark in the engineering profession and proved beyond a shadow of a doubt that women can be engineers. Still only 43 years of age, she will continue proving it for many more years. She is living proof that you can achieve whatever goal you set for yourself.

"Tell your story to the public . . . what you have and what you propose to sell. Promise them not only bargains but that every article will be found just what it is guaranteed to be.

—*Timothy Eaton,* founder of Eaton's Department Stores (Statement made in 1869. Nothing has changed.)

He Can Do Anything

Ken Church

They say you can take the boy from the farm but you can't take the farm from the boy. As a person who was raised on a Prairie farm I know that statement is true. As further proof, I offer this story of Ken Church.

Ken was raised on a small farm near Ryerson, Saskatchewan. Like all farm kids he milked cows, cleaned pig pens and wished chores were easier. As a youngster Ken was very inventive. At age 13 he built a pea-shelling machine that could fill a 3-gallon pail in 5 minutes. *"Neighbours from miles around would bring washtubs full of peas to our house for shelling. My mother knew then that someday I'd invent something important."*

Ken graduated from the Saskatchewan Institute of Applied Arts and Science, a technical school in Saskatoon. In 1981 he did something about helping farmer's kids who have to clean pig pens. He formed a company called *"Feroex"* in Gimli, Manitoba. Using a sophisticated method of introducing fibreglass into plastic, he created a grid hog flooring of plastic, raised and supported by fiberglass reinforced joints. The flooring was easier to clean, easier to install, and durable. Dealers came from around the world and bought. Ten years later, they're still coming and buying.

Ken's company has branched out into a number of other products. In 1984 a Winnipeg window manufacturer asked Ken to develop a window frame using his specialized method. Bigger plastic companies had told the manufacturer it couldn't be done. Ken tackled the project, mastered it, and his strong flexible window frame won first prize at the 1985 International Plastics Show in Atlanta, Georgia.

Now Ken has developed another highly specialized technical product. It's fibreglass rods, 40 km long, spooled on reels. The rods go down the centre of fibre optic cables to give the cable strength and still provide flexibility.

With the world's emphasis on recycling waste material, Ken is leading the way in recycling waste plastic. He buys waste plastic foam from Canadian and U.S. auto manufacturers, brings it to Gimli and recycles it by manufacturing his hog grids with it. Ken boasts, and rightly so, that, *"We are one of the very few manufacturers in North America who recycles plastic into a manufactured product. Most recyclers produce plastic pellets which they sell to manufacturers. We go pick up the waste plastic, bring it here and manufacture."*

Ken Church has achieved a lot in ten short years. He was nearly wiped out in 1983 when fire destroyed his plant. Like most fledgling businesses he was only partially insured. Somehow he managed to rebuild and survive. By 1987 he was ready to really expand. This time into a big new 30 thousand square foot modern plant. What's his key to success?

"I always wanted to have my own business. I'm very strong on technology and that is the strength of our company. Our products are technically advanced over existing products."

Ken's company now employs 42 people and sales this year should top four million dollars! He's still only 40 years old. I have a strong feeling that over the next few years we'll be hearing a lot more from this Saskatchewan farm boy.

"So to each of you—I say I believe in Canada—a Canada undivided. A Canadian I was born, a Canadian I will die."
    —*The Rt. Hon. John G. Diefenbaker*

She Does the Un-Do-Able!

Kaaydah Schatten

The story of Kaaydah Schatten begins as an all too common Canadian tragedy. Born on an Indian Reserve at Campbell River, British Columbia, one of six children, parents alcoholic.

She moved to Nanaimo and became an honours high school graduate. At 18, just as things were going well, Kaaydah was badly injured in a car accident, lost a hip and one lung and spent a year in a wheelchair. But she fought back, took the seven thousand dollars she received in an insurance settlement and invested in real estate. She also trained as an accountant.

At 26, (1980) she was worth five million dollars! Then, her investments crashed and she was wiped out. She bounced back, invented a new method of cleaning ceilings of commercial buildings, brought her method of cleaning ceilings to Toronto and founded *"The Ceiling Doctor"*, a company which cleans ceilings and ceiling tiles in offices. It became an immediate success so she decided to franchise. In just seven years she now has 80 franchises in Canada, the U.S., Japan, Ireland and Germany. She told me her company is a pioneer in Germany.

"We were the first Canadian company to franchise in Germany. Most foreign franchisers in Germany are from France. It's a very tightly controlled industry over there. We expect to do quite well."

What is the key to her successful operation?

"We operate lean and mean. Other franchise companies of my size would have a staff of twelve to twenty. I have four, but pay them well. Also being female I do more research than my male counterparts."

Up till now the franchise business in North America has been a male domain. Kaaydah is one of probably only six major franchisers. Jenny Craig and Mary Kay being two of them. She has no partners. Her personal net worth is, *"about 5 million dollars"*. Plus her company is worth, *"Price Waterhouse recently did an evaluation for me and set its value at 10 million"*.

At 36, Kaaydah owns four luxury cars including a Maseratti and a Jaguar. (She recently sold her Rolls Royce.) Wears designer clothes and travels first class. Happily married, her husband sold his medical practice to work with her in the company. They have three children whom she is already grooming to bring into the business someday.

Kaaydah makes achieving sound so simple. *"In a nutshell, the key to achieving is belief in yourself, your creator, and an unnerving persistence to do the un-do-able. Everyone thought I was crazy seven years ago. Now I'm being touted as some kind of an expert"*.

Never standing still, she has a new invention, *"A type of screw-head that may revolutionize the industry. We're still working on it"*.

As busy as she is she works actively to promote Indian Culture and the status of Native people. Because, as she says, *"If I could make it from the reserve to a luxurious life in the big city, others can"*.

Twenty-one years ago Kaaydah was active as a founding member of GreenPeace with Paul Watson, Robert Hunter and the man who later became world famous as the promoter of *"Live Aid"*, Bob Geldorf.

Kaayday Schatten, she's another Canadian Achiever.

Come Hell or High Water

Gordon Bell

"It's very important that you really stick with it because, there are lots of ups and downs. So you have to decide that you're going to stick with it come hell or high water."

That's the advice of Gordon Bell the man, who with his family, has built *"The 3 Valley Gap Resort"* near Revelstoke, B.C.

It's a dream come true for Gordon and Ethel Bell. Back in the 50's Gordon was a young entrepreneur building houses in Regina. He built the small seven unit motel at 3 Valley Gap because he fell in love with the area the moment he saw it. It's located in one of the most spectacular scenic spots in B.C., surrounded by mountains, tumbling waterfalls, a sparkling mountain-fed lake, and a lovely beach where hardy folks can challenge the lake's icy waters. It is truly a paradise location.

Today Gordon has transformed those seven small motel units into a modern, bustling 117 unit motel with gas bar, restaurant, dining rooms, banquet centre, indoor swimming pool, gift shop . . . you name it!

The main attraction is a genuine, reconstructed frontier town that you just have to see to believe. Tourists come from all over the world for the nightly outdoor barbeque and authentic cowboy entertainment.

Being located in an isolated area has created many problems. None of which has ever fazed this most ingenious achiever. Like the time a few years ago when B.C. Hydro wanted 450 thousand dollars to run a power line to accommodate Gordon's increasing demands. Of course there would be substantial monthly Hydro bills as well. So instead, Gordon built his own hydro generating system by running 8000 feet of submarine cable under the lake, three and a half miles of overhead power line up a mountain to a dam he'd built. He installed turbines and generators and now produces all of the electricity required. In fact, he can produce a surplus amount which he's negotiating to sell to B.C. Hydro. They require it to accommodate nearby homes that are springing up. Although there is ample water in the lake, Gordon ran 1000 feet of pipeline to a natural spring high on a mountain. Gravity provides 80 lbs. of pressure thus eliminating the need for water pumps.

Spend an hour talking with Gordon Bell and you quickly unerstand why he is a success. People look at Gordon today and envy his achievements. But they shouldn't. Everything he has he's worked darn hard for and earned honestly.

"Money was terribly hard to borrow for this project. Back thirty years ago the bank rate was 5%. We had to pay 12%. Not because there wasn't any money around, it was because nobody but us believed in this project."

The Gordon Bell story is one I enjoy telling because it confirms my belief that there is no land on earth more spectacular or magnificent than Canada, and there is no country in the world that offers more opportunity.

"There are no limits to the majestic future which lies before the mighty expanse of Canada with its virile, aspiring, cultured and generous-hearted people."

—Sir Winston Churchill

You're Bound To Succeed

Albert Cohen

While interviewing the late Albert Cohen, founder of General Distributing, Winnipeg, the company that introduced ball point pens and Sony to Canada, I asked him the usual. . . "what advice do you have for other Canadians wishing to achieve in business?" *"It's simple,"* he said and pulled out a ball point pen (what else). Then he drew a triangle on the back of a napkin and wrote three words. . . *"Follow this triangle faithfully and you're bound to succeed."*

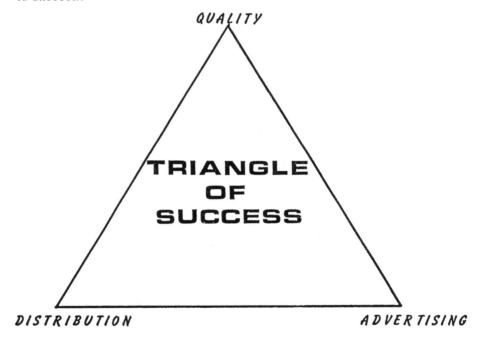

"When business is good it pays to advertise; when business is bad you've got to advertise."
    —*Anonymous*

Sometimes It Pays to Quit

Raymond Waechter

During the 1950's Raymond Waechter was working in Montreal as a salesman for a building supply dealer. He was being paid a good salary but he wanted a commission on his sales. His boss refused, so Raymond decided, after a lot of thought and deliberation, to start his own business.

Today, 'Boiseries Raymond' employs 150 people and has annual sales in excess of $26 million.

In addition, 'Boiseries Raymond' has the largest showroom in North America specializing in wood-finishing products. And... surprise... all of Raymond's 35 sales people are on commission.

"You know, the salary I made with that company was very good. For that time. I even had a company car. But I was always very ambitious and I wanted to employ myself in a better way. So I said to my boss; 'I will give you back your company car and you will pay me in commission alone. I will take care of my own expenses.' He refused, and that is why I started my own business."

Raymond was only 22 years old!

Now, after 33 years of operating his own business does he have any regrets? *"Of course not! By owning my own business I know there is no way I could have made what I made as a salesman. Even if I had been paid commission."*

What would Raymond recommend to people who want to go into business for themselves? What are the pitfalls? *When you make your first $100,000, don't go out and have a good time in Las Vegas, or buy yourself that big boat to show off how important and successful you are. Plough the profits back into the company so it can continue to grow. What made us a success... if we go back and look at it over the years... is that simple formula: all the money we made was kept in the company. So that today, at age 55, I am semi-retired, and I sold part of the company to younger people.*

"I even named one of them president of the firm. I guess what I could say is: work hard while you are young so you can enjoy life at retirement.

"Another suggestion I would give to people today is not to entirely sell your company; retain some control."

Raymond and his wife, Pierrette, began their spiral to business success very simply: they bought a piece of land in east Montreal in 1958 and set up a lumberyard. It was a business that Raymond already knew, but in the beginning it was not easy. While Raymond was delivering lumber in his station wagon, Pierrette was taking care of business in the office.

But the big break came when the Waechters decided to specialize. They quit selling just raw lumber and began to focus on wooden doors, stair railings and moldings. It was a bold move and led to what would have been a modest and profitable business to one that has done much better.

With all the trials and tribulations of establishing a business in a very competitive field, does Raymond have any regrets? *"My only regret is that we did not establish our branches in Quebec City and West End Montreal earlier."*

The commission sales pitch: a lot of people starting out want the comfortable cushion of the guaranteed salary. What is the motive for those who are on commission alone? Isn't it pretty scary? *"One thing I have always stressed to my sales people is that he or she is in business for themselves. The profit they make is up to them. There is no limit to how much they can make. I believe in that motive. It worked for me. Everybody in my company is happy with that system.*

"Sometimes the owner of a company takes the attitude that if a certain salesman is earning a lot of money, he should reduce his territory or cut his commission or do something to 'make him work harder' to earn his commission. That is not right. I always say if a salesman earns more money I make bigger profits on his ability. So why cut him down? It's crazy!"

Raymond Waechter is a Canadian Achiever who has discovered a formula that works for him. Perhaps in his commissioned staff are other achievers. The formula worked for Raymond.

"It's not where you are. It's where you're headed that matters."
—*Joey Smallwood*

Paging Mr. Success

Charles Sirois

Charles Sirois, born in the small Quebec town of Chicoutimi, always had a gift for mathematics. He studied economics and finance at Laval University in Quebec City. When he graduated, he had no money but a lot of ambition and he looked around for what he thought would be a promising business. Of all things, he landed on the idea of Beepers, those portable Pagett machines that many doctors and messengers carry around, usually attached to their hips, to be paged at any instant by the sound of a beep.

Sirois, who grew up speaking only French, started off modestly with a Pagette service in a Quebec City Hospital, and later he expanded into the telephone message business.

By 1985, Sirois still did not speak English very well, but he had cornered more than forty percent of the Canadian paging business. Then he scored his big scoop. December 23, 1985 he bought "T.A.S. Pagette", Canada's largest paging company based in Toronto. That acquisition made Sirois, still under 30 years old, Canada's undisputed "Mr. Pagette".

Always on the move, he merged his company with B.C.E. and formed "B.C.E. Mobile", now one of the world's largest mobile communication companies doing business all over the world. Charles is that company's second largest shareholder. His own personal company, "Intermedia Financial Corp." is a merchant with offices in Canada, France and several other countries.

Still a young 36 years old, Charles married Therese, also from Chicoutimi. They have a boy, 15, and a girl, 12. When I asked Charles what he figured his net financial worth was he chuckled and said, *"It all depends on the market, as high as 250 million. Today, (January 14, 1990) probably only 100 million."*

He's another Canadian Achiever.

The carrot always wins over the stick.

She Follows Her Own Path

Vera Bates

"Go for it. If you really want to do something in life, do it. I don't care if you're a man or a woman. I'm not a feminist by any means. I just feel you should go and do what you want to do in life. If you're scared to because of what people might think, well, to heck with you!"

That, Vera Bates told me, is her philosophy towards life. She means it, and she lives by it.

Formerly of Fonthill, Ontario, when she received a degree in nursing, folks said she'd go a long way. And she did. Vera went to New York to become a successful fashion coordinator. Then to Jamaica to manage a hotel. Along the way, she became conversant in five languages. As if three careers weren't enough, Vera returned to Canada and Prince Edward Island to become a sheep rancher, and a highly respected one at that.

Redcliffe Farm became the home of the famed *"Redcliffe Polled Dorset Sheep"*. A breed that brought her acclaim throughout the Maritimes. Not surprisingly, Vera wasn't content with winning ribbons, attending international conferences, or judging or speaking *"sheep"*. She turned her home into a 'guest house' that welcomes visitors from every country.

"I've had some really interesting guests from all around the world."

Recently she sold off her sheep. *"For the time being"*, she told me, *"to have more time to return to my first love . . . sculpting. I am sculpting the Anne of Green Gables series and then making the original dolls. I'm making reproductions of antique dolls."* You can bet they will quickly become much sought after collector's items.

Vera Bates is an Achiever who follows her own path and her own advice, *"Go for it"!*

"You have a great country up here. And a great people too."
—*William Jennings Bryan*

Knowledge is Power

Pierre Ducros

51-year-old Pierre Ducros had an unusually disciplined education while growing up in Montreal. His French-born father sent young Pierre to the Military College in nearby Saint Jean and then he was off to Ontario's Royal Military College in Kingston. After a degree in engineering from Montreal's McGill University and a stint in the Canadian Navy, Ducros joined IBM in 1964 and quickly moved up the ladder in the rapidly-expanding computer company.

Working with him at IBM were two close friends; Alain Roy, who Pierre knew from Military College days, and Serge Meilleur. In 1973 the trio decided to leave IBM and go on their own. They formed the *DMR Group"*, (the first initial of their last names). Using knowledge gained at IBM their company specialized in helping corporations set up their own software systems to meet their particular management needs.

As Pierre Ducros explained to me, *"It was not our purpose or intention to expand as rapidly as we did. We began offering consulting services in data processing and management ... it just grew."*

They now have offices coast to coast in Canada and seven other countries. Combined they employ 2,097 people, (January 1991) of which 1300 are here in Canada. Pierre, Serge and Alain are excellent examples of intrapreneurs wanting to become entrepreneurs and doing it.

"We left many good friends at IBM. It is a very good company. We are still friends, we just wanted to become entrepreneurs."

And boy, have they done it. Sales this year, (1991) are expected to top 200 million dollars. They are Canadian Achievers.

"Aim High . . . in Canada you can reach the sky."
—*D.D.*

Stopping Thieves the World Over

Peter Matiowsky

Peter Matiowsky was born and raised in the Seech District of Manitoba. He moved to Calgary and for the next 20 years did a variety of things including selling insurance, working in the oil fields and for 16 years worked as a glass man for "Custom Glass", a company specializing in home window renovations. That's where he soon picked up on a common theme: people are very concerned about the security of their homes. Many of Peter's customers were looking for more effective ways of burglar-proofing their doors and windows, so he started thinking about ways that he could help.

In 1974 Peter decided to capitalize on this, risk it all, and start his own company "Environmental Glass Service". Peter tested several normal household doors and found that they could be kicked in easily. He came up with the idea of putting a steel plate inside the door, attached to a dead bolt lock. Such construction makes the door much more difficult to break in, giving a thief the option of kicking noisily at the door and attracting a lot of attention, or completely abandoning the idea of robbing that particular house.

From there, Peter branched out to windows with break-resistant glass, and windows with special security bars. Peter feels the profits his business earns are only part of his reward. He enjoys pitting his mind against that of a criminal, especially when Peter is the winner.

Environmental Glass Service products are sold through locksmiths under the trade name "Intrud-A-Shield". Peter has been satisfied to let the company grow at its own pace.

"But now", he told me, *"my 28 year old son Kevin is running the show. He has big plans to market our product world-wide."*

Soon they'll be thwarting criminal minds and stopping thieves in their tracks, the world over.

"Anybody can cut prices, but it takes brains to produce a better product."
—*P.D. Armour*

Canada's Future is Bright

Dan Wilton

When I first met 17 year old Dan Wilton of Winnipeg, it was hard to believe he's was only 17. Dan exudes confidence and maturity. The kind of person you want leading Canada into the next century, I met Dan through Junior Achievement, the excellent organization which gives young people the opportunity to expand their horizons. In 1989 Dan was selected to give the keynote address in front of 1600 of Canada's business leaders at the annual Junior Achievement Captains of Industry dinner in Toronto. Can you imagine being asked, at 17, to speak to 1600 of Canada's senior business leaders who each paid $275.00 to hear you? I spoke with Dan just before his address and asked him how he felt?

"I'm a little bit nervous because many of the people in the audience are legends in the business world."

Someone wise once said ... "courage is being scared silly and still proceeding". Well, Dan proceeded to the dias and knocked them out with a speech that left a lasting impression. What impressed everyone was his confidence in the future of Canada, *"my address deals mainly with the future of the Canadian entrepreneur. I think it's quite bright. I have a lot of confidence in Canada. I think it's a great country."*

Canada's future is indeed very bright. Particularly with bright young Canadians like Dan Wilton and all of the other young people at Junior Achievement.

Courage is being scared silly and still proceeding.

Beating the Japanese to the Chip

Waldemar ("Wally") Pieczonka

In 1972, Waldemar ("Wally") Pieczonka came to a crossroads in his life: The company he had been working for had lost faith in the future of the silicon chip industry as it related to their present development. Wally had not lost faith, went to work on his own, and made a name for himself.

Born in Poland, Wally and his family emigrated to Canada in 1938 where they settled on a farm in Saskatchewan. He received a Ph.D in solid state physics in 1960 and went to the United States to work for IBM for four years. He then returned to Canada to work for Westinghouse Canada but in 1972 the Canadian branch of the Pittsburgh giant withdrew from the silicon chip business. It had already dropped its interest in that part of the industry in the U.S. in 1968.

But Wally felt there was a great future in silicon chips.

"I decided to take the risk and start my own company."

The company was called Linear Technology, later renamed Gennum Corporation. Linear's sales in the first year of operation were about $500,000. Sales by Gennum in 1991 will exceed $20 million.

"We had the conviction that we could succeed. What we did was to pioneer the application of silicon chips in a niche market—the hearing aid industry. In this field we now have about 65 percent of the world market."

Not bad for a little Polish boy from Saskatchewan!

"It took a lot of persistence to sell into the Japanese market. To convince them that they weren't the only ones who could make micro-chips. At first they were cool to the idea but when they realized we had a good product they went for it. I must admit it was quite a coup and it felt great to be able to pull it off."

Pull it off is right! Gennum Corporation employs about 200 people and deals mainly with American companies, including his old bosses, Westinghouse!

His advice to young entrepreneurs? *"Have confidence in yourself. Start early on your ideas and don't waste time sitting on the fence waiting for something to happen that might not. Or waiting too long so somebody else runs with the same idea."*

Wally admits it is sometimes difficult to get financing, but if you have a good product and your own track record is clear, you will succeed.

"Be persistent. Don't take no for an answer. Be organized. Many businesses fail because they don't keep on the main track. Maintain a narrow focus on your product and—like they say in the telephone commercial—you don't win by working harder but by working smarter."

Good advice from Wally Pieczonka, a Canadian Achiever who gambled personally and won with an idea that his American bosses had no faith in.

Soar Like An Eagle

Peter Legge

"I think you have to first of all come to grips with how gifted you may or may not be. And are able to work within that framework.

"Secondly, my strongest advice would be, don't bite off more than you can chew. Try very hard not to go into debt... don't run too fast. Be more like the turtle than the hare. Allow things to grow slowly. Things will never happen as fast as you can dream or visualize them. The marketplace will not likely glom onto you that fast and grow as fast as you want. You have to keep pushing and do it slowly. You have to take risks. You have to be entrepreneurial... and keep an eye on your debt."

That's the answer Peter Legge gave when I asked his advice to would be entrepreneurs. He also said...

"The first priority is... get into your own business. The second priority is... produce a good product and sustain it. My background is selling and marketing; that's what I really focused on."

Peter is certainly very qualified to give advice. Not only is he an outstanding business success, he shares his success with others around the world as a leading motivational speaker.

Peter Legge is not your average motivational speaker. He has a proven track record to back up what he says.

Peter's family emigrated to Canada from England in 1954, when he was 12 years old.

His ability to entertain and perform began at age 12 when he realized he could make people laugh. In fact, he was actually very good at it. Eventually he decided to pursue a career in entertainment which took him back to England where he hosted a very successful comedy show for the BBC.

His desire to succeed in the business world brought him back to Vancouver where he pursued a successful career in the broadcasting industry. But Peter had the same uncontrollable itch so many achievers have. He wanted to own a company.

"I really have to say I backed into it... There was an opportunity to buy a company that didn't have many assets or much money but it was something that I could call my own and that I could run."

The company he bought in 1976 published 'TV Week' Magazine. It was doing sales of 70 thousand a year and barely surviving. Now 15 years later, Peter's company "Canada Wide Magazines"is virtually a publishing empire publishing 13 magazines with 1991 sales expected to top 15 million dollars.

"I think what really got us going in the first place was my ignorance of what I was doing. I didn't know I shouldn't be doing it so I went ahead and did it. If I had to make those same decisions today, knowing what I know about the publishing business and its complexities, I probably wouldn't go into the business."

Peter attributes his phenomenal success to three factors... persistence, patience and a positive attitude. He often paraphrases former U.S. President Calvin Coolidge who said *"Nothing in the world can take the place of these three factors... talent will not, education will not and genius will not."*

Peter puts 100 percent into everything he does. People who hear him speak leave the meeting wanting to *'soar like an eagle'*. In fact, that's the title of his address and motivational cassette. I have his cassette in my car and listen to it whenever I need a good stiff jolt to get my adrenalin flowing.

"There is no limit whatsoever to your ability to be successful in Canada."
—Mel Steinke

Canada Week

Broadcast June 22, 1990

We are very fortunate to live in Canada. This most wonderful of all countries. Millions of people around the world would gladly change countries with you and me in an instant. If you doubt me just ask any immigration officer. As Canadians we are protected by our Charter of Rights and Freedoms. It's in place to protect everyone. As Canadians we are guaranteed the right to worship, or not, as we wish. In the place of worship of our choice. Freedom of the press and other media is ensured and our right to gather in peaceful groups as well as our right to freedom of association is protected. Canada may not be 100% perfect but it's as close to perfect as you'll find anywhere in the world. I challenge anyone to name a country that offers more opportunity to achieve. In Canada you can achieve any reasonable goal you set your sights on. In Canada you can achieve. I know, I meet Canadian Achievers every day. From all walks of life, every corner of Canada. It's a great country—the very best. So, next week I hope you'll place a Canadian flag in your window to remind yourself and passersby that it's our birthday. Canada—the greatest country in all of the world is 123 years young, growing, and full of vitality!

An Underwater Entrepreneur

Bill Blakey

An intrapreneur is an employee working for a company. An entrepreneur is an employee risking personal capital. It's rare to meet someone who is accomplished at both at the same time. That was the case of 42 year old Toronto advertising executive and Northern Ontario resort owner/operator Bill Blakey.

As an advertising intrapreneur he worked at one of Canada's largest agencies, 'McCann Erickson Event Marketing'. Bill was the best. His projects included General Motors sponsorship of the '88 Calgary Winter Olympics, the annual 'Arnold Palmer Cadillac Golf Classic', The Molson Indy. Plus many other major national events. I think you get the picture.

For relaxation, and as a means to get away from it all, Bill took up scuba diving. *"They can't reach me by phone when I'm underwater."*

Not one to do things in half measures, Bill became proficient to the point that he began teaching diving as his hobby. Soon, the hobby became a profitable business to the extent that five years ago he bought "The Will Robb Lodge", a run down hunting and fishing lodge on Georgian Bay and began fixing it up for the exclusive use of scuba divers. *"It needed a lot of T.L.C. to return it to rentable condition. It's in great shape now. In fact, I just bought the marina next door."*

Word spread among scuba divers about Bill's lodge and you can imagine the rest. The lodge is fully booked months in advance. It was a lot of work for Bill, juggling two successful careers. *"I really enjoy it. It's something that opens a lot of doors. It requires a lot of time during the summer but I know that somewhere down the road there will be a final pay off and it will have all been worthwhile."*

Well, it appears that the pay off is coming faster than even he imagined. On January 11th, 1991, he resigned from the advertising agency, obtained a cellular telephone franchise, agreed to consult for three major clients and will devote more time to his hobby which has now become his profession.

Bill is fulfilling the dream of most of us. It did not come easy, nothing worthwhile ever does. Someone once said . . . that if achievers are distinguished by anything it is by the simple fact that they 'act' on thoughts most of us at one time or another have had. . . . That certainly fits the description of Bill Blakey, another Canadian Achiever.

She Bucked A Trend
In The Automobile Industry

Marlene Buck

Marlene Buck is one of Canada's very few female car dealers. When her husband Dave died in 1986, Marlene stepped in as president of the dealership, Dave Buck Ford in Vancouver.

Winnipeg-born Marlene had never worked in the automotive business, and hadn't worked at all for ten years when she took over. But she was determined to keep the business in the family, so she took a condensed course in the car and truck business and took over.

She has a staff of 95 and under Marlene's eye, the dealership's 28 year reputation for reliable sales and service is firmly intact. Marlene makes a special point of stressing the importance of women customers when talking to her staff. She feels strongly that women don't want to be treated any differently than men, and they deserve attention and respect.

She told me, *"women are usually better buyers than men because they do their homework."*

Marlene has taken a very active role in the automotive industry. She served three years on the board of the Auto Dealers Association of Greater Vancouver. She is now their immediate past president (1991).

Her philosophy towards achieving is, *"You have to be totally committed to what you are going to do. Be sure to hire good people. Maintain a high energy level."* Her high energy level will see total sales at her dealership this year (1991) of ... *"somewhere between 35 and 40 million. That sounds like a lot but a store like ours has a huge overhead."*

How does she manage her time? *"Well I've really learned to control myself. I've become much better. I'm cutting back. I seldom work weekends now, except when I have to. I'm out of here by seven every night. I've improved a great deal."* Now she is only working 50 to 60 hours per week. Some improvement.

Marlene Buck had a goal firmly in mind then she set out with determination, hard work, and a few ideas to get her there ... and has. She's another Canadian Achiever.

End of the Decade ... Entertainment

Broadcast Tuesday, December 26, 1989

Canada is blessed with an abundance of outstanding entertainers. To cover their achievements of this decade in this short space is impossible. A few highlights were the Royal Winnipeg Ballet celebrating their fiftieth anniversary. They are North America's second oldest ballet company. The Irish Rovers and Tommy Hunter celebrating their 25th anniversary. Watching Anne Murray host along with Kenny Rogers, the Country Music Awards from Nashville. As expected, Anne stole the show. Other outstanding entertainers are Judith Forst, the world-class soprano with the New York Metropolitan Opera. She prefers to live in her hometown of Port Moody near Vancouver and commute to New York. David Foster and his stirring composition for Rick Hansen's *"Man in Motion"* world tour ... Two years later David raised goose bumps again with his stirring theme for the Winter Olympics. Karen Kain celebrating her 20th anniversary with the National Ballet. k.d. Lang accepting a Grammy award. Andre-Phillippe Gagnon knocking 'em dead on the Johnny Carson show. Bryan Adams touring the world reminding his young audiences that he is Canadian, and darn proud of it. Howie Mandel, Martin Short, Michael J. Fox, young Canadians who found their mark and represented Canada so well in this decade.

And for sheer home entertainment ... Scott Abbott and Chris Haney who gave the world *"Trivial Pursuit"*. There was nothing trivial about our Canadian entertainers in the past decade. And there won't be in the next one either.

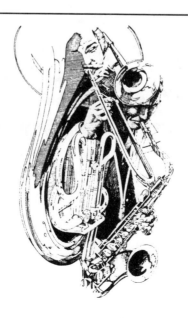

End of the Decade ... Sports

Broadcast Wednesday, December 27, 1989

Canada is a nation of athletes. We excel in so many sports that it's impossible to cover them all here in 90 seconds. Elizabeth Manley stealing the show, and winning a silver at the Calgary Olympics, Wayne Gretzky setting a new NHL record. Then watching another Canadian achiever Gordie Howe congratulate Wayne even though it was Gordie's record Wayne had broken. In golf, Dave Barr, in tennis Carling Bassett. Speedskater Gaetan Boucher winning two gold and a bronze. Alex Baumann the swimmer with a Canadian flag tattooed over his heart winning two gold and a silver. Carolyn Waldo winning two Olympic gold in synchronized swimming. While we're still in the water ... Vicki Keith swimming long distances to raise money for Variety Village. Canadians also excelled in the ultimate endurance sport ... mountain climbing ... when Sharon Wood of Canmore, Alberta, became the first North American woman to reach the top of Mount Everest. Al Howie set a world record in the New York Marathon running 1,300 miles in 17 days, 8 hours, 25 minutes.

Our athletes have certainly given us so many achievements to be proud of this past decade. Congratulations to all of them ... they are Canadian Achievers.

End of the Decade ... Science & Medicine

Broadcast Thursday, December 28, 1989

Canada became recognized as a leader in space technology when the world, watching on television, saw the Canadarm with a big bold Canadian flag in full view manipulate successfully on board the U.S. Space Shuttle. Earlier, on October 5, 1984, Marc Garneau became the first Canadian astronaut to enter space. In medicine we rejoiced when University of Toronto chemistry professor John Polanyi won a Nobel Prize for research. The need for research funds was brought home forcefully in 1981 when a young one-legged runner, Terry Fox set out on his Marathon of Hope. Raising funds for cancer research. The challenge was taken up and completed in 1985 by another young one-legged runner Steve Fonyo. The world was soon to learn about another young Canadian and his dream to raise funds and awareness of spinal research. Rick Hansen's *"Man In Motion Tour"* through 34 countries. While these major events were occurring, thousands of other equally important events were happening in Canada. In Bathurst, New Brunswick three volunteer machinists designed an artificial arm so that Scotty Morgan, a youngster living in King City, Ontario, could play hockey. Their design is now being shared around the world. Yes, Canadians in the field of science and medicine have recorded enormous achievements this past decade.

End of the Decade ... Canadian Business

Broadcast Friday, December 29, 1989

Forbes Magazine in the U.S. reported that Canada has more billionaires per capita than any other industrialized country. We also rate quite high as millionaires. Earlier this year it was my pleasure to present, on behalf of the Miramichi region, an achiever's award to K.C. Irving. Although he's one of the world's wealthiest men, he still has not lost touch with the people around him. Most self-made people are like that. Jimmy Pattison, self-made billionaire from Luceland, Saskatchewan is the same.

Although this decade has been good to some businesses, it has taken its toll on quite a few. Max Ward and Robert Campeau come quickly to mind. But where would Canada be if it wasn't for risk takers like Max Ward, who started with a bush plane and built it into a world class airline? Robert Campeau at age 16, started sweeping floors in a Sudbury steel mill and ended up becoming the largest retailer in North America. Look what they built along the way. Think of the thousands they have employed. The last decade saw the emergence of many new entrepreneurs. Men and women with the same fire and drive that set Campeau and Ward apart. Let's hope our new budding entrepreneurs don't back off and start playing it safe. If they do, Canada will lose. Our country was built by people with vision ... risk takers ... We can't allow complacency to set in. So this Canadian Achiever year end tribute is to all of the risk takers ... good luck in the 90's.

Real Estate ... It's The Real Thing

Raymond Aaron

Buying a home can be the best investment you will ever make. Do it when you are young and it could become the cornerstone to your financial independence.

Thanks to a $3000 real estate investment Aline and I made in 1962 we were able to buy a radio station in 1979. Here's how it happened ... We were married in 1956 and rented until 1962. During that time we built absolutely no equity whatsoever. In 1962 we scraped together $3,000 as downpayment on a $12,000 bungalow in the Mountain Gardens area of Burlington, Ontario. In 1967 we sold it for $24,000 and bought a new 5 bedroom home in Burlington for $42,000. In 1979 we bought radio station CKAY in Duncan, B.C. We sold our home during a depressed market for $130,000 and used the money to swing the deal on the station. Since then we have never looked back. That's what can happen with real estate. In fact, four of the largest fortunes in Canada are centred around real estate investments; the Irvings in the Maritimes, the Reichmanns in central Canada, the Ghermezians in Alberta, and the Belzbergs in B.C.

Although real estate prices fluctuate through good times and bad, they almost always recover. Raymond Aaron knows that:

"There are two types of problems in real estate. Chronic and acute. The chronic never goes away; the acute always goes away. Recognizing this fact is part of what I teach in my real estate courses."

Raymond wasn't always an expert on the subject. He took his lumps too. *"When I was 21 and just out of university I raised $50,000 and started making a soft drink from apple juice that foamed like beer. I got terrific publicity in Maclean's, The Toronto Telegram and Marketing Magazine. But I was going head-to-head with Coca-Cola and we just didn't make it. We were out of business in nine months."*

Although he is not ashamed of his failures, Raymond is also extremely proud of his successes. By buying and selling real estate in Ontario, Alberta and British Columbia, he became a millionaire in less than five years.

"I tried working for other people and a couple of other ventures on my own. But I felt empty. I started giving real estate courses based on what I called 'The Contrarian Principles of Wealth'. By that I mean, when most people are doing one thing, you do another."

Raymond gives as an example—when the economy is soft, interest rates are high and prices are low, buy. When "the problems go away", sell. Seems a fairly simple and logical philosophy. Why doesn't everybody follow it? If Raymond has his way, millions of Canadians will. Many thousands have already heard his "12-Hour Real Estate Course", which he started offering in 1983.

Speaking to groups of 20 to 700, Raymond extols the wisdom he has learned first-hand. *"I have bought upwards of 1,000 properties, sold some, and retained about 300. These transactions, which form the basis of my income, allow me to travel and lecture. This is the side of the business I love most. Ever since I was a little boy I could tell stories and hold an audience. For me, it's fun. And at the same time I am fulfilling my mission: making Canada a better country by providing educational services."*

Born into a middle-class family in Toronto, where his father, Joseph Aaron, was a cabdriver, Raymond excelled in school, graduating from the University of Toronto with an Honours B.Sc. in Nuclear Physics. He aimed at a career in industry but hated it. *"I felt so empty. Even when I was operating my own businesses, I still did not feel fulfilled."*

Teaching mathematics still didn't satisfy his desire to succeed, while also putting something back that would help others. In that regard, he opened a real estate bookstore in 1984 and launched the Library Club two years later.

"The Club now has about 2000 members. Every two months members receive a book or a tape or other useful financial information which they would not come across themselves."

To what does Raymond credit his success.

"My father instilled in me to take your time and build slowly and carefully. He went from cabby to fleetowner and in 1960 established the Canadian Natural Hygiene Society. He ran the Boston Marathon in his 50's."

Raymond's advice for people investing in real estate in the 90's? *"Invest in the bad times. In my book 'You Can Make a Million in Canadian Real Estate' in 1987, I predicted a Recession in 1990. I also predicted we will have a false short-term recovery followed by a real Depression between now and 2000. After that, when the world returns to real value, we will experience a long spell of good times."*

Raymond Aaron has a staff of seven working at his Raymond Aaron Group office in Newmarket, Ontario. *"Most of their work involves setting up appointments and lecture tours for the real estate seminars. It's an all-Canadian company. My carriage is hitched to the Canadian horse. I love this country!"* He's another Canadian Achiever.

Times Are Changing

You must remain flexible because times are changing. Big companies are down sizing by either laying off or offering generous early retirement packages.

We live in a volatile world where mergers and corporate takeovers are commonplace. When such events occur, people often lose their jobs.

Fewer people also remain with the same employer throughout their careers. In the book "When Smart People Fail", the authors Hyatt and Gotlieb project that a typical young person entering the job market today will work for 10 different employers an average of 3.6 years each, changing his or her career 3 times prior to retirement.

Times are changing. You must change with the times. New technology means new opportunity.

"Golfer Arnold Palmer has never flaunted his success. Although he has won hundreds of trophies and awards, the only trophy in his office is a battered little cup that he got for his first professional win at the Canadian Open in 1955.

In addition to the cup, he has a lone framed plaque on the wall. The plaque tells you why he has been successful on and off the golf course. It reads:

If you think you are beaten, you are.
If you think you dare not, you don't.
If you'd like to win but think you can't,
It's almost certain you won't.
Life's battles don't always go
To the stronger or faster man.
But sooner or later, the man who wins
is the man who thinks he can.

—Soundings, The Economic Press

Irish Prayer

In closing this book let me share with you this wonderful Irish prayer which has been my inspiration. I trust you will share it with your friends . . .

Take time to *work*
   Work is the price of success
Take time to *think*
   Thinking is the source of power
Take time to *play*
   Playing is the secret of perpetual youth
Take time to be *friendly*
   Friendliness is the road to happiness
Take time to *love* and *be loved*
   Loving & being loved is the privilege of the gods
Take time to *share*
   Life is too short to be selfish
Take time to *laugh*
   Because, laughter is the music of the soul

Index

Ed Gould

I am deeply indebted to the professional manner in which Ed Gould worked with me on this project. When it appeared the book was mired in my indecision, Ed came on board, took control, and you see the results. As you read the stories in this book you will discover a common piece of advice offered by most *"Canadian Achievers"*. That advice is "surround yourself with good people, and rely on their judgement". I'm happy to say that is exactly what I did when I convinced Ed to join this project.

Over the years Ed has authored 14 books. I featured him as a *"Canadian Achiever"* in 1989 when he published his excellent book "Entertaining Canadians". It has become an important reference book. I urge you read it. You will find it most entertaining.

The Perfect Gift

Give a copy of this important book to Friends, Relatives, Young People or Students Visiting From Other Countries, Local Schools, Service Clubs, Libraries, Corporate Gifts.

Fire them up with confidence in Canada, and enthusiasm for the future. Let them read first hand how Canadians from every walk of life have seized opportunity and shaped a successful career.

A unique, personal, permanent and positive gift. A reminder to them of the important achievements of to-days' Canadians.

Please send me_____books @ $17.95, $3.00 shipping/handling and 7% G.S.T.

NAME:_____

ADDRESS:_____

CITY:_____PROVINCE:_____

POSTAL CODE:_____ PHONE:_____

FAX:_____

_____Cheque/Money Order enclosed. (no COD's or Phone Orders)

_____ VISA _/_/_/_/_/_/_/_/_/_/_/_/

_____ MASTERCARD _/_/_/_/_/_/_/_/_/_/_/_/

Expiry Date _____ / _____

DREW PUBLICATIONS
202-2006 Main Street
Vancouver, BC V5T 3C2
(604) 879-1500 PH
(604) 879-8278 FX

Multiculturalism and
Citizenship Canada

Multiculturalisme et
Citoyenneté Canada

A look
at Canada

If you have attended any of my speaking engagements, you know that I always close my address by inviting the audience to join in the singing of this most beautiful song about this most beautiful country. It's only fitting that I close my book the same way.

O Canada

O Canada!
    Our home and native land!
True partiot love
    in all thy sons command.
With glowing hearts
    we see thee rise.
The True North
    strong and free!
From far and wide
    O Canada
We stand on guard
    for thee.
God keep our land
    glorious and free!
O Canada.
    we stand on guard for thee.
O Canada.
    we stand on guard for thee.

O Canada!
    Terre de nos aieux
Ton front est cein!
    de fleurons glorieux!
Car ton bras
    sait porter l'épée.
Il sait porter
    la croix!
Ton histoire
    est une épopée
Des plus
    brillants exploits.
Et ta valeur.
    de foi trempée.
Protégera nos foyers
    et nos droits.
Protégera nos foyers
    et nos droits.

Notes